D0945439

Southern Literary Studies
Fred Hobson, Editor

Nationalism and the Color Line in George W. Cable, Mark Twain, and William Faulkner

Barbara Ladd

Nationalism and the Color Line in George W. Cable, Mark Twain, and William Faulkner

LOUISIANA STATE UNIVERSITY PRESS
Baton Rouge and London

Copyright © 1996 by Louisiana State University Press
All rights reserved
Manufactured in the United States of America
First printing
05 04 03 02 01 00 99 98 97 96   5 4 3 2 1

Designer: AMANDA MCDONALD KEY
Typeface: PALATINO
Typesetter: IMPRESSIONS BOOK AND JOURNAL SERVICES, INC.
Printer and binder: THOMSON-SHORE, INC.

Library of Congress Cataloging-in-Publication Data

Ladd, Barbara.
    Nationalism and the color line in George W. Cable, Mark Twain, and
William Faulkner / Barbara Ladd.
        p.   cm. — (Southern literary studies)
    Includes bibliographical references (p.   ) and index.
    ISBN 0-8071-2065-0   (alk. paper)
    1. American fiction—Southern States—History and criticism.
    2. Cable, George Washington, 1844–1925—Political and social views.
    3. Faulkner, William, 1897–1962—Political and social views.
    4. Twain, Mark, 1835–1910—Political and social views.   5. American
    fiction—White authors—History and criticism.   6. National
    characteristics, American, in literature.   7. American fiction—West
    Indian influences.   8. Southern States—In literature.   9. Afro-
    Americans in literature.   10. Race relations in literature.
    11. Racism in literature.   I. Title.   II. Series.
    PS261.L33   1996
    810.9'975—dc20   96-21711
                                                            CIP

Grateful acknowledgment is made to the Manuscripts Department, How-
ard-Tilton Memorial Library, Tulane University, New Orleans, La., for per-
mission to publish excerpts from Robert Underwood Johnson's letters to
George W. Cable in the George Washington Cable Collection. Portions of
Chapter 2 were first published as "'An Atmosphere of Hints and Allusions':
Bras-Coupé and the Context of Black Insurrection in *The Grandissimes*,"
Southern Quarterly, XXIX (Spring, 1991), 63–76. Portions of Chapter 4 were
first published as "'The Direction of the Howling': Nationalism and the
Color Line in *Absalom, Absalom!*," *American Literature*, LXVI (1994), 525–51,
copyright by Duke University Press, and are reproduced by permission.

In time they could not even locate the
direction any more of the howling.

—*Absalom, Absalom!*

CONTENTS

Preface

The idea of nationalism has been of fundamental importance in the construction of history in the modern world. In fact, one scholar has called it "the pathology of modern developmental history." Not everyone is so condemning. Ernest Gellner—always critical of the widespread belief in the "naturalness" and inevitability of nationalism—defines it straightforwardly as "the political principle which holds that the political and the national unit should be congruent." It is considerably easier, however, to define *nationalism* than to define or delineate the boundaries of the "nation," upon which the principle depends. The most famous definition may be Joseph Stalin's: "A nation is a historically-evolved, stable community of language, territory, economic life, and psychological make-up manifested in a community of culture." This definition is not the most reliable. Like most, it raises a number of questions—about the nature of a "community" (of "language" or of "culture"), or of a "territory" (which might be geographical, temporal, or even illusory). There is also some disagreement about whether a nation is better described as "historically-evolved" (which it is) or as "pre-historical" in origin (which it also is). Can one choose one's nation? For many statists, the answer is yes: nationality is "a status freely chosen, *de jure*, by the individual who has reached the age of majority, and on behalf of minors, by their legal representatives." For others, however, the nation has more in common with systems of kinship and religion than with the state and is marked by its fatality. In other words, one cannot choose a nation to be born in, although most modern nation-states do have methods for naturalization. Benedict Anderson defines the nation as "an imagined political community . . . imagined as both limited and sovereign" and agrees with Gellner and others that many modern "nations" are constructions of "nationalism," not vice versa.[1]

Anderson's definition is the most useful for the purposes of this study, which explores the impact of postbellum United States nationalism upon three U.S. writers often classified as "southern" (a classification none of them properly "chose")—and therefore assumed to be somewhat less than, or at least *other* than, "representative" of the most "national" qualities of the United States (it being considered by most literary historians a *good* thing to be more or less representative of one's nation, and essential to the proper determination of a writer's place in literary history).

I hope to suggest that there is a problem here, not so much with the representativeness of any or all of these writers as with the fact that the United States has been conceptualized (misconceptualized, I think) as "a" nation, when in fact the modern nation-state—and, certainly, *this* one—is made up of many nations (geographical, temporal, and illusory); it is not so much a stable community of culture or language as protean, in process. A century ago, Ernest Renan defined the nation as "a continued plebiscitum."[2] Since that time the linguistic and cultural, like the economic, boundaries between nations have become even more shifting, each day's (or moment's) plebiscite the outcome of the voting of different constituencies, or a differently constituted constituency.

In this study I argue that the work of George W. Cable, Mark Twain, and William Faulkner explores the tensions associated with the return of the South to a more nationalistic, deeply racist, and increasingly imperialistic United States in the half century following Reconstruction. Writers like these, aware of the implications of defeat in a nationalistic

---

1. Tom Nairn, *The Break-Up of Britain: Crisis and Neo-Nationalism* (London, 1977), 359; Ernest Gellner, *Nations and Nationalism* (Ithaca, 1983), 1, 8 (Stalin quote); Karl Renner, quoted in E. J. Hobsbawm, *Nations and Nationalism Since 1780: Programme, Myth, Reality* (New York, 1990), 7; Benedict Anderson, *Imagined Communities: Reflections on the Origin and Spread of Nationalism* (Rev. ed.; New York, 1983), 6.

2. Ernest Renan, "What Is a Nation?," trans. E. J. Leonard, in *Cyclopedia of Political Science, Political Economy, and of the Political History of the United States,* ed. John J. Lalor (Chicago, 1883), II, 929.

culture, which sees itself as redemptive, as the vanguard of progress, have constructed the South as dangerous territory—a kind of national "id" (to state the case too strongly). In their work the relationship of the southerner (who is often not only an agent for the defeated South but also an ironically "representative" American to the extent that all Americans *experience* identity as divided whatever their ideologies dictate) to the ideal of progressive and redemptive nationalism can range from cynical or self-doubting resistance to unreflective dedication. In any case, the South provides a powerful site for the critique of U.S. nationalism in the work of white southern writers.

The power of the South and the southern author to challenge the ideology of nationalism is apparent in the ways these writers construct the South's relationship with Europe and, for two of them—George W. Cable and William Faulkner—particularly in the ways they construct the South's relationship with European slave colonies and their creole offspring throughout the Caribbean. The relationship of the United States to a declining European empire was of particular interest to many American writers in the years following the Civil War. But the southern writer's construction and use of that relationship is very different from Henry James's, Constance Fenimore Woolson's, Edith Wharton's, or the work of any number of other emigrés from the northeast and mid-Atlantic areas of the United States, many of whom were no less troubled than the white southerner by the implications of U.S. nationalism. The most obvious difference is that the American Innocent Abroad was seldom represented as southern, even by the southern author. The southerner was more likely to be constructed as an agent for decadence in the New World than as a representative of American Innocence in the Old. (Basil Ransom of Henry James's *The Bostonians* is an example.) The postbellum southern author understood the United States differently—many have said more tragically—than others.

If the most immediate cause of this difference stems from the experience of southern secession and defeat in the Civil War, part also stems from the very different historical relationship between the southern states and Europe, and between southern states and creole slave colonies in the New World. The vast Louisiana Territory was ceded to the United States by France only in 1803, a little more than fifty years prior to the Civil War. The legacies of French and Spanish colonialist cultures remained strong throughout the nineteenth century (and still

remain) in the Deep South and down the Mississippi along what has
been called the "French Arch," which extends from "Quebec, along the
St. Lawrence, through the Great Lakes and the various tributaries of
the Ohio, Illinois, and Wisconsin river systems, then down the Mississippi to New Orleans," and links Canada with the Deep South.[3]

My argument is complicated by the fact that I am attempting to
comprehend the very complex relationship of the South (with its more
intricate historical and ideological ties to Europe and to colonialist slave
cultures) to the post–Civil War United States by focusing on differences
between colonialist and nationalistic policies with respect to the relationship among the races in the New World. For example, colonialist
governments encouraged a policy of assimilation between their own
agents (explorers, landholders, trappers, and so on) and other populations on the frontier. This policy forged cultural ties between the distant metropole and colonized populations, and presumably made governing those populations easier.[4] On the other hand, U.S. nationalism
(like most, but not all, nationalisms) discouraged the assimilation of
slave and indigenous populations and, after the cession of Louisiana
in 1803, enforced an increasingly intense policy of segregation throughout the Deep South and along the western frontier. (There is no superiority assumed here of "assimilation" or "segregation." Although the
policies were different, both were underwritten by racism, and either
one could work to liberate or to oppress, depending on the context.)
The reasons for the difference can be traced to the ideology of U.S.
nationalism itself, which is founded on ideals of cultural (which has
been understood in some eras as racial) homogeneity as a condition of
unity. In a racist and xenophobic culture, the creation of a "creole" caste
makes sense only when a region is defined as a colony, or a borderland.
When a nationalistic United States expands its own territory into what
used to be a "colony," when it pushes back the frontier, the creole caste
has to be either assimilated completely by the national culture or dis-

---

3. Arnold R. Hirsch and Joseph Logsdon, eds., *Creole New Orleans: Race and Americanization* (Baton Rouge, 1992), 6.

4. I say "presumably" because of the fact that New World revolutions were largely
creole revolutions, which suggests that the formation of an identity as "Creole" (or "born
in the colony," without any necessary racial designation) fostered independence movements. See Benedict Anderson's analysis in *Imagined Communities*, 47–65.

placed in order to preserve the integrity/unity/homogeneity of the nation, which supposedly comprises the state.

Slaveholding cultures in the Deep South from 1803 forward produced complex responses to the dual traditions of colonialist assimilation and nationalist segregation. The anxiety during the 1830s and again in the 1850s about the threat to slavery represented by free blacks (who in the Deep South were largely Creoles of mixed white and black ancestry) stems in part from the reality of assimilationist, or colonialist, legacies in a nationalistic culture. Creoles of color had owned property (including slaves), possessed certain rights of inheritance, and claimed legitimacy through a white European ancestry; they were encouraged, by government representatives from the homeland if not by white Creoles themselves, to "aspire" to the status of white Creoles. Governor William C. C. Claiborne struggled with the contradictions between this reality and official U.S. policy for a number of years in Louisiana before persons of mixed ancestry were "redefined" as part of the black or "slave" race during the 1830s.

It is significant that so many white southern writers of British descent have used this particular geographical site and this historical moment—the moment of the confrontation between nationalistic *Américains* and colonialist Creoles or European immigrants—to explore the anxieties associated with the return of the southern WASP to the Union after the Civil War. In so much of the literature of the late nineteenth century, the southerner is constructed as "Creole," the racial ambiguity of the term denied as whites insist that, when capitalized, the word refers only to "a white person born in the New World of French or Spanish ancestry," and the plot defined around the question of creole assimilation to the nationalistic mission of the United States. One sees evidence not only in the work of George W. Cable but also in novels and short stories written by many other Deep South writers (Grace King, Marion Baker, Kate Chopin, and others, including William Faulkner). But if the white southerner's insistence that "Creoles" are "white"—and only "creoles" (lowercase) are mixed—is intended to protect the southerner from being aligned too closely with former slaves or with colonialism in the New World, the creole metaphor also marks the southerner as a dangerous border figure, someone who might look like an American and claim to be so (with greater fervor than other Americans at times) but who carries within him- or herself traces of the displaced and who might at some point act traitorously to undermine the progressive nation. In the same way that the existence of an intermediate "black Creole" class that linked black and white and red populations undermined the U.S. policy of racial segregation, the existence of even a "white Creole" population undermined U.S. nationalism insofar as it represented an intermediate stage between European "encroachment" in the New World and the development of a New World nationalism on British foundations.

In short, all three of the authors I am studying—Cable in *The Grandissimes,* William Faulkner in *Light in August* and *Absalom, Absalom!,* and even Mark Twain in *Pudd'nhead Wilson and Those Extraordinary Twins*—are engaged in an effort to uncover the cultural implications, specifically for the southern author, of the legacy of French and Spanish colonialism in the Deep South and along the Mississippi River. It may be surprising that I have included Mark Twain in this study, but he, too, is engaged with questions raised by race- and nation-mixing on the frontier, although he is certainly more interested in the border communities associated with the frontier sections of the French Arch than in the cultivated Creole. Both he and Cable are concurrently engaged in a related—but very different—exploration of the impact of the failure of the official assimilationist ideal of Reconstruction upon the United States (and upon the southerner). If, as I argue, after the cession of Louisiana to the United States, the Deep South and Mississippi River areas were the chief sites of a deeply embedded cultural conflict between a nationalist principle of segregation and a colonialist principle of assimilation, these postbellum southern authors appropriated this conflict as a means to explore their own complicated literary situations in the increasingly nationalistic United States.

I am not, like Benedict Anderson, whose book *Imagined Communities* has been so important to my study, a political theorist, nor am I a historian like Winthrop Jordan, Joel Williamson, or so many of the scholars to whom I am indebted, and I am certainly no literary theorist. I am a reader of literary texts and propose to read some literary texts in what I hope is a useful way. My approach, which is not political in any narrow sense of the term, nevertheless attempts to engage the political imaginations—or to engage the literary imaginations politically—of three white southern authors, who are very different kinds of writers, writing after the end of the Civil War. But the implications of this approach are more broadly psychopolitical or psychocultural to the extent that I am chiefly interested in the intersections between political history (particularly with respect to ideas of race and nationalism in the United States), constructions of identity, and questions of literary form or coherence. Furthermore, I shall not be as interested in the polemical statements made by any of these authors as in their "literary" statements. I choose to focus on the literature rather than on essays or interviews or other forms of discourse because of the fascinating complexities of the cultural work that literature does. The essay or opinion or position or endorsement made by a literary figure may be interesting and may even illuminate a work of dramatic (or literary) narrative, but the capacity of dramatic prose narrative, chiefly the novel, to function as an arena or a field for the dramatization of conflict and change, to formalize and to transfigure what has been variously described as dissonance, difference, indeterminacy, or polyphony is vastly greater. Hence my focus on the novel and on the ways the story of its composition (its drafts and revisions) or the composition of its stories by various tellers emerge as distinct kinds of language in which one might read and interpret the ideological voices and voicings of the text. "Political readings" of literature (and of anything else) often beg the very questions the "literary" produces. I like the way Dominick LaCapra puts it:

> The great temptation in recent "political" readings has been to interpret all cultural artifacts predominantly if not exclusively as symptomatic expressions of dominant discourses and historical pressures and to mention forces that question or contest these discourses and pressures only en passant (if at all). Hence "realism" may be taken as symptomatic of early market capitalism, "high modernism" of imperialism, and "postmodernism" or "poststructuralism" of contemporary consumer, multinational capitalism. The problem in this kind of approach—aside from the fact that it pours seemingly new wine into decidedly old bottles—is the replication of a dominant, indeed an imperial and domesticating discourse in what may be intended to be a critique of it.[5]

On the other hand, it sometimes seems that the hermeneutics of contestation—otherwise known as "oppositional criticism" or "the school

5. Dominick LaCapra, *History, Politics, and the Novel* (Ithaca, 1987), 2.

of subversion"—has constructed all American literature (all worth reading) and all American writers (worth reading) as "subversive," and necessarily liberating. The reality is more complex. Literature is not always subversive; and subversion can be the very opposite of liberating. Recently, Sacvan Bercovitch has suggested that "the classic American authors . . . were imaginatively nourished by the culture, even when they were politically opposed to it."[6] I should like to borrow this idea for the purposes of this project because it underscores what I believe to be a truth too often ignored: these "southern" authors, for all their resistance to ahistorical American nationalism, for all their renegade "pessimism," for all their engagement with what one critic refers to as "doubled, divided, and crossed selves," are paradoxically "representative" of the complex experience (if not always the ideology) of the United States. Where nationalism is subverted in their work, it is often subverted in the service of a more inclusive, more viable, humanism that many practitioners of oppositional criticism would find objectionable. I have tried, throughout this study, neither to deify nor to demonize the writer or the literature. The writers I discuss here were critics of racism, but they were also racist; they were critics of U.S. nationalism, but they were also—at particular moments and within particular discursive contexts—committed to U.S. nationalism. They were deeply aware of the divisions and crossings and fragmentations of identity in the United States, and if they sometimes embraced the improvisational or the expedient or the subversive as liberating, they sometimes feared it and sought the kind of wholeness and autonomy promised by nationalist ideology.

The method of the study is broadly New Historicist. I am not, like traditional historicist critics, a believer in the transparent referent. This study will consequently be less focused on the putative "event" of history than on the construction and reconstruction of the event. I read literature historically, but with the New Historicist's stronger sense of the constructedness of history as of literature, of its appropriation by the present, than traditional historical critics.[7] Nor does my historicism

6. Sacvan Bercovitch, *The Rites of Assent: Transformations in the Symbolic Construction of America* (New York, 1993), 16.

7. Stephen Greenblatt has defined anthropological literary criticism, or his brand of New Historicism, as concerned with "the interpretive constructions the members of a society apply to their experience" because the literary text exists as "part of the system

derive from Hegelian ideas of history as progressive. In fact, one of the objects of this study is the conflict between a faith in historical development (exhibited by nationalisms everywhere) and challenges to that faith. My leanings are, therefore, more toward Michel Foucault, for whom "evolution" is less compelling a trope for history than "disjunction."[8]

Following Bakhtin, I claim that novels are polyphonic and dialogic, not necessarily dialectic. I am interested in this work in the gaps, the interruptions, the incoherences, the juxtapositions of seemingly disparate narratives for what they reveal in the form of counternarratives or countermemories. For a writer like Cable, wrenched from romantic historiography to dramatic fiction by a genteel aesthetics that sought transcendence of the local by the universal, the gaps are strategic whispers to the reader of the truth of racial division and racial violence that lay beneath the romance of white reconciliation. For Mark Twain, these gaps, in texts like *Pudd'nhead Wilson and Those Extraordinary Twins*, function to much the same purpose, although with the added dimension of literary experimentation with narrative form and structure to explore the frontiers of identity (for I do believe that Mark Twain's late works are experimental, even if somewhat less than entirely successful) in the service of reconceptualizations of racial, sexual, and national identities. And for William Faulkner, issues of narrative incoherence become central to stories of racial, sexual, and national identity with respect to form and to theme, to his vision of the nature of narrative and its relationship to the construction of the subject.

---

of signs that constitutes a given culture." See Stephen Greenblatt, *Renaissance Self-Fashioning: From More to Shakespeare* (Chicago, 1980), 4.

8. Michel Foucault, *L'ordre du discours* (Paris, 1971), 58; Alan Sheridan, *Michel Foucault: The Will to Truth* (London, 1980), 129.

ACKNOWLEDGMENTS

I have incurred a number of debts during the years I have been working on this book. My work has been greatly facilitated by research grants from the Emory University Research Committee. A summer grant enabled me to travel to a number of library collections; and another grant reduced my teaching load during one year, giving me much-needed time to write. Walter Menerey and his staff in the special collections department at Tulane University have provided much assistance, as have the librarians at Columbia, Princeton, and Harvard, where I spent time researching this project. I first became interested in the impact of Deep South and Caribbean history on William Faulkner in a course taught by Evan Carton at the University of Texas at Austin. Louis D. Rubin, Jr., has helped me in ways too numerous to name. His scholarly and critical work has been invaluable; his example has been inspiring. Everett Emerson has supported and encouraged me throughout the writing of this book, not least by inviting me to housesit for Hillary, Khatmandu, and the roses—and to use his study—while he and Katherine were in Italy. Anne Jones's criticism helped me to clarify many ideas, and her enthusiasm kept me inspired during a very busy season. The comments of those anonymous readers who were invited by Emory to read a draft of the manuscript were of great help to me in the final stages. As will be immediately apparent, the work of Lewis Simpson and Eric Sundquist, different as it is, has been of great importance to the project.

Nationalism and the Color Line in George W. Cable, Mark Twain, and William Faulkner

1

Race and National Identity in the Work of White Writers

" ... died in the blood ... "
—Edward Williams
Virginia, More Especially the South Part Thereof, Richly and Truly Valued (1650)

The man of mixed blood is among the most intriguing figures in U.S. literature, where he has appeared less frequently than his sister, at least in the work of white writers.[1] Everyone is familiar with the female version: beautiful, accomplished, vulnerable, a tragic kind of American geisha.[2] However idealized this

---

1. African American writers have used the figure of the man of mixed blood often, and in ways very different from those devised by white writers. In the work of Frederick Douglass, Harriet Jacobs, Frances E. W. Harper, Pauline Hopkins, Charles Chesnutt, Jean Toomer, Zora Neale Hurston, Ralph Ellison, Toni Morrison, Alice Walker, and many others, the man of mixed blood figures prominently and hardly resembles white creations like the dark Honoré Grandissime or Charles Bon. Certainly, in African American literature as in Anglo-American literature, the octoroon is an alienated figure. But in much African American literature, he or she is also an index of racial progress, and the drama often moves the character from an alienated condition to an identification with and commitment to the African American community. One has only to think of Charles Chesnutt's "The Wife of His Youth" and *The Marrow of Tradition,* or Frances E. W. Harper's *Iola Leroy.* For a good discussion of the use of the mixed-blood figure in African American literature, see Dickson D. Bruce, Jr., *Black American Writing from the Nadir: The Evolution of a Literary Tradition, 1877–1915* (Baton Rouge, 1989), 11–55.

2. The terminology used in the Deep South and West Indies to classify people of mixed racial ancestry according to the percentage of African "blood" is elaborate: there are recognized differences in status between mulattoes, quadroons, and octoroons. In contrast, in the Upper South and throughout the rest of the United States, the word *mulatto* can function as a catch-all term reflecting the legal traditions of the United States,

legend—and a number of writers (as well as their critics) hardly acknowledge it as anything but the strictest realism—she has exerted a real imaginative hold on the minds of white Americans, for obvious reasons. In the literature of abolition, as well as in historical novels written long after emancipation, she is usually a virtuous and beautiful young woman, with connections to "aristocracy" through her white father, and sometimes through her African mother as well, virtually indistinguishable from the idealized white heroines of any number of Victorian romances except that in the one detail—her legal status as slave—she becomes vulnerable to sexual injustice in a way the white heroines never are vulnerable. The figure of Cassy in Harriet Beecher Stowe's *Uncle Tom's Cabin* is perhaps the best-known example of the character, but she appears as a central figure (if not the protagonist) in most abolitionist novels. According to many commentators she was the best fuel antislavery writers had for igniting public sentiment against slavery.

The fact remains that readers of U.S. literature have yet to devote much of their attention to the man of mixed blood. Jules Zanger describes the "tragic octoroon" as "a beautiful young *girl*." Sterling Brown does the same. The white reader's "favorite character" is "wretched because of the 'single drop of midnight in her veins,' [and] desires a white lover above all else. For this she 'must go down to a tragic end.'"[3] It may well be that the male octoroon is simply more disturbing in some ways, or more disturbing in particular ways, because of the more explicit challenge he makes to cultural and political legitimacy in a society that restricts women from direct participation in many of its institutions. In any case, the tendency to describe the "tragic octoroon" as female has led scholars to attempt to define the male octoroon, where he does appear, in similar terms: in terms of his romantic or sexual inclinations with respect to white women; in terms of the sexuality and emotionalism whites associate with Africa as it figures in the work of white Americans. Scholars tend to treat the male octoroon in one of

which classifies people as either black or white. In this study, I use the word *octoroon* (strictly speaking, a person with one-eighth African ancestry) to refer to any figure who is described in a literary text as being "deceptively" white.

3. Jules Zanger, "The Tragic Octoroon in Pre–Civil War Fiction," *American Quarterly*, XVIII (Spring, 1966), 63. Italics mine. Sterling Brown, *The Negro in American Fiction* (Washington, D.C., 1937), 144.

two ways—as a sterile or sexually ambiguous figure or as the sign of uncontrolled sexual impulse, and they often perceive him as a representation of white sexual anxieties.[4] Such logic, based as it is on a psychological methodology, may indeed contain a great deal of truth, but it is also a curious distortion of the paradigms of gender as they determine the construction of political and economic roles in the post–Civil War South (and just about everywhere else), where sex never exists independently of politics, where masculinity (as well as femininity) is defined in terms of political and economic entitlements and disentitlements of certain kinds, where rights to own land and to govern are inseparable from certain sexual rights, and fundamentally, where the figure of sexual transgression, especially across racial lines, serves as a sign of frightening political and economic upheaval.

The renowned bestiality of the man of mixed blood is best illustrated

4. The miscegenation story has been read as the American equivalent of the European story of lovers doomed by class differences, as a means for exploring "the archetypal theme of guilt and resolution" or, less often, as a tool for exploring existentialist themes of metaphysical alienation. See William Bedford Clark, "Cable and the Theme of Miscegenation in *Old Creole Days* and *The Grandissimes*," *Mississippi Quarterly*, XXX (Fall, 1977), 598; and Judith Berzon, *Neither White Nor Black: The Mulatto Character in American Fiction* (New York, 1978), 122. Others look for political or moral reasons: James Kinney claims that the miscegenation story written after the Civil War serves as much to focus the white reader's attention on the plight of black Americans as the pre–Civil War instance served to argue on behalf of abolition or in some cases to serve as proslavery propaganda. See his *Amalgamation! Race, Sex, and Rhetoric in the Nineteenth-Century American Novel* (Westport, 1985), 20. Jules Zanger is more interested in the psychocultural plight of the northern white reader, asserting that the story of the tragic octoroon appeals to the northern reader's sense of moral superiority, and points out that the interesting displacement of culpability from the aristocratic southerner to a brutal working-class overseer over whom he has no control is an index of the subversive appeal of the aristocratic southerner for those readers (63–68). At any rate, most scholars seem to agree that the sufferings of a nearly white character elicit among white readers an awareness of common human bonds; whether those common human bonds are tightened and twisted in the service of political, moral, or philosophical messages is, however, a matter of some disagreement.

See George Fredrickson's *The Black Image in the White Mind* (New York, 1971), where he discusses the determination among whites to see Africa as site of "licentiousness" and Africans as "the original Sodomites of the old Testament," savage "beasts" who desired white women above all else (276). See also Joel Kovel, *White Racism: A Psychohistory* (New York, 1970); and Lawrence J. Friedman, *The White Savage: Racial Fantasies in the Postbellum South* (Englewood Cliffs, N.J., 1970).

with references to certain overtly racist Reconstruction novels written by the likes of Thomas Dixon, Jr., and Robert Lee Durham. There is no question that in the work of these writers he has been characterized by an inclination to sexual excess and violence associated with images of "African" savagery, his white skin nothing more than a mask to hide the destructive fires associated with the heavily sexualized "dark continent," a place that ostensibly exists prior to history and political order. But as Joel Williamson points out, Dixon and Durham were men of their time—the late 1880s and the 1890s, when a particular political and economic order was supposedly threatened by the demands of African Americans for property and political rights and when actual sexual threats to white women were very few indeed. What did happen during the 1890s was the removal of black men from farms and from their families, as Whitecaps in the Deep South became more determined to possess the valuable land farmed by black tenants. A generation of black wanderers, unfamiliar men who turned up in towns and cities looking for work, was the most immediate consequence; and their presence aggravated the insecurities of white people in economic trouble. Not surprisingly, it was this decade that saw the creation of the "black beast" in fiction and rhetoric, as well as the rise of radical racist doctrines of the African American as sexual savage. Prior to this decade, the fear of African Americans had centered on the possibility of insurrection and murder.[5]

In U.S. literary history, the figure of the mulatto is one of the white writer's best tools for exploring the pressing issue of his own political identity, his own capacity for assimilation to a national ideal, particularly where the figure exhibits little or no physiological evidence of African ancestry. The earliest example of this use of the figure is found in a work by a Frenchman, Gustave de Beaumont. *Marie, ou l'Esclavage aux Etats-Unis: Tableau de moeurs américaines*, a little-known book first published in France in 1835, is interesting for this study because of the way it makes clear (from a French point of view) some of the most important differences between colonialist France and the nationalistic United States with respect to policies of racial assimilation versus segregation.

5. Joel Williamson, *The Crucible of Race: Black-White Relations in the American South Since Emancipation* (New York, 1984), 80–84.

During 1831, Beaumont traveled with his more famous friend Alexis de Tocqueville through the United States. His trip was prompted by the July Revolution of 1830 in France, a revolution that made the liberal Louis Philippe, formerly duc d'Orléans, a constitutional monarch. Beaumont, the son of French aristocrats, was split between his loyalty to his family and friends and his faith in the liberal-democratic cause. To avoid (or to displace) the conflict and to serve his country, he and Tocqueville came to the United States to study the politics, the manners, the customs—and the prison system. Alexis de Tocqueville produced from this nine-month trip the classic *Democracy in America;* Beaumont produced the less well-known work that would be translated as *Marie, or Slavery in the United States: A Novel of Jacksonian America.*

Although the French had written previously of U.S. slavery, this was, in Jean Fagan Yellin's assessment, "the first such novel based on direct observations of American life."[6] It is composed of the recounting, by one disillusioned Frenchman, Ludovic, to the traveler Beaumont who is enthusiastic about the new country he is exploring, the story of Ludovic's tragic romance with the beautiful Marie, daughter of an American Puritan and a Spanish creole woman who is discovered to have had a mulatto great-grandparent; this means that she, the mother, is an octoroon. Marie, of course, is only one-sixteenth black. Despite the distance of the "taint," Ludovic makes it clear to his listener that Marie and her brother George, regardless of their gifts of intellect and character, cannot escape the nationalist ideology of race that ties them and their descendants permanently to the slave caste. Their own father, a white American Puritan and patriot of the first degree, instills into them a sense of the tragic nature of their birth.

This Puritan paterfamilias, Daniel Nelson, is unflinching in his adherence to the nationalist principles of racial homogeneity: "Your ardor" for Marie, he tells the outraged Ludovic, "leads you astray . . . beware of the consequences of a generous emotion. If you contemplated reality with a less prejudiced eye, you could not endure the sight, and you would realize that a white man can never marry a woman of color." "What, then," asks Ludovic, "is the origin, among a people exempt from prejudice and passion, of this false idea which makes a sin of

6. Jean Fagan Yellin, *The Intricate Knot: Black Figures in American Literature, 1776–1863* (New York, 1972), 89.

misfortune, and of this pitiless hatred which pursues a whole race of men from generation to generation?" Nelson responds:

> The black race is despised in America because it is a race of slaves; it is hated because it aspires to liberty.
>
> Common practice and law alike say the Negro is not a man, he is a thing.
>
> He is an article of trade, superior to other merchandise; a Negro is worth ten acres of well-cultivated land.
>
> For the slave, there is neither birth, marriage, or death.
>
> The child of a slave belongs to the slave's master, as the fruits of the soil belong to the owner of the land. The loves of a slave leave no more trace on society than does the breeding of plants on our gardens; and when he dies, the only thought is to replace him, as one replaces a fruitful tree destroyed by a storm. . . .
>
> The principle once admitted, these consequences follow: The child born in slavery knows no more of family life than does an animal. The maternal bosom nourishes him as the teat of the wild beast feeds her young. The touching relationships of mother with child, of child with father, of brother with sister, have neither sense nor moral value to him, and he does not marry, because, belonging to someone else, he cannot give himself to anyone.
>
> *Ludovic:* But why do not the American people, enlightened and religious, recoil in horror from an institution which offends the laws of nature, morality, and humanity? Are not all men created equal?
>
> *Nelson:* No people are more attached than we to the principles of equality; but we will not allow a race inferior to ours to share in our rights.

However oversimplified a portrayal of the U.S. sense of chattel slavery, this is a revealing debate between constitutionalism and the principles upon which consensus is established ("common practice and law alike") and a more Romantic conception of "laws of nature, morality, and humanity." It is a profound, and distorting, adherence to constitutionalism and consensus that the Frenchman attributes to the Anglo-American. And it is that Anglo-American constitutionalism that finally isolates Marie and George, who are given by the French author certain inherited traits that doom them to ostracism by Anglo-America. Even though Marie is—Ludovic tells us in horror—"American by reason of her mind," and lives "in the midst of a moral and religious world," she possesses "in her great dark eyes a flash of that ardent light which scorches the Antilles" and is elsewhere attributed with the qualities of Mediterranean cultures.[7] It is finally the French displacement from its North American holdings only twenty-five years prior to Beaumont's visit that offers the most revealing context for the depiction of the octoroon heroine as a particularly "European" figure, a depiction that will continue in the work of U.S. writers and becomes particularly useful to southern white writers of the post–Civil War era, when issues of the white southerner's own capacity for U.S. citizenship were of great interest. It is the conflict between European Romanticism and Anglo-American "common practice and law alike" that creates the tragedy of *Marie*.

Marie internalizes the principles of U.S. redemptive nationalism. Beaumont defines her as a complicitous victim of the ideology that would make of her a pariah. Her sense of the "taint" is religious, metaphysical, to be atoned for through sacrifice and service to the poor and the outcast. She works at the Baltimore Almshouse.

Her brother is not so resigned. George Nelson is twenty when we first meet him, a young man who "bore upon his lofty brow the mark of a firm and noble character," a young man whose "upright soul revealed itself through the frankness of his gaze." He and the narrator Ludovic become fast friends. It soon becomes apparent that George Nelson is truly heroic, determined to own his heritage and to fight for the lives and the political viability of those whom the nationalistic U.S. government would displace: the Cherokees removed by political machinations to Michigan from their lands in Georgia, the Ottawas, the men of mixed blood like himself, and the African slaves of the southern states. The outcome is tragic, of course: George dies working among African and Native American insurrectionists in the West. In a letter to his Puritan father he asserts, "I do not know if my blood is tainted, but I am sure of the purity of my heart." Marie, who has followed her brother, dies as well, leaving her devoted Ludovic to mourn at her tomb, unable to follow the advice of a priest to return to France, for that is a "sacrifice beyond [his] strength. As long as one drop of blood flows in [Ludovic's] veins, it will feed [his] sorrow."[8]

7. Gustave de Beaumont, *Marie, or Slavery in the United States: A Novel of Jacksonian America*, trans. Barbara Chapman (Stanford, 1958), 57–58, 41. All subsequent citations are to this edition.

8. *Ibid.*, 32, 171, 179.

The Frenchman undergoes a great deal of conflict during the course of the narrative between his more Romantic ideals of "liberté, egalité, fraternité" and the reality of "common practice and law alike" in the United States. Initially, he joins his friend Nelson in attempting to "teach the Indians the principles which are the bases of all civilized societies . . . the advantages of an agricultural life, the benefits derived from the industrial arts," but he soon becomes aware that his Catholicism is not compatible with Nelson's Presbyterianism and searches out a Catholic priest for guidance. Soon disillusioned (characteristically) by "the pettiness in [the priest's] greatness," Ludovic pursues the political life, only to be disappointed once again by the discrepancy between claims and realities. At last he reaches the understanding he seeks:

> Through having lived so long outside society, I had become unfitted for it, and my imagination had for so long fed on dreams of an ideal perfection that it could no longer enter upon the ordinary paths of humanity. I bore the yoke of habit, despicable and powerful. . . .
>
> A very short time sufficed to show me that the sickness within me was without remedy; I did not persist in fighting it: I recognized its extent and submitted. Without passion, without despair, I returned to this wilderness, the only place which suited my state of mind. I could live no longer among men; and this solitude offered my heart at least the interest of my most grievous memory, and also the dearest of my life.
>
> Now I present the strange spectacle of a man who has fled the world without hating it, and who, though retired into the wilderness, never ceases to think of his fellow men, whom he loves, and far from whom he is forced to live. It is very sad to feel the need of society, and to have had the unhappy experience of being unable to live in it. The chief source of all my errors was my belief that man is greater than he is.

The import of Ludovic's final understanding is that Beaumont, his listener, returns to his "dear fatherland" prepared to accept the less-than-ideal conditions of that world. The author-auditor, who began his journey in an attempt to escape the conflict between his emotional ties to his aristocratic family and friends and his commitment to the principles of equality, ends by comprehending (as the French reader is supposed to comprehend) the delusion produced by New World nationalism (the delusion of an autonomous and unified self, at home in a world defined as "new" or without history), the delusion of "seeking [in the United States] a *country* which might make me happy."[9]

9. *Ibid.,* 182–85, 187, 12–13. Italics mine.

Here, in a story by a French traveler in the United States, lies the germ of the idea that would continue to define the mixed blood in U.S. literature: the idea of the figure as carrying, within himself or herself, the repressed history associated with the establishment of the nationalistic United States in the New World, "repressed" because the United States did not in fact establish itself in any virgin wilderness but on a continent trodden by many different peoples, by Native Americans, by Africans, by colonists from France and Spain, and by their creole descendants. As the bearer of that history—the one who, in the words of Quentin Compson, "owns the terror"—the mixed blood enacts the conflicts through which the white and southern observer defines himself and his relationship to the American project; Faulkner would use the word *design*.[10]

"Louisiana to-day is Paradise Lost. In twenty years it may be Paradise Regained. . . . It is the battle of race with race, of the picturesque and unjust civilization of the past with the prosaic and leveling civilization of the present." With these lines, Edward King began "The Great South," a series of essays commissioned in 1873 by *Scribner's Monthly Magazine*, edited by Dr. Josiah Holland and devoted to the fostering of greater understanding between white persons north and south. As Louis D. Rubin, Jr., observes, King's series on the South was instrumental in setting the stage for "the final abandonment of Reconstruction" and the return of political authority in the South to the southern white man.[11] At this point (toward the end of Reconstruction), there was unfortunately a waning of national interest in the condition and the future of the African American. Within this context, the implications for the white South of King's opening lines are supposed to be optimistic. But the principle that underlay the construction of New Orleans

10. Throughout most of this study I have used the masculine pronoun, not out of any acceptance of the idea that it is inclusive of both male and female (which it is not), but as a means to underscore the reality that it is the enfranchised male, the politically and economically empowered male, whose identity is most directly at issue in all of these texts. The relationship of the white southern woman (or the white American woman or black woman) to race and to nationalism is very different. Rather than obscure this reality by using gender-neutral language, I choose to acknowledge it.

11. Edward King, *The Great South*, ed. W. Magruder Drake and Robert R. Jones (Baton Rouge, 1972), 17; Louis D. Rubin, Jr., *George W. Cable: The Life and Times of a Southern Heretic* (New York, 1969), 14–17.

(and the South) as a "paradise lost" that might be regained is the old one that pits the American nation against the senility of Europe and the savagery of Africa in a battle of the forces of progress against those of degeneration and decadence. According to the principle of U.S. self-definition, the United States—as culmination of British political and cultural development—possesses a redemptive power through which the tragedies of history might be transcended; and the focus of U.S. efforts in the years following the Civil War was the American South, where the residue of history and magnificent opportunities for uplift lay very close to hand. Any such construct bears trouble in its wake. The impact of this nationalistic ethos upon the South, and upon both African American and Anglo-American, was (and remains) complex.

The "Great South" series ran in *Scribner's* from November, 1873, to December, 1874, with a final installment in April, 1875. At its close, Dr. Holland wrote happily that King had "spread before the nation the wonderful natural resources, the social condition, and the political complications of a region which needs but just, wise, and generous legislation, with corresponding goodwill and industry, to make it a garden of happiness and prosperity." [12]

Perhaps, but Dr. Holland may have been too optimistic. If the rhetoric of southern redemption makes it clear that there is no place in the garden of the U.S. future for the former slave, except as menial, the place imagined for the white southerner is equally, if differently, problematic. Behind the rhetoric of the defeated South as potential "garden of happiness and prosperity" lay the related (and deeply seated) fear, on the part of southerners as well as northerners, of a southern moral wilderness that might be beyond reclamation and might, in fact, continue to threaten the integrity of the United States.

Such fears had been expressed as early as the beginning of British settlement in the New World. In comparison to the cold colonies to the North, Virginia was an Eden, represented to potential settlers in Britain as a New World paradise where little labor would be rewarded with great profits, where "your foot can hardly direct itself where it will not be died in the blood of large and delicious Strawberries." [13] As might

---

12. Paul H. Buck, *The Road to Reunion, 1865–1900* (Boston, 1937), 131–32.

13. Edward Williams, *Virginia, More Especially the South Part Thereof, Richly and Truly Valued,* in *Tracts and Other Papers Relating Principally to the Origin, Settlement, and Progress of the Colonies of North America,* ed. Peter Force (New York, 1947), III, n.p.

be expected, southerners were soon saddled with a reputation for laziness. And implicit in laziness, as all good Puritans know, is moral degeneration and death both bodily and spiritual. The development of the South as a slave power in what was supposed to be a redemptive New World paradise did not help matters, either. By the Revolutionary era, Thomas Jefferson, southern slaveholder and revolutionary committed to what Lewis Simpson terms "the polity of the free mind,"[14] was himself expressing some doubts concerning the capacities of slaveholders, used to wielding power despotically, to attain the sense of an autonomous and free self required for maintaining a republican form of government. In Query XVIII of *Notes on the State of Virginia*, Jefferson writes: "There must doubtless be an unhappy influence on the manners of our people produced by the existence of slavery among us. The whole commerce between master and slave is a perpetual exercise of the most boisterous passions, the most unremitting despotism on the one part, and degrading submissions on the other. Our children see this, and learn to imitate it. . . . The man must be a prodigy who can retain his manners and morals undepraved by such circumstances."[15]

The doubts revealed by Jefferson's *Notes on the State of Virginia* and other written work with reference to the capacity of the slaveholder for self-mastery offer a testimonial to Jefferson's consciousness of the experimental nature of the U.S. system and the very high stakes that accompanied the mission in the eyes of the young citizen who was not unaware of the dangers of breaking with time-honored hierarchies in order to champion human liberty.[16] Winthrop Jordan, in *White over Black: American Attitudes Toward the Negro, 1550–1812*, notes that there existed a general "feeling, which had [by Jefferson's day] been strengthening for more than a century, that the arrangement of society was becoming disorderly and rather the opposite of hierarchical." The new

14. Lewis Simpson, *Mind and the American Civil War: A Meditation on Lost Causes* (Baton Rouge, 1989), 14.

15. Thomas Jefferson, *Notes on the State of Virginia*, ed. William Peden (New York, 1972), 162. The subtitle of Beaumont's *Marie* is no mere irrelevancy. The degeneration, during the Jacksonian era, of the original Revolutionary ideals of individual self-sufficiency, restraint, personal moral and political agency, and the evolution of a more speculative, expansionist, and exploitative nationalism have everything to do with the Puritan father's racial discourse in the novel.

16. Simpson, *Mind and the American Civil War*, 1–32.

United States of America had provided a means for the subordinates of Britain to overturn a hierarchy buttressed by an ideology of the social order as governed by a "Great Chain of Being," a tradition inherited by the American revolutionary himself and one that would continue to influence the way the new citizen interacted with Europe and with Africa. Under the circumstances it should not be surprising that the insurrectionary Anglo-American might project his own fears about the consequences of social and political transgression upon the black slave, about whom he harbored deep suspicions anyway, suspicions that the darker skin of the African served as outward evidence of a spiritual and intellectual depravity.[17] The new citizen would, with respect to his own involvement with subordinated or marginalized groups, seek either to reconstitute what he perceived as a natural hierarchy or to excise the "disorderly" forces that could no longer be subordinated because of the republican ideology. Speaking very generally, the northern states opted for an ideology of nationalism, U.S. exceptionalism, and segregation; the southern states, economically dependent on slavery, opted for the attempted re-creation of a stable hierarchical order patterned to some extent on European models and which limited the claims of citizenship to white men.

The southerner—as committed to republican political ideology as the northerner—would never be entirely comfortable with his decision. He would continue to struggle with a conception of social order which, however expedient, led to the inevitable conclusion that his capacity for self-government, his capacity for redemption by the U.S. project, was undermined by his alliances with a subordinate and potentially insubordinate group of people who were held to possess, in conjunction with the human desire for liberty, a "contaminating" spiritual and intellectual depravity. In other words, the dependence of the U.S. slaveholder upon his slave became a source of his own degeneration.

Even though the origins of the idea of a barbaric and barbarizing South can be traced to the colonial period (and the impact of colonialism upon the image of the South ought not to be underestimated), the manifestation of the idea in the nineteenth century owes a great deal to the

17. Winthrop Jordan, *White over Black: American Attitudes Toward the Negro, 1550–1812* (New York, 1977), xiii, 216–65, 3–43.

rhetoric of the abolitionists and to the fundamental racism that coexisted with the opposition to slavery for most of these nineteenth-century white Americans. Charles Eliot Norton, who visited the South in 1855, expressed graver concerns about the moral effects of slaveholding on the slaveholders than he expressed about the effects of slavery on the slaves. In a review for the *Atlantic Monthly* a few years later, he describes the Deep South, those states bordered by the Gulf of Mexico, as "this new Africa" where the African "multiplies" and "the white man dwindles and decays" chiefly for reasons of climate. Of most concern to Norton, however, is the future of the free states of the Union. He quotes from the author of the book he is reviewing: "The predominant influence of the blacks in the Cotton States is already (even putting aside the results of slavery) exhibiting itself in a lowering of the whites"; and he clearly fears the dangerous proximity of "the mixed and degenerating population of the Slave country" to those free states with a small black population and supposedly greater industry and backbone.[18] Ralph Waldo Emerson articulated similar sentiments, yet with the important difference of greater Transcendentalist faith in the capacity of white men, that is, New England white men, to transcend slavery and its legacies. In 1853 he had written that "the secret, the esoterics of abolition—a secret, too, from the abolitionist,—is that the negro & the negro-holder are really of one party." Not long afterward he returned to the idea: the abolitionist, he writes, "thinks . . . that it is the negro in the white man which holds slaves. He attacks . . . slaveholders north & south generally, but because they are foremost negroes of the world, & fight the negro fight."[19] And of course some, like William Lloyd Garrison, advocated northern secession from the Union in order to preserve itself from dangerous contact with the slave power to the south.

18. Charles Eliot Norton, Review of *The Laws of Race, as Connected with Slavery*, by Sidney George Fisher, *Atlantic Monthly*, VII (February, 1861), 253–54.

19. Ralph Waldo Emerson, *The Journals and Miscellaneous Notebooks of Ralph Waldo Emerson*, ed. William H. Gilman *et al.* (16 vols.; Cambridge, Mass., 1960), XIII, 35, 198. After the war, as well, Emerson's reservations about the moral and intellectual capacities of the South remained in place. "Even the poor prisoners that starved & perished in the Libby & Andersonville prisons . . . [drew] out into the daylight the cruelty & malignity of the Southern people, & [showed] the corruption that slavery works on the community in which it exists" (*ibid.*, XV, 458).

There was one very prominent white abolitionist, however, who was not so convinced of the innate inferiority of persons of African or southern descent nor of the exceptionalism upon which U.S. nationalist ideology grew increasingly to rest, and whose understanding of individual and social life was deeply historical. Richard Hildreth, the nineteenth-century American historian who usually can be found in the margins of any discussion of George Bancroft, is the author of the first abolitionist novel produced in America by an American—*Archy Moore, the White Slave; or, Memoirs of a Fugitive,* a work that defined the genre as it was practiced by antislavery authors, at least up until the Civil War, and that placed the debate over the moral degeneration of the slaveholder within the context of the debate over U.S. exceptionalism and romantic nationalism.

Jean Fagan Yellin tells us that it was during a visit to Florida that Hildreth must have read both Gustave de Beaumont's *Marie* and Tocqueville's *Democracy in America,* and that *Archy Moore,* along with the companion polemic *Despotism in America,* were written by the time Hildreth returned to Boston a confirmed abolitionist. *Archy Moore* was taken for quite some time as an autobiographical work. Yet Richard Hildreth was a white descendant of a prominent New England family, trained as a lawyer. He was also a Whig in an era of Jacksonian Democracy—a political allegiance that accounts for a good deal of the conservative perspective on nationalism and on the evils of slavery that one finds in the novel. In particular, he was philosophically opposed to what he characterized in the introduction to his *History of the United States of America* as "romantic nationalism." Surely he meant to evoke George Bancroft, arguably the most popular historian of the United States during the nineteenth century, a Jacksonian Democrat who served under the Polk administration as secretary of the navy, a man who often employed the rhetoric of romantic nationalism in his own six-volume *History of the United States.* For Bancroft the Declaration of Independence was "the beginning of new ages" and the United States a "youthful nation" that had turned away from the corruptions of history and "with prophetic promise toward the boundless future." It is a familiar rhetoric, but Hildreth, more cautious, proposed in his history "to set forth the personages of our colonial and revolutionary history, *such as they really were in their own day and generation . . . with their faults as well as their virtues, their weaknesses as well as their strengths"* [italics added].[20] This was not a popular ideal during the era of nationalist chauvinism, and although Hildreth has been criticized by many contemporary historians for an inability to assimilate his material, to make it readable, one suspects that the problem is more than one of style, that Hildreth's conservative Whig vision was not congenial to the mid- and late nineteenth century, nor to our own.

Archy Moore, the hero of Hildreth's novel, is the illegitimate slave son of one of Virginia's most "aristocratic" planters, Thomas Moore, and is virtually indistinguishable from a white man. His hair is brown and curly, his eyes blue, his skin a shade or two darker than that of his white brothers. He is remarkable among his white siblings for his intellect, gentleness, and nobility of both mind and spirit. While he is still a young man living on his father's plantation, he marries his half sister (without his father's knowledge). When that father, who wants to set up his quadroon daughter as his own mistress, discovers that she is married to the slave son, he has the son beaten and sold to eliminate him as a rival. But through a series of lucky accidents, the son has received an education and can pass as a white man. Archy Moore sails for the Old World and ends up as a captain on a British ship during the War of 1812, where he distinguishes himself for valor and leadership. Eventually he takes up residence in London and twenty years later returns to the South as Archer Moore, a wealthy British citizen, to seek his quadroon wife Cassy and their son Montgomery. He finds everyone intact: his wife has apparently escaped sexual brutalization (although Hildreth's commitment to life-as-it-is may be the source of an interesting vagueness on this point), and his son has become a successful businessman in a New York countinghouse. With the help of a southern reprobate, the honest and good-hearted gambler Colter, the family escapes the clutches of slave dealers and treacherous Yankees to settle happily in London, where Archer Moore watches his five grandchildren grow up free and happy.[21]

This first treatment of a man of mixed blood by a U.S. antislavery

20. Yellin, *The Intricate Knot,* 101; George Bancroft, *The American Revolution* (Boston, 1874), 31–32, Vol. III of Bancroft, *History of the United States from the Discovery of the American Continent* (Boston, 1874); Richard Hildreth, *History of the United States of America* (New York, 1880), vii.

21. In W. D. Howells' *An Imperative Duty* (New York, 1892), the white husband takes his racially mixed wife to live in Europe to escape American racism.

writer does differ from the earlier one by Beaumont and later ones by white southerners in that here the man of color is the protagonist of the work and never shares that status with any white hero. Although he has two white brothers, they are both unworthy—one brutal, the other sickly—and do not take up much of the story. As a result, readers identify directly with the man of color, as they do not in later works by post–Civil War southern authors. In other words, in this early abolitionist text the mixed blood is the character whose search for identity defines the narrative. As Kenneth Burke might say, in order to find an identity, he enrolls himself in a band and casts off an old identity, in this case "slave"/property, in favor of a new identity as citizen. He participates, then, in a drama of regeneration through citizenship, a drama that engages race but that also takes as its model the revolutionary drama of U.S. self-making.[22] It is significant that Archy Moore is regenerated upon the high seas in the name of Britannia rather than in America.[23] Hildreth was as confirmed an Anglophile as Bancroft was an Anglophobe, suspicious of the direction of the growing nationalism in the United States (although he was also very nationalistic) and very much on the side of Britain in the War of 1812. Through Archer Moore, Hildreth comments upon political and moral corruption in the United States, upon the pre–Civil War relationship of the United States and Britain, and upon the aristocratic ideal, which he would replace with a middle-class ideal.

But in a novel so full of the migration of white younger sons westward from the worn-out plantations of Virginia and South Carolina

22. Kenneth Burke, *The Philosophy of Literary Form: Studies in Symbolic Action* (Berkeley, 1973), 38.

23. Alfred H. Kelly, in "Richard Hildreth," in *Marcus W. Jernegan Essays in American Historiography*, ed. William T. Hutchinson (Chicago, 1937), writes that the War of 1812 made Hildreth "the complete sectionalist, the complete Federalist, the complete Anglophile": "it is the Jeffersonian administrations that offer Hildreth the golden opportunity for a complete synthesis of every sentiment of partisanship. Sectional prejudice merges naturally with party hatred, dislike of France, and vituperance against slavery. To attack Jefferson is to attack the South, that center of radical Democracy, slavocracy, and Francophilism. To defend New England is to defend Federalism, to sympathize with England in her war against autocracy.... And at last he [Hildreth] thrusts aside even the restraints of patriotism and accepts openly the secessionist position of the Junto, which would have disrupted the Union in the interest of Federalist New England" (37–38). This context accounts for Archer Moore's flight to Britain and his activities in the War of 1812.

toward the fertile lands of the Mississippi Delta, Archy Moore's eastward flight is noticeable and makes perfect sense. On the most practical
level, the Fugitive Slave Laws, which began to be instituted in the late
eighteenth century, would make security difficult within the borders of
the United States. But in sending the hero eastward, onto the Atlantic
and further eastward into Great Britain, Hildreth allows Moore and the
U.S. reader to engage *British* history in a way that more "national"
literary heroes of the day would not, and to comment somewhat ironically on the U.S. project of nationalistic expansion westward and southward, a project bound up with the spread of slavery. In Hildreth's
novel, as in his historical writings, the ideology of liberty evolves from
the British origins of the American nation, and anti-British nationalism
threatens U.S. republicanism itself. Hildreth never shirked from acknowledging the U.S. debt to England for "our language and our literature, our social customs and domestic manners, our laws and, in a
considerable measure, our systems of legislation and principles of
government."[24]

Hildreth, through his octoroon hero, has much to say respecting the
irresponsible husbandry—moral, economic, and ecological—of the
southern planters, and he does so through numerous descriptions of
the natural world and the relationship of the plantation to the world
of nature. In fact, the human tragedies in *Archy Moore* are, without
exception, the result of moral failures that are themselves largely constructed around the inevitable failure of the plantation as a viable economic institution. The plantation in its very nature is wasteful of both
natural resources and human potential. In Hildreth's novel the South,
represented by the plantation, is the theater of U.S. moral, spiritual,
and civic degeneration, where both land and humanity are betrayed by
greed and despair, where ruined and abandoned houses abound, where
it is common practice among financially strapped Virginia planters to
"eat a nigger" every year, even if the "nigger" is a planter's own child.

In most ways Archy Moore, as the estranged son of a corrupt and
corrupting father, seems to function as a touchstone for the white novelist's own political and social values and as an instrument for social
and political criticism that reaches outside the slavery issue. The re-

24. Richard Hildreth, review of *Travels in North America, in the Years 1827 and 1828*,
by Captain Basil Hall, *American Monthly*, I (1829), 532.

generation of Archy Moore from slave to citizen aboard a British war-ship operates as an ironic reversal of the degeneration of white south-erners from masters to slaves of various passions, and it is a striking indictment of the ideal of political self-creation that was so readily as-sociated with the expansionist nationalism of the era. (One should re-call here that expansion was fueled to some extent by the desire to extend the slave territories southward and westward toward the Ca-ribbean, Texas, and Mexico.) In this text, the U.S. slave becomes captain and citizen not through enacting the U.S. expansionist myth but through traveling eastward to reclaim a civilization that seems on the verge of being lost in the New World. When the American octoroon, a slave despised and servile, is transformed into a British captain, he identifies completely with his adopted homeland. Upon his return to the United States, he comes as an Englishman, having lost, it would seem, all traces of the African features that threatened to make him distinguishable as a slave in Virginia. As a young man contemplating escape, Archy Moore dreamed of passing, and feared it; as an older man returning to the South, his identity as a white man and a British subject is never questioned. Aside from the questions this raises about Hildreth's racism (questions Yellin discusses in her book), what better testimony of the power of citizenship to transform the lowly? What better evocation of the ideal of America as it existed in the mind of an early nineteenth-century Whig?

Whether Hildreth was simply exhibiting an unconscious color preju-dice or attempting a comment on the arbitrariness of racial distinctions, it is obvious that where the man of mixed blood is concerned Hildreth, like many of the white authors who follow him (at least until the advent of scientific racism, which had already begun to take root in some cir-cles), steps easily from issues of race and caste to issues of class and citizenship.[25] Archer Moore the Englishman is no longer in any respect Archy Moore the unacknowledged and illegitimate octoroon son of a white man. During his travels through the South as a well-to-do En-glishman, he encounters ruin, dissipation, and viciousness. In this novel, the southern planter is greedy, imprudent, lustful, violent, mean,

25. "The fact of the matter," writes Benedict Anderson, "is that nationalism thinks in terms of historical destinies while racism dreams of eternal condemnations," dreams that "have their origin in ideologies of *class* rather than those of nation;" *Imagined Com-munities*, 149.

and drunk with his own unchecked power (a description that will do quite well for the man of mixed blood as he will appear later on in the work of some radical racist writers). The plantation is in ruins, with "the roof of the mansion house . . . all tumbling in." At this point, Moore seems curiously, but happily, alienated from his Virginia plantation origins, touring the ruined sites of adolescent joys and suffering with little emotional involvement. He is entirely anglicized in a way that permits his lengthy commentary upon the civic degeneration of the South to be read as the comment of the political fatherland upon the barbarism of the United States. Visiting the two graves of his parents, in different graveyards upon the ruined plantation, he muses that "these silent graves, already half obliterated, no less than the fast-mouldering ruins of what had once been the seat of opulence and plenty, seemed plainly to testify, that not by such means were families to be perpetuated, prosperous communities to be founded, or permanent triumphs over nature secured."[26]

He is no longer victim, but he does retain some memory of his previous identity as touchstone for his creator's conservative values. The octoroon, the young man forbidden even to acknowledge his relationship to his own father, is regenerated by the political fatherland into the fine gentleman his Virginia father failed to become. For all of Hildreth's conservative belief in human imperfectability, Archer Moore's ending is that of a Whig's fairy tale. A male Cinderella, scorned and abused in his youth by his wicked relations, he is rescued by tradition and elevated above them.

Although stories of the slaveholder's mixed-race children were immensely popular prior to the Civil War, most were written, as one might expect, by northern writers like Richard Hildreth to the extent that they were committed to, or at least not opposed to, stirring public sentiment against slavery.[27] The white southern writer tried to avoid the subject. After the Civil War, however, mixed-blood characters begin to appear

---

26. Richard Hildreth, *Archy Moore, the White Slave; or, Memoirs of a Fugitive* (New York, 1969), 247–48. All subsequent citations are to this edition.

27. Many were unlike Hildreth, however, in that their opposition to slavery was based on a faith in American exceptionalism. There was, in other words, an abolitionism based on conservative political principles as well as an abolitionism founded on the tenets of redemptive American nationalism.

with some frequency in the work of white southerners like George W. Cable, Joel Chandler Harris, Grace King, Kate Chopin, Mark Twain, and, later, William Faulkner. The issue of passing was of particular interest to many of these writers. They often dealt with characters traditionally classified as quadroons or octoroons, not solely to indicate that they had more white ancestry than black but also to suggest their origins in the colonialist slave cultures of the Deep South and the Caribbean, where they were associated with a distinct caste of free persons of mixed blood relatively unknown in the slaveholding areas of the Upper South—Creoles of color. Consistent with this cultural legacy, in many of these Deep South texts the octoroon is initially attributed not with an African origin but with a European (a French or Spanish) one; the figure seldom carries any tell-tale sign of African ancestry. It is well into *The Grandissimes,* for instance, before the young German-American Joseph Frowenfeld learns that his dark and elegant landlord Honoré Grandissime is anyone other than a Spanish Creole. We don't learn of Armand's ancestry until the very end of "Désirée's Baby." In Alice Morris Buckner's *Towards the Gulf: A Romance of Louisiana,* we are never sure if the innocent young wife carries the "fatal drop" or not. And William Faulkner's Charles Bon is a white Creole for a long time before he is revealed (or "reconstructed") as black. These "mistakes" or "indeterminacies," or "reclassifications" of characters, these shifting or obscured color lines, point to questions and anxieties that the white southerner had about his or her own future in a nationalistic and increasingly imperialistic United States.

The most salient feature of the octoroons as they are constructed in these texts is their capacity to delineate the political and cultural repressions and displacements, the submerged or forgotten history that underlies the dream of U.S. national unity. In so many of these texts, the personal history of the octoroon—his or her origin in a slave culture, alienation from the father, even the memory of a dead, sometimes anonymous, or monstrously rendered mother—is a psychologized recapitulation of the nationalist narrative; the octoroon's tragic fate—death or exile to Europe—is the fate that always attends the past in any dream of U.S. redemptive nationalism. In most of these texts, the figure is inscribed with the threatening characteristics of the displaced colonialist culture. He or she is almost always "aristocratic," a true product of a European-style and colonial class system, often superfluous both economically and politically, completely unsuited to the economic and political life of the U.S. republic. The presence of the octoroon, as a sign of transgression of U.S. racial as well as cultural ideology, is associated with the southern white protagonist's review, critique, and confirmation of his or her own political and cultural entitlements. In the octoroon the white author creates alternative political and cultural selves that for one reason or another have to be rejected, scapegoated, or otherwise silenced, but are versions nevertheless of the postbellum white southerner in terms of the political and cultural history of the Deep South.

The reasons for the assignment of a French or Spanish origin to the octoroon in the work of Cable, Faulkner, and others do stem directly from the history of colonization and miscegenation in the Deep South—especially Louisiana, which is the octoroon's site of origin in so many of these works—and particularly from the very different methods of classifying the offspring of Anglo- or Euro-African liaisons there. Prior to the Louisiana Purchase in 1803, racial classification in the creole Deep South was much more complex than in the Anglo Upper South, where the status of a mixed-blood child followed that of the mother, from the very beginning of the eighteenth century. The consequence is that the figure of the mixed blood was classed officially and metaphorically as part of the race that was defined as "slave," or as a legal/political nonentity.

In the Deep South, however, traditions were different. Until the Louisiana Purchase, racial classifications were in some ways based upon the status of the father. Children of white fathers were more easily manumitted in the Deep South, and fathers acknowledged those children more frequently than in the Upper South. Children could inherit from the white father's estate more easily. Furthermore, legalized marriages between white men and black women were possible, if very rare. Throughout the Caribbean (and in New Orleans), these children of European colonists and African women constituted a separate caste. They were recognized by law as well as by sentiment as bearing some legitimacy as carriers of European "blood" or "culture," although one would not want to overstate this point. They could, and often did, fight against slaves during insurrections. Many identified strongly with the European homeland, sometimes being sent to France to be educated and in many cases emigrating to France, where they bore even less of the stigma of slave descent, it having been decreed at one point that any slave or former slave who once set foot in the French homeland would be forever free.[28] The consequence is that the mixed blood possessed some power of economic and political agency in these cultures and often exercised a considerable economic and political role with respect to the colony's relationship to the homeland.

The cession of colonial Louisiana to the nationalistic United States in 1803 overturned this system of caste in the Louisiana Territory. The greatest difference between France and the United States with respect to racial policies derived from the fact that the French government, like many colonialist governments, found it useful to pursue a policy of

28. Gwendolyn Midlo Hall's recent *Africans in Colonial Louisiana: The Development of Afro-Creole Culture in the Eighteenth Century* (Baton Rouge, 1992), especially her chapter "The Pointe Coupee Post: Race Mixture and Freedom at a Frontier Settlement," is invaluable for an understanding of race mixing and passing on the French colonialist frontier, as is Virginia R. Dominguez, *White by Definition: Social Classification in Creole Louisiana* (New Brunswick, N.J., 1986).

For discussions of the traditions of classifying children of black/white liaisons in the Deep South and the West Indies and the political and economic consequences of the arrival of the United States into the Louisiana Territory, see also Adele Logan Alexander, *Ambiguous Lives: Free Women of Color in Rural Georgia, 1789–1879* (Fayetteville, Ark., 1991); Ira Berlin, *Slaves Without Masters: The Free Negro in the Antebellum South* (New York, 1974), 97–98, 160–65; Carl Degler, *Neither Black nor White: Slavery and Race Relations in Brazil and the United States* (New York, 1971), 226–45; Laura Foner, "The Free People of Color in Louisiana and St. Domingue," *Journal of Social History*, III (1970), 406–30; Jordan, *White over Black*, 167; Kinney, *Amalgamation!*; John G. Mencke, *Mulattoes and Race Mixture: American Attitudes and Images, 1865–1918* (East Lansing, Mich., 1979), 1–36; James Roark, *Black Masters: A Free Family of Color in the Old South* (New York, 1984); Charles Barthelemy Roussève, *The Negro in Louisiana: Aspects of His History and His Literature* (New Orleans, 1937), 25, 239; H. E. Sterkx, *The Free Negro in Antebellum Louisiana* (Rutherford, N.J., 1972).

The following discussions focus specifically upon the coming of the United States into the Louisiana Territory: Alice Dunbar-Nelson, "People of Color in Louisiana," *Journal of Negro History*, I (1916), 361–76, II (1917), 51–78; Donald E. Everett, "Emigrés and Militiamen: Free Persons of Color in New Orleans, 1803–1815," *Journal of Negro History*, XXXVIII (1953), 377–402; Thomas Marc Fiehrer, "The African Presence in Colonial Louisiana," in *Louisiana's Black Heritage*, ed. Robert R. MacDonald, John R. Kemp, and Edward F. Haas (New Orleans, 1977); and Roussève, *The Negro in Louisiana*, 25, 47–48, especially the speech by Robespierre included in the appendix and entitled "Speech on the Condition of the Free Men of Color in the French Colonies," 173–74; and a series of documents under the heading "Legislation Restricting Free People of Color," 175–78.

assimilation between its own agents on distant frontiers and other populations. This practice had produced an intermediate "black Creole" caste, which provided the home government (as well as white Creoles, *i.e.*, white persons born in the colonies) with assistance in the acculturation of alienated populations (slaves and natives) in the colony, but which did not threaten the "integrity" (the status quo) of the colonialist government, because of the distance between the homeland and the colony (and for other reasons). On the other hand, the United States was not acquiring a new colony. The nationalistic United States was acquiring the Louisiana Territory to be a part of its expanding nation, and the racist ideology of U.S. nationalism (like most nationalisms) had never been particularly hospitable to assimilation. What happened was the attempted replacement of an assimilationist and colonialist policy toward racial relationships with a segregationist and nationalist policy that demanded one prove title as white in order to be assimilated to any degree whatsoever into the redemptive New World nation.[29]

Initially, Creoles of color seem to have had some hopes that the new U.S. government in Louisiana would augment their status, but the segregationist ideology of the United States not only prevented any such thing from happening but also tended to eradicate the distinctions of caste already in existence. Creoles of color were in a difficult situation. They negotiated with Governor Claiborne and his successors for a number of years in an effort to preserve some of their traditional rights of caste. The segregationist United States had, however, no place for them except as "free blacks" or (to use the legal term) "free men/women of color," a class of persons the United States was already in the 1820s beginning to persecute in various ways. Many Creoles of color emigrated to France during this period.

Whereas white racial purity had been an important commodity prior to the cession, it became absolutely essential afterward. White Creoles

---

29. For a discussion of the different policies of nationalist and colonialist expansion, especially as worked out in the Deep South context, see Joseph G. Tregle, Jr., "Creoles and Americans," in *Creole New Orleans*, 131–85; and Gwendolyn Midlo Hall, "The Formation of Afro-Creole Culture," in *Creole New Orleans*, 58–87. See also the introduction to Pt. 2 of this work, entitled "The American Challenge," 91–100. For a discussion of nationalism and its connections to ideas of "race" as well as for a good discussion of race in the creole New World, see Anderson, *Imagined Communities*, 141–54.

had to insist on it if they could do so—and they would do so, vehemently. "Creolism," or the worship of the supposedly "pure" white inheritance of the Creole elite, originated in the West Indies in the revolutionary years of the late eighteenth century, when blacks and mulattoes rebelled against slavery and French rule. Ironically, it seems to have functioned as a means of legitimation. Because Europeans as well as Americans had doubts about the capacities of mixed races for self-government, the reputation of a Creole as "white" thus carried with it an important kind of cultural validation.

But creolism increased in Louisiana during the years following the cession. Louisiana Creoles began to insist that the word itself, where capitalized, always referred to the white descendant of a French or Spanish colonist, with the emphasis on "white." In actuality, "creole" (capitalized or not) had long been used in both North America and South America in several different ways to classify various groups of people (as well as to classify plants, architecture, language, art, religion, political authority, and just about everything else) with respect to their place via New World colonies and Old World powers. In France's Caribbean holdings (which included Louisiana and therefore much of the Deep South) during the seventeenth and eighteenth centuries, the word was used irrespective of race to designate someone (or something) born in the colonies rather than in the French or Spanish homeland.[30] And it makes sense, of course, that in an outlying colony, where the government of the homeland finds it useful to pursue a policy of assimilation, the possession of wealth (and by extension of economic and political power) by members of an intermediate racial caste would in some instances work to break down taboos regarding intermarriage between whites and certain members of that caste. Under the new American government, however, assumptions about race, culture, and politics were becoming vastly different.

Despite the insistence of some Creoles upon white racial purity (and despite the fact that many *were* "white" even by U.S. standards), the association of "creole" with suggestions of colonialist race mixing persisted in the American context. As late as 1854, some American politicians in Louisiana attempted to ensure their victory by charging that

30. Hirsch and Logsdon, eds., *Creole New Orleans*, 60, 98, 132–34; Dominguez, *White by Definition*, 12–15, 93–94, 121–25, 149–51.

their creole opponents possessed African ancestry, a charge that was by that time a de facto basis for political disfranchisement. Alexander Dimitry, one of the oldest and most "elite" of New Orleans Creoles, found his own son-in-law, George Pandely, removed from office because of a supposed trace of African inheritance.[31] But the association of Creoles with the slave population was not always so exclusively focused on *biological* "traces and taints." More often it seems to have derived from the tendency of Anglo-Americans (many of whom were already uncomfortable with the presence of slavery in the United States) to associate Creoles—regardless of whether they believed those Creoles to be biologically "tainted" or not—with the colonialist site of slavery, miscegenation, and political and cultural degeneration. As European, as Roman Catholic, and even as victims of slave insurrections, of seizures of property and torture, Creoles were carriers of "traces and taints" that Americans feared as challenges to their own redemptive mission in the New World. At one point during Thomas Jefferson's reelection campaign in 1800, a U.S. representative from South Carolina wrote home that the antislavery French were about to launch an invasion of the southern states from bases in St. Domingo—an indication that the creole threat was not solely based on the specter of black revolution. For a time, terrified of the consequences on their own slaves of contact with refugees from the black and mulatto revolutions of the West Indies, Americans prohibited immigration into ports at Charleston and New Orleans. Not only were black Creoles feared but white ones as well, for they carried servants with them. Even if servants were prohibited from entering the ports, these white refugees would talk of what they had experienced. It was sometimes the fear of the effects of rumor, of talk, that made Americans distrust even white Creoles. They, too, carried "news" that might threaten the supposed peace of the U.S. slave states. John Rutledge in 1787 reported to the Fifth Congress on the insurrectionary activities of West Indian slaves, concluding in righteous U.S. fashion that "sufficient for the day is the evil thereof" and advising that southern states "shut their door against any thing which had a tendency to produce the like confusion in this country."[32]

There is, no doubt, something biblical about Rutledge's style, but

31. Hirsch and Logsdon, eds., *Creole New Orleans*, 98.
32. Jordan, *White over Black*, 388.

there is something equally biblical about the general U.S. fear of rumor, of news from either "senile" Europe or "savage" Haiti; that is because there was something biblical about the way the New World nation envisioned itself as redemptive, as innocent, as untouched (or "unconfused") by history. The ethos of national innocence made it perfectly logical to link Creoles and slaves as constituting an intricately interconnected challenge to the mission of the United States. In 1804, for example, while debating the kind of government most appropriate to the newly acquired Louisiana Territory, disagreement hinged on the effect of granting a republican form of government to subjects of European monarchy. If they were not "ripe for liberty," the consequences for the United States could be dire. An exchange between Benjamin Huger, a U.S. representative from South Carolina, and John Jackson, from Virginia, demonstrates very clearly exactly what those consequences were imagined to be. Huger, arguing that Creoles were unfit to rule themselves, asserted that they "ought to be looked upon as a certain portion of people among us [i.e., slaves] and treated as such." Jackson objected to the analogy but took the opportunity to issue a plea for freedom: "I believe," he said, "that man is the same, whether born in the United States or on the banks of the Ganges, under an African sun or on the banks of the Mississippi, and that a love of liberty is implanted in his nature." [33] This is, no doubt, an instance of one of the early skirmishes in the U.S. debate over southern slavery, but it is more relevant to this argument that blacks would be implicated in that debate as rhetorical surrogates in what was supposed to be a discussion of the fitness of Creoles for republican self-rule. Black surrogacy makes sense, of course; it was supposed at this time that the white Creole created the man of mixed blood, educated him, gave him rights withheld from men of African descent, and in that way paved the way toward the terrifying revolutions that eventually replaced white with supposedly degenerate mulatto governments in Haiti. (Similar suppositions would be made with respect to the relationship between the white American slaveholder and the slave during the mid- and late nineteenth century in the United States.)

Under the circumstances, it is no wonder that white Americans like Huger feared Europe's presence in the New World—Europe was seen

33. *Ibid.*, 389–90.

as the source of those mulatto governments, since it was presumably French revolutionary idealism and the political pressure of France, as well as Great Britain, to abolish slavery in the Caribbean colonies that had led to those revolutions. Both France and Great Britain even went so far as to recognize the mulatto government of Haiti, the second independent republic in the New World, the first being the United States. For slaveholders and speculators for whom manifest destiny, the Monroe Doctrine, and the "benevolent institution" of slavery were concepts essential to the understanding of the U.S.'s messianic mission, such recognition may have been only one more example of Old World complicity with African insurrectionists in a threat against the political and economic integrity of the United States.

It is within this context of anxiety that we should perhaps understand the speed with which the coming of Claiborne and the U.S. government into the Louisiana Territories resulted in a redefinition of the mixed blood as part of the "black," hence "slave," population. In effect, an even more repressive segregationist system supplanted a well-developed system of assimilation that would have enabled those descendants of white fathers to "aspire" (but probably never to attain) to something resembling the status of the European colonist.

It is evidence of the persistence of history that despite U.S. attempts to classify the mixed-blood figure as "black," to redefine the status according to the condition of the mother, traces of the mixed blood's disturbing associations with another, competing, "white" cultural authority remain. One result is that this figure is always destabilized; whether male or female, the octoroon is seldom a figure whose "place" is clear. In U.S. literature, it is often a feature of the plot that the quadroon or octoroon is not *immediately* recognizable as such, although the damning revelation of African ancestry, when it does come, brings with it a perception that the evidence was always there. This is not the case in French or Spanish Caribbean literature, where the mulatto's associations with a distinct social and legal caste, with distinct privileges, the occupying of an intermediate position on the social ladder between black and white, all gave a certain visibility. In the U.S. context, however, one of the few stable features of the figure is his/her alienation from both black and white communities; in that sense, the mulatto is a relatively empty figure, a kind of repository for qualities and associations, capable of taking on changing roles, revealing him- or herself within different contexts, depending on the anxieties or the needs of the creators. Nevertheless, the associations of the mixed blood with a French or Spanish cultural identification did not disappear completely with the legal distinctions. Despite the redefinition of the octoroon by the coming of the "one-drop" rules in the 1830s (and even more stringent "one-drop" rules in the Redemption era and early twentieth century), Anglo-Americans seem to have remained fascinated by the complex dramatic and rhetorical possibilities surrounding the claims of the Louisiana or Caribbean "octoroon" to political and economic legitimacy in ways that were not at all identical with their fascination for slave figures or free blacks.

This particular historical and discursive context exerted a real fascination for postbellum southern writers. In it they found the same issues that would reappear in the discourse surrounding the reconstruction of the South in their own eras: race and nationalism, assimilation and segregation, black surrogacy or the moral "contamination" of the slaveholder by the slave, as well as the cultural effects of racial hybridization or amalgamation versus what might be termed racial purity, homogeneity, or (even more insidiously) "integrity." In George W. Cable's postbellum generation, and perhaps largely through Cable's work and influence, there developed a tendency to represent the defeated South as "creole," to attempt to read the reconstruction of the postbellum white southerner in terms of the nationalization of white Creoles during the cession years. On their surfaces, texts like *The Grandissimes* or the stories of *Old Creole Days* are optimistic reconciliation tales, where white Creoles become American or are displaced by others who do. But the complexity of the historical discourse about "Creoles"—"real" or metaphoric Creoles, political or literary discourse—in the American context, the very indeterminacy of the word *creole* itself, especially where its racial referents were concerned, permits what Foucault might term the excavation of a counternarrative, a narrative that ran submerged in the story Cable may have wanted to tell of our nation's progress toward redemptive unity, toward a kind of political millennium wherein history would be transcended. It is a counternarrative of division and recalcitrance and defeat by history; Faulkner's *Light in August* and *Absalom, Absalom!* will pursue this counternarrative with as much diligence as Cable's texts pursue the reconciliationist dream of reunification and transcendence of tragic history.

As I have already suggested, the term *creole* has operated as a kind of traveling (and changeable) stage upon which the national drama of race and nationalism in the Deep South is enacted. When Cable, followed by others, appropriated the term in the 1870s to define the South's own complex relationship to colonialism, to slavery, and to U.S. ahistorical nationalism, he seems to have been unprepared for the outrage his characters would elicit from the elite (stipulated as white) Creoles of New Orleans, who were concerned not only about what they perceived as caricatures of themselves but also by Cable's suggestions of race mixing among the Creole population, a suggestion it had long been essential to deny. Hence Cable's scrupulous acknowledgment in *The Creoles of Louisiana* that Creoles (capitalized) define themselves as the *white* descendants of European colonists. But the mere necessity for such insistence belies its problems, as Cable concedes when he writes that "there seems to be no more serviceable definition of the Creoles of Louisiana than . . . that they are the French-speaking, native portion of the ruling class." [34] He is even more direct about this in an entry written for the ninth edition of the *Encyclopedia Britannica*, where he says that the "better class" of Creole in New Orleans appears to be white although (with a syntax admirably complicated in what may be an attempt not to offend) "the name they [Louisiana Creoles] have borrowed from [the West Indies] does not necessarily imply, any more than it excludes, a departure from a pure double line of Latin descent." [35]

The newly intensified debate in the 1880s and afterward over the definition of *creole* reminds us that once again, in the post–Civil War era, the question of who might be or become an American had resurfaced, and the implicit racism of the U.S. national mission made it once again necessary that the color line be reaffirmed. The speed with which Claiborne and the U.S. government divested Creoles of color of their hopes for citizenship after the Louisiana Purchase—it took a few decades—is surpassed by the speed with which the United States divested freedmen of their hopes after the Civil War. It took less than one decade to decide that the freedman would not become an active par-

34. George W. Cable, *The Creoles of Louisiana* (New York, 1885), 41–42.
35. *Encyclopedia Britannica*, 9th ed., s.v. "New Orleans."

ticipant in national life except through the mediation of former white masters. During the post-Reconstruction years and into the twentieth century, southern legislatures proposed and often passed "one-drop" rules that made antebellum "one-drop" rules seem remarkably liberal. The cultural debate about the capacities of the former slaveholder continued, however, in much the same fashion as the debate over the capacities of the white Creole during the years following the cession. The questions were the same: the impact of slavery on the moral fiber of the former slaveholder, the former slaveholder's fitness for self-government, and the impact of the former slaveholder's assimilation upon the body politic. An editorialist for the New York *Tribune* summed up a too-familiar argument: "Wherever slavery existed, there the moral sense was so blunted and benumbed that the white people as a whole is to this day incapable of that sense of honor which prevails elsewhere."[36]

Despite the persistence of some suspicion that the former slave-holder was, like the Creole who so often represented him in the dis-course, tragically touched—morally if not genetically—by the history of colonialism and slavery, *i.e.*, compromised by his intimacy with the savage and the senile, the rhetoric of southern redemption was largely inspiriting. In an 1882 address to the graduating class at the University of Mississippi, Cable called for southerners to transcend the past, to put history behind them. In this talk, he objected to the phrase "New South," suggesting that we aim for the "No South": "Does the word sound like annihilation? It is the farthest from it. It is enlargement. It is growth. It is a higher life."[37]

Yet neither the reality of political and economic life in the South nor the literature of the period bears out the promise of Cable's optimistic rhetoric. (Cable's own literary work doesn't even bear out the promise of his rhetoric.) The white southerner's return to the reunified nation during the significantly named Redemption era that followed Recon-struction was less a transcendence of southern history in a redemptive national body than a return to the white southerner of the rights to reconstitute, or attempt to reconstitute, a racial order which imitated,

36. New York *Tribune*, Unsigned editorial, August 30, 1879.

37. George W. Cable, "Literature in the Southern States," *The Negro Question: A Se-lection of Writings on Civil Rights in the South*, ed. Arlin Turner (New York, 1958), 44.

in some respects, that of antebellum years. And, predictably enough, it was less a redemption from than a renewal of certain racist assumptions about the proper relationship between black and white in the United States. It also revealed the continuing assumption that it was the white southerner's particular history and nature that would fit him to deal with the dangerous African American. In this assumption there is something of the idea that Emerson had attributed to the abolitionist— that "the negro & and negro-holder are really of one party." [38]

It might have been expected that the fundamental racism of the U.S. culture would result in just this kind of "redemption," the return of the African American to a semislave status and the return of the white South to a marginal status with respect to a national mission imagined in terms of its capacity to transcend history. The politics of Redemption struck a deal with the white southerner, of course, but it was a deal that led, within a few years of the Rutherford B. Hayes election in 1876, to the South's increasing political, economic, and cultural isolation and to a growing—because related—southern hysteria about the dangers of "amalgamation." This hysteria seems to have developed from the white southerner's awareness, at least on some level, that the color line was little more than a reflection of the political, cultural, and economic alienation of selected populations; that he himself was, in some respects, alienated by that very color line from the U.S. national mission; and that to be alienated in the United States was, whatever the color of your skin, to be "black." Lest this sound a bit extreme, we might recall that it is the putative "blackness" of the mysterious stranger who appears white that preoccupied the white southern writer, as it preoccupied the U.S. court system during these years.[39] This preoccupation was based on the belief that political and economic equality for the freedman would inevitably lead to "social equality," to the "contamination" of white bodies with black blood, to the further "degeneration" of "white" civilization in the South. These terrors themselves reflected doubts on the part of the white southerner as well as the rest of the nation about the white southerner's capacity to accomplish the transcendence of history that was required before he could be effectively

38. Emerson, *Journals and Miscellaneous Notebooks*, XIII, 198.

39. See Eric Sundquist's discussion of the *Plessy* v. *Ferguson* case and its impact on American literature of the era in "Mark Twain and Homer Plessy," *Representations*, XXIV (Fall, 1988), 102–28.

redeemed. They also reiterated the issues of assimilation versus segregation that had preoccupied the nation during the original cession of
the Deep South to the United States and echoed against a new reality—
the reality of imperialism—which ironically placed the white American
abroad in the same position in which the white southerner had been
placed on the domestic front.[40]

The variations played upon the conventional miscegenation story by
Anglo-southerners writing after the Civil War are many and revealing.
Consistent with the burgeoning "science" of human descent, the terms
of the debate shift from the political and cultural toward the biological.
Rebecca Harding Davis, born in Alabama and raised in West Virginia,
is perhaps best known for the 1861 short story "Life in the Iron Mills,"
and is hailed as the first U.S. naturalist, writing thirty years before
Stephen Crane and Frank Norris. In her *Waiting for the Verdict*, published in 1867 at the dawn of Reconstruction, a young mulatto slave is
purchased by a kind Quaker woman and sent to France to be educated
as a physician. It is interesting that the French physician retains no trace
of the African ancestry visible when he was a child. The "yellow" complexion and sullen demeanor of the slave Sap have been transformed
into the "sallow" complexion and melancholy of the foreign Dr. Broderip, a transformation which suggests not only that presuppositions
about racial traits determine the ability to see evidence of racial ancestry but that a fundamental likeness exists between the slave and the
sickly foreigner. Dr. Broderip anticipates in many respects the "tragic
mulatto" as he will begin to appear in white texts. He is a physically
stunted, sexually ambiguous figure whose love for a white woman
(slightly mixed with Native American "blood") is doomed by her own
racism and that of the culture she shares. At last Dr. Broderip acknowledges his African inheritance and dies in the Civil War, attempting to
serve black soldiers and refugees.

In *Chita*, the traditional mulatto plot device of a beautiful foundling
who is raised as white by unsuspecting foster parents and later exposed
as bearing the "fatal drop" of black blood is suggested repeatedly, but

---

40. One might look at the portrayal of the American abroad in the work of Heming-
way, Fitzgerald, and other American writers of the 1920s for confirmation. No longer is
the American an "innocent," but carries with him/her the sins of American imperialism.

Lafcadio Hearn's story finally backs off from the recognition scene and confirms that the child is actually white. (Hearn was charged with stealing the idea from Cable, who treated the same issue of black/white indeterminacy in "'Tite Poulette.") In *Towards the Gulf,* the white Creole's doubts about the purity of his wife lead him to see in his child's "dark skin and willful ways" the sign of African ancestry. Despite his conviction, however, his sister sees only the "old Morants," the features of the original French ancestors, and the text leaves the question of ancestry entirely open. In some respects this novel is reminiscent of Kate Chopin's "Desirée's Baby," with the important qualification that in Buckner's novel ancestry does remain indeterminate.

By the end of the century, however, a new variety of radical racism had blossomed and the fiction associated with the agenda of radical racism would be different as well. Although they often retain their blood ties to aristocratic southerners, it is not the practice of radical racist writers to acknowledge in any direct way the likeness of the mixed-blood figures to whites or their ties to Western culture. Some of the most racist white authors writing during this period clearly attempt to emphasize the innate unlikeness supposedly hidden beneath the surface similarities. Their men and women of color become threats to the U.S. mission of cultural and political regeneration by being associated with Africa as the site of the primitive, of savagery as alternative to civility. These mixed bloods are frightening creations, sometimes more simian than human in their appearance and behavior, capable of acquiring nothing more than a thin veneer of civilization that can crack at any moment, unleashing primitive rage and violence against whites. These characters seem designed for the express purpose of terrifying white racists with their interesting schemes for substituting black supremacy for white and in that way undermining all of civilization, which is understood to be a white and Western invention. The Reverend John Durham, in Thomas Dixon, Jr.'s 1902 novel *The Leopard's Spots,* comes right out with it:

> My boy, the future American must be an Anglo-Saxon or a Mulatto. We are now deciding which it shall be. The future of the world depends on the future of this Republic. This Republic can have no future if racial lines are broken and its proud citizenship sinks to the level of a mongrel breed of Mulattoes. The South must fight this battle to a finish. Two

thousand years look down upon the struggle, and two thousand years
of the future bend low to catch the message of life or death.[41]

The sexual threat so apparent to today's readers is present in this passage, but Reverend Durham is using it less out of any real sexual anxiety than in an effort to serve his own political interests. The "mongreli-
zation" he fears most comes from the addition of black voices and votes
to local and state governments. The "racial line" of most importance to
him is the line between governor and governed. In fact, the primary
issue in this passage is political rather than sexual. References to "racial
lines" and "mongrel breed," though suggesting sexuality, possess more
force as descriptions of the way southerners saw Reconstruction governments. In this work, mulatto becomes a metaphor for governmental
corruption, and the emotion tapped by the sexual suggestions in the
language is directed toward a political goal.

In Robert Lee Durham's *The Call of the South,* the octoroon, John
Heyward Graham, threatens the entire U.S. government by fathering a
very dark child with his white wife, who happens to be the daughter
of the president. It is possible that Durham's story is a response to the
widespread white hysteria that followed Theodore Roosevelt's decision
to invite Booker T. Washington to dinner. This act outraged the North
Carolinian Josephus Daniels as an "insult" to the South and an appall-
ing demonstration of the doctrine of "social equality," which could
lead, in his mind, nowhere but to marriage between black men and
white women. Robert Lee Durham was also a North Carolinian. His
novel, published in 1908, carries a dinner invitation extended by a U.S.
president to a black man to what the white racist considers its inevitable
consequence: the marriage of a white woman and a black man and the
birth of a very dark child, which results in the mother's insanity and
the death by shock of the president, who is the child's grandfather.

There are fascinating psychological complexities in the story.[42] A
psychoanalytic critic might note that not least among the complexities
are the echoes of the name Robert Lee Durham in the octoroon hero
John Heyward Graham—Graham's white father's name was John
Graham Heyward. But one does not necessarily have to return to the

41. Thomas Dixon, Jr., *The Leopard's Spots* (New York, 1902), 200.
42. See Joel Williamson's psychoanalytic reading of Thomas Dixon in *The Crucible of Race,* 158–76.

psychological paradigm at this point; names are as much political and cultural insignia as references to a psychosexual subject. Of Graham, Durham writes that "beneath [his] creditable but thin veneer of civilization there slumbers in his blood the primitive passions and propensities of his immediate ancestors, which are transmitted to him as latent forces of evil to burst out of his children and grandchildren in answer to the call of the wild."[43] On first sight, one might conclude that those "passions and propensities" must be "African" ones, but the hero's "most immediate ancestors" are almost all white. Furthermore, there is also the interesting exchange between the words "wild" in the text and "South" in the title. Under the circumstances, the "wild man" may well be the rebellious white father who leaves his home in order to deal honorably with the black woman he has impregnated. The "wild man" might be more a sign of the exiled rather than the black beast or rapist. As is the case with any number of "white" men in the South, the octoroon son's most predominant "passion" does seem to be his love of the military and he does have a "propensity" to want to keep his good name unbesmirched. Furthermore, his most immediate, and most discussed, ancestor is his white father, a landowning and politically valuable southerner from whom he may have inherited those "passions and propensities," if not the cultural legitimacy that would make his desires attainable.

Whatever Durham's intentions, his octoroon character is not an unsympathetic one. His greatest suffering stems from his knowledge of the "drop of black blood" that dooms any attempt he makes to serve his country as soldier or as father or to further his own fortunes. No doubt the presupposition of African inferiority is present in these texts on many levels, but so is the suggestion that the slaveholding history of the South may render the white southerner himself unfit for any future in a republican society.

This complex history of cultural displacement is of particular relevance to selected works by George W. Cable, Mark Twain, and William Faulkner where the mixed blood becomes the means through which post–Civil War white southerners dramatize their own recalcitrance. What the trope of mixed blood makes possible for writers like these is the

43. Robert Lee Durham, *The Call of the South* (Boston, 1908), 119–20.

configuration of the southerner as a carrier of the repressed history of the United States. The power of that trope as it is used by these writers is illustrative of the nexus of anxieties associated with both race and "nation" in their work and in the culture that produced it. All three authors construct the southerner as a dangerous border figure, someone who might look like an American and claim to be so (with greater fervor than other Americans at times) but who carries within him- or herself traces of the displaced and who might at some point act traitorously to undermine the progressive nation. The preoccupation with race and national genealogy in the work of Cable, Twain, and Faulkner reveals the conflict between the legacy of the colonialist slave culture and the republican ideal of self-ownership, self-mastery. Cable's *The Grandissimes* is a site for conflict between discourses about race and nationalization in the post–Civil War South. Mark Twain's works, particularly *Pudd'nhead Wilson and Those Extraordinary Twins,* function in the same fashion, even though the terms and context of the discourse are drawn more from the border South than from the Deep South. And William Faulkner's "Red Leaves," *Light in August,* and *Absalom, Absalom!* carry the discourse well into the twentieth century.

2

George W. Cable and American Nationalism

" . . . whisperings of hidden strife"
—*The Grandissimes*

George W. Cable is most often described as a reformer-turned-novelist, a writer whose work was inspired and, as time passed, more and more controlled by a limited political agenda. The most well known of Cable's editors, Richard Watson Gilder, along with many other contemporaries of Cable, thought his work too "preachy." During the writing of *The Grandissimes,* another of his editors, Robert Underwood Johnson, admonished Cable for his inclination to "go pamphleteering."[1] With a few exceptions, the opinions of twentieth-century critics have not been substantially different—Cable is more reformer than artist.[2]

There is no disputing that Cable was very much a reformer. He was committed to political and economic equity for African Americans, to prison reform, and particularly to alleviating the brutalities of the Convict Lease System. In "My Politics," he writes that "I meant to make *The Grandissimes* as truly a political work as it ever has been called," asserting that the novel records "as plain a protest against the times in which it was written as against the earlier times in which its scenes

1. Arlin Turner, *George W. Cable: A Biography* (Baton Rouge, 1966), 98.

2. See Violet Bryan, *The Myth of New Orleans in Literature: Dialogues of Race and Gender* (Knoxville, 1993), 12; Griffith T. Pugh, "George W. Cable as Historian," in *Writers and Their Critics: Studies in English and American Literature* (Tallahassee, 1955), 29; Edmund Wilson, *Patriotic Gore: Studies in the Literature of the American Civil War* (New York, 1962).

were set."[3] *The Grandissimes* was set in 1803 and 1804, against the background of the cession of the Louisiana Territory from France to the United States. It was written in the late 1870s, against the background of the Hayes-Tilden Compromise and the return of governmental authority in the South to the white man, but in comparing *The Grandissimes* to later works like *Pudd'nhead Wilson and Those Extraordinary Twins, Light in August,* and *Absalom, Absalom!,* it is important also to remember that it was written and published very early in the Redemption era, when the freedman's rights had not yet been so thoroughly eroded, when it was still possible for men like Cable to imagine that white governments might in fact be persuaded to deal honorably with blacks. Cable's flaw (or perhaps his virtue) may have been his capacity to believe that the white man of his generation could be reconstructed, through reason, into American assimilationistically conceived.

The record of his disappointments is long. In 1875, when angry whites in New Orleans forcibly removed from Girls' High School a number of pupils who were known or suspected to be of African ancestry, Cable (newly reconstructed) was outraged and wrote a letter to the New Orleans *Bulletin* in which he attacked the motivations for any such violent attempt to ensure segregation in the public sphere. In this letter Cable addressed the fears of white "contamination" one by one: no child spent so much time at school that any parent need worry about loss of moral authority, schools could be counted upon to remove any child who might exert some negative influence, and no one had worried about the negative consequences of intimate contact when white and black children had played together during slavery or when slave-women had nursed white children. The crux of his argument, however, hinged on a distinction between "social" and "public" contact. The integration of public schools, of public transportation, of government offices and agencies ought not to threaten social segregation of the races. No child would be forced to associate socially with anyone. Americans would remain as free to choose their personal associates as they had ever been.

He signed the letter "A Southern White Man," and provoked angry responses from other southern white men, including his employer,

---

3. George W. Cable, "My Politics," in *The Negro Question: A Selection of Writings on Civil Rights in the South,* ed. Arlin Turner (New York, 1958), 14.

William C. Black, and friends like Page Baker. Baker wrote: "The only condition under which the two races can co-exist peacefully is that in which the superior race shall control and the inferior race shall obey. . . . African proclivities are towards savagery and cannibalism. . . . For our part we hope never to see the white boys and girls of America forgetful of the fact that negroes are their inferiors."[4]

One basis for this disagreement can be found in the fact that nationalistic political ideology in the United States vested the private citizen with such a degree of agency and representative power in his (and more and more "her") own person that arguments such as Cable made in his letter about the separation of public and private spheres must have seemed specious. U.S. nationalist ideology is built on the presumption of a distinct but analogical relationship between private world and public world. The citizen was understood to be an agent of the nation-state—enfranchised, autonomous, and stable—and it was as difficult at the time for Anglo-American whites to imagine former slaves as possessors of political and cultural agency in the United States as it had been in 1803 for them to imagine the free Creole population of the Louisiana Territory in that way, and for some of the same reasons. However, under the influence of the pseudoscientific racism that had recently become visible on the horizon, Anglo-Americans had become more likely to cite reasons that had to do with the former slave's "innate" racial characteristics than with his lack of education and training for citizenship. During the final years of Reconstruction, white Americans were becoming more and more fearful of the possible cultural consequences of social contact with people they took to be representatives of "savagery and cannibalism."

After this experience Cable kept silent for a while, but by 1884 he had decided to return to the battlefront. He did so in an address to the Alabama Historical Society, in which he pointed out the abuses of the Convict Lease System and traced the corruptions of Reconstruction not to the impact of the freedmen or the carpetbaggers but to the influence of slavery in its training of white southerners in the vices of "shameless hard drinking, the carrying of murderous weapons, murder, too, and lynching at its heels, the turning of state and county prisons into slave-pens, the falsification of the ballot, night riding and whipping, and all

4. Turner, *George W. Cable*, 76–78, 77.

the milder forms of political intolerance." The cries of the wounded continued for weeks. Then, in January, 1885, he published in the *Century* "The Freedman's Case in Equity." In spite of a deliberate effort to dispel the "huge bugbear of Social Equality," it was on that very issue that opponents attacked, charging Cable with advocating intermarriage. By this time, the mid-1880s, the threat of race mixing had become the preoccupation of many white Americans, and it would be on this point that Cable's opponents would continue to assail him. In 1889, while in Nashville, Cable dined with a black family. The Nashville *American* responded:

> Mr. George W. Cable, just before he took his departure for the East, was entertained by J. C. Napier, colored, where he spent a most agreeable evening in the society of our colored elite. Mr. Cable has often urged social equality of the races, and we are glad to see him following his own advice on the subject. In the South, however, a man must choose the race with which he associates and Mr. Cable having signified his preference for the negro race over his own should be left undisturbed to his choice. We do not mean to say that Cable lowered himself by accepting the hospitalities of Mr. Napier, colored; on the contrary we think he found his proper level.[5]

Although Cable was no doubt very prudent not to say so directly, he seems, to his credit, not to have had any particular horror of social equality or race mixing. Cable himself was a man of many divisions. His father, George Washington Cable, was the son of a Virginia family with German origins. In 1811 the Cables moved north to Pennsylvania, where they set their slaves free, and then to Indiana. Here George Washington Cable met his wife, Rebecca Boardman, of New England ancestry. But the son of this very northern European ancestry would later claim to be himself a "Creole." Perhaps in claiming this title he sought some relief against the charges that he had vilified creole customs and creole morals in his literature, but as Louis D. Rubin, Jr., points out, Cable (born and raised in New Orleans) "remained in many ways an outsider, the child of American interlopers, and a kind of real-life Frowenfeld in the Creole-cum-American city." Like Joseph Frowenfeld, Cable was a strict Protestant moralist who may have possessed "a certain susceptibility to the voluptuous" but who was nonetheless a Prot-

5. Cable, "My Politics," 20; Turner, *George W. Cable*, 71, 268.

estant moralist. The fascinations of Cable's literary work may owe a great deal to the divisions between his "susceptibilities" and his right-eousness.[6] No doubt his liberalism on the issue of miscegenation finds its source not in his Protestant morality but in his upbringing among and identification with Creoles, whose objections to miscegenation were not so much based on fears of "blood taints" as on fears of ob-scuring the distinction between "slaveholder" and "slave," making slave labor unstable, inheritance more complicated, and challenges to slave status more likely. In short, in the creole Deep South, the color line had been (prior to the encroachment of the United States) less im-portant for its preservation of "race purity" in the sense in which sci-entific racism would understand it than for its ability to stabilize eco-nomic and social relationships on a colonial frontier, to disarm the implications of the "border."[7] But finally, Cable's "susceptibility to the voluptuous," along with his passionate devotion to political and civil justice for the freedman, coexisted with a fundamental ethnocentrism which held that the "Anglo-Saxon life and inspiration" of the United States was responsible for elevating the savage and transforming the degenerate.[8] Thus, Cable's deep fascination for history coexisted with a vision of a redemptive futurity founded in "Anglo-Saxon life and inspiration."

Cable, like the Creoles he depicted, was more elitist on the basis of class than on the basis of race. His decision to reenter the war zone in 1884 had been prompted by seeing a well-dressed black woman with a child forced into the company of black convicts in the "colored car" on an Alabama train. And Cable's high-handed manners with servants irritated Sam Clemens when the two men traveled together on the "Twins of Genius" tour.[9]

6. Rubin, *Life and Times*, 20–22; Jay Hubbell, quoted *ibid.*, 26.

7. See n. 28, Chap. 1. One of the best treatments I have found of the origins and history of the color line, including methods of "passing" is Joel Williamson's *New People: Miscegenation and Mulattoes in the United States* (New York, 1980), especially the first chapter, "Genesis" (pp. 1–61). For legal and historical sources which show that disputes often centered on issues of inheritance, see Harriet Spiller Daggett, "The Legal Aspect of Amalgamation in Louisiana," *Texas Law Review* XI (February 1933), 166, 174–84; also Dominguez, *White by Definition*, 57–89. For comparison with the Upper South, see A. Leon Higginbotham, Jr., and Barbara K. Kopytoff, "Racial Purity in Colonial and Antebellum Virginia," *Georgetown Law Journal*, LXXVII (1967–89), 1967–2021.

8. Cable, *The Creoles of Louisiana*, 1.

9. George W. Cable, "The Freedman's Case in Equity," in *The Negro Question: A*

Cable's fiction is not as good as Mark Twain's. It is certainly not equal to Faulkner's. But it is not bad. Cable had a flair for dialect, for atmosphere, and could (when encouraged) write powerful dramatic scenes. But more important for this study, he possessed a rich historical sensibility, which is finally as central to his literary output as his political principles. Despite his commitment to "the great nation of futurity," he remained deeply aware of the powerful legacies of history in the present and of the importance of a knowledge of history to any dream of the future.

The extent of the white southerner's engagement with history has often been discussed, albeit at a relatively high level of generalization, especially by literary critics. C. Hugh Holman, as a young scholar, identified the characteristics of southern literature as follows: "A sense of evil, a pessimism about man's potential, a tragic sense of life, a deep-rooted sense of the interplay of past and present, a peculiar sensitivity to time as a complex element in narrative art, a sense of place as a dramatic dimension, and a thoroughgoing belief in the intrinsic value of art as an end in itself." In a later essay, Holman expressed some regrets that he had participated in what he had grown to see as a distorting categorization of southern literature and called for a renewed commitment to discovery and revision among southernists. Others have maintained a deep faith in the identified characteristics of southern literature as "fixation on place, the past, and history." [10]

I do not want to argue with the importance of history in southern literature. What is interesting is that so many critics—even those, like Cleanth Brooks, deeply engaged in historical analysis—have spoken less of "history" and more of "memory," a development of critical perspective related to the ideology of "realism" in American literature, a perspective that translates complex cultural experience into the familiar

Selection of Writings on Civil Rights in the South, ed. Arlin Turner (New York, 1958), 67–68; The Love Letters of Mark Twain, ed. Dixon Wecter (New York, 1949), 235.

10. C. Hugh Holman, "Ellen Glasgow and the Southern Literary Tradition," in Southern Writers: Appraisals in Our Time, ed. R. C. Simonini, Jr. (Charlottesville, 1964), 123; as well as his "No More Monoliths, Please: Continuities in the Multi-Souths," in Southern Literature in Transition: Heritage and Promise, ed. Philip Castille and William Osborne (Memphis, 1983), xiii–xxiv; and Cleanth Brooks, "Southern Literature: The Past, History, and the Timeless," also in Southern Literature in Transition: Heritage and Promise, ed. Philip Castille and William Osborne (Memphis, 1983), 3–16.

(and I mean the word to be taken literally as "family-like") terms of personal psychology. Within this economy, historical forces are relegated to the margins of human experience, and one loses contact with the capacity of public or official historiography to construct identity, to shape the way subjectivity is experienced and utilized.

If Cable is more optimistic about human potential than the southern writer is usually imagined as being, and if he is more interested in the capacity of art to promote human and social development than in its intrinsic value, he is nonetheless very southern in his sense of the impact of history upon the present. In one of his most interesting letters to Cable, Robert Underwood Johnson defined *local color*, which he would have Cable avoid: "By too much 'local color' Mr. Gilder and I mean descriptions of local customs and characters not necessary to the story which distract from the thread of the plot—the tendency to tell all the truth . . . too many facts about the characters—in other words a historical tendency." In short, he and Gilder associated the "historical tendency" with local color as distinctly unimportant to the extent that it was concerned with the particularities of history rather than with the "universality" of the modern, the national, character. For Gilder and Johnson (as for many other readers of that era and our own), Cable's biggest problem was the tendency either to become obscure in his foregrounding and use of local and regional (*i.e.,* culturally repressed) history and values or to become polemical—to violate the tenets of ahistorical realism by failing to follow the principle W. D. Howells would articulate a few years later, when he suggested that "our novelists . . . seek the universal in the individual rather than in the social interests."[11]

But Cable's original inspiration to write came not from Henry James, nor W. D. Howells, nor even from Hawthorne, Hugo, and Turgenev (repeatedly recommended to him by his *Scribner's* editors as writers who avoided the inartistic), but from Charles Gayarré's boldly inartistic series of lectures entitled *Romance of the History of Louisiana,* published in 1848. Despite Cable's later disagreements with the testy creole historian over what Gayarré saw as unflattering portrayals of the Creoles,

11. Robert Underwood Johnson to George W. Cable, March 13, 1880, in the George Washington Cable Collection, Manuscripts Department, Howard-Tilton Memorial Library, Tulane University, New Orleans, La.; W. D. Howells, "Dostoevsky and the More Smiling Aspects of Life," in *W. D. Howells: Selected Literary Criticism,* ed. David J. Nordloh (Bloomington, Ind., 1993), II, 35.

Gayarré's call in that lecture series for a Louisiana-born-and-bred Sir Walter Scott who might make history accessible to "the intelligence of the many" fired Cable's literary imagination in the early 1870s. In an 1872 essay for the New Orleans *Daily Picayune*, Cable announced his decision to take up the task of "mining" Louisiana's colonial history for those "gems" that lay "like those new diamonds in Africa, right on top of the ground." In doing so, he acknowledges Gayarré directly as "the historian" who "in following the annals of colonization . . . has uncovered the mines of romance."[12]

Cable was well prepared for the job of mining Louisiana and Caribbean colonialist history. His interest had been long and his reading thorough. In "My Politics," he reports having read Hume's *History of England* at the age of ten.[13] As a young man he read George Bancroft (not Richard Hildreth), whose romantic U.S. nationalism would remain a shaping influence on both Cable's life and literature. The notebooks he kept during the 1870s are filled with details from numerous historians, explorers, and chroniclers of the Caribbean and Deep South; St. Méry, De Pauw, Fortier, Duvallon, the Duke of Saxe-Weimar-Eisenach, and many others provide not only fascinating sources for some of the details of his early work but also sources for our understanding of its ideological or discursive agenda.[14] On the other hand, Cable's early

12. Charles Gayarré, *Romance of the History of Louisiana* (2nd ed.; New Orleans, 1879), 16–17; George W. Cable, "Drop Shot," New Orleans *Daily Picayune*, February 25, 1872.

13. Turner, *The Negro Question*, 2.

14. Cable was a habitual researcher. In early 1876, he asked Richard Watson Gilder for a copy of Benjamin Franklin French's *Historical Collections of Louisiana*, a compilation of documents related to the settling and development of Louisiana. He also requested a copy of Poole's *Index to Periodical Literature* at the same time. See George W. Cable to Richard Watson Gilder, April 21, 1876, in George Washington Cable Collection. As early as 1872, he recorded in a letter to his mother that he had plans to listen to a reading of Gayarré's *History of Louisiana*, which he had already read. George W. Cable to his mother, July 4, 1872, in Lucy Leffingwell Cable Biklé, *George W. Cable: His Life and Letters* (New York, 1928), 43. His research among the archives of New Orleans for his series "Churches and Charities of New Orleans" (New Orleans *Daily Picayune*, February 14, 18, 25, March 3, 10, 17, 1872) is discussed in Turner, *George W. Cable*, 47–48. See also copious notes from *De Bow's Review*, the 1812 *Directory of New Orleans*, and various reports written by administrators at Charity Hospital in his Ledger-Book in the George Washington Cable Collection. This notebook indicates that he also read in François Barbe-Marbois, *The History of Louisiana, Particularly of the Cession of That Colony to the United States of America* (Philadelphia, 1830); Pierre-Louis Berquin-Duvallon, *Vue de la colonie espagnol du Missis-*

reading in literature seems limited to *Uncle Tom's Cabin* and Sir Walter Scott's *The Lady of the Lake.*

Cable's literary landscape was about to be changed. Two years before Cable announced his intention to write historical romance, Dr. Josiah Holland had founded *Scribner's Monthly Magazine* with the stated purpose of promoting reconciliation between North and South, of "holding out a helping hand to our brethren at the South" and "helping to develop a Southern literature." As part of this project, Edward King came to New Orleans in 1872 to begin research for his "Great South" series. He met Cable not long after his arrival, and through King the young romancer came to the attention of *Scribner's.* In a few early submissions Cable seemed to provide something very close indeed to what Josiah Holland and Gilder were looking for in a "new" southern literature—the "color" and charm of southern "jadis," or the suggestion of the "once upon a time," the antique, the relic. Cable was praised for his use of dialect and setting, for his strong sense of character, for the "bright and witty" style in which he told his tales. He seemed destined to become an exemplary southern author in *Scribner's* literary stable.[15]

In Cable's "best" work, it was intimated again and again, the unfortunate legacies of history—colonialism, slavery, miscegenation—were safely subordinated to the optimistic discourse of redemptive U.S. nationalism. But too often Gilder found in the stories "coarse suggestions" and "touches of horror" that were objectionable. He disliked, for example, the fact that 'Sieur George, an aging creole speculator and gambler of unknown origins, proposes marriage to a young ward left in his care, a proposal that leaves the girl no alternative except to flee to a convent. Apparently, the American sense of decorum was violated by the contrast between Monsieur George's ostensible assumption that marriage to him would be the best way to ensure the young lady's continued respectability and the reality of what most middle-class

---

sippi, ou des provinces de Louisiane et Floride Occidentale en l'année 1802 (Paris, 1803); Charles Mackey, *Life and Liberty in America, or Sketches of a Tour in the United States and Canada in 1857–1858* (New York, 1859); François-Xavier Martin, *History of Louisiana from the Earliest Period* (New Orleans, 1827); Duke of Saxe-Weimar–Eisenach, *Travels Through North America* (2 vols., Philadelphia, 1828); and others referred to in the following discussion of Bras-Coupé. He also perused the Louisiana *Gazette* and the New Orleans *Times-Picayune.* See the discussion of his reading in Turner's *George W. Cable,* 48–51.

15. Turner, *George W. Cable,* 67–68.

Americans considered to be his probable motivations, in light of his obscure origins and speculative character. For Gilder, literature should be not only "true," "robust," and "artistic," but also "decent" and "just."[16] Unfortunately, the "historical tendency" was at the bottom of Cable's desire to write fiction, and history had been neither "decent" nor "just."

Without underestimating Richard Watson Gilder's astute editorial instincts, it is clear that the pressure Cable experienced from his editors between the beginning of his career in the early 1870s and the mid-1880s affected his work deeply and negatively. In essence, there were certain areas in which he was asked not to work, and those were precisely the areas where he most wanted to work—in the history of slavery and the color line and the growth of U.S. nationalism upon the foundation provided by that history. In a rather famous assessment, Edmund Wilson claimed that "the slow strangulation of Cable as an artist and a serious writer is surely one of the most gruesome episodes in American literary history."[17]

The obscurity and the confusions of Cable's texts stem directly from the strategic displacements by which he not only tried to avoid treating too directly but also tried to avoid sidestepping too shamelessly the implications of the colonial history of Louisiana, slavery, and miscegenation for the present. The "touches of horror," "coarse suggestions," and confused relationships function integrally in the texts as commentaries on the optimistic nationalism that was supposedly governing the progress of the plots. One may recall here the mysteries surrounding the genealogy of 'Tite Poulette even at the happy ending, or the legacies of the slave trade in "Jean-ah Poquelin." In short, Cable's "fault of eddying about his point" as well as the muted "touch or two of horror" are more often than not products of his highly strategic ironic subver-

---

16. Richard Watson Gilder, "The Nationalizing of Southern Literature: Part I—Before the War," New York *Christian Advocate*, July 3, 1890, p. 426. Whenever Cable broached the subject of interracial sexual relationships, for example, he risked being charged with "coarseness"; whenever he attempted to sketch the character of a drunken preacher (as in "Posson Jone'") or a gambler who would gamble with the future of a young innocent ("'Sieur George"), he risked treading on the pieties of the Reconciliationist agenda. "Write something intensely interesting," Gilder wrote at one point, "but without the terrible suggestion you so often make use of" (Turner, *George W. Cable*, 67).

17. Wilson, *Patriotic Gore*, 579.

sions of the conventional reconciliation plot with its distancing frames and clear, uncomplicated closure around a happy ending.

It is within this context that Cable conceived, wrote, and revised *The Grandissimes,* which is without doubt one of the most important novels published in the United States during the late nineteenth century. Louis D. Rubin, Jr., calls it "the first modern southern novel," to the extent that it attempts to deal "honestly with the complexity of Southern racial experience." And in the *Columbia Literary History of the United States,* Eric Sundquist notes that Cable is capable of lifting his fiction "above sheer regional interest" and reaching deeply into "mythic, psychological realism." It is also one of the first works to explore from a Deep South perspective the tensions associated with the assimilation or nationalization of the southerner after the reunification of the North and South in 1865. That it was written by a white southern liberal (a rare breed in the first few years after Reconstruction) makes it particularly interesting as a predecessor of later works by Mark Twain and William Faulkner, both of whom held more liberal perspectives on race than many of their contemporaries.[18]

Insofar as the plot is concerned, the most important players in *The Grandissimes* are the white Honoré Grandissime, the wisest and most capable of all the Creoles of New Orleans, and Joseph Frowenfeld, the German-American immigrant to "the little Creole city" and a somewhat naïve spokesman for the ideals of U.S. nationalism. It is in the encounter of these characters with the imagined future as embodied in the white Clotilde and Aurora Nancanou—the most beautiful, the most innocent, indeed "the best blood of the Province"—and with the very heavy legacies of the past represented in this text by the black and mulatto characters that the novel takes shape.[19]

Much of the reconciliationist plot of the novel as published concerns the development of a romantic relationship between the white Honoré—that finest flower of Grandissime stock—and Aurora de Grapion Nancanou, who years previously had been deprived of her for-

---

18. Rubin, *Life and Times,* 78; Eric Sundquist, "Regions and Regionalism," in *The Columbia Literary History of the United States,* ed. Emory Elliott *et al.* (New York, 1988), 515.

19. George W. Cable, *The Grandissimes* (New York, 1880), 19. All subsequent citations are to this edition.

tune through the punctilio of a member of the Grandissime family, Agricola Fusilier, the closest thing to a villain in the work. The task set for Honoré is how to effect the greatest justice. He can return Aurora's estate, win her love, and cope with the guilt of ruining his own family fortunes through mere "love of woman," or he can retain the title to her estate and cope with the loss of Aurora, as well as with the suspicion that in placing the claims of his family before those of his beloved, he has sacrificed the greater for the lesser justice.

Honoré's private difficulties with respect to the conflicting demands of his family and Aurora are set within the context of a general review of titles of all kinds connected with the transfer of legal authority from France, where Civil Law prevailed, to the United States, where property rights and rules of control and inheritance of property had more or less been determined according to the principles of English Common Law, a legal code that deals very differently with issues of family law and property, particularly where gender is involved. Civil Law considers the fundamental social unit to be the family and has traditionally controlled the way property is passed from one generation to another by restricting the capacity of the testator, *i.e.*, the paterfamilias, to disinherit his descendants. Under English Common Law the fundamental social unit is the individual, and a testator (acting on his or her own behalf as an individual) has greater power of disinheritance, as beneficiaries have additional grounds on which to dispute a will. Furthermore, although in many respects married women possessed less control over their own property under English Common Law, inheritance through female lines was possible in ways it was not possible under Civil Law, precisely because of the freedom granted to the testator as an individual.[20]

The import of these differences is particularly striking along the color line. In French Louisiana, a white father could legitimate by no-

20. For good discussions of the traditional differences between English Common Law and Civil Law in provisions for inheritance, see Phanor J. Eder, *A Comparative Survey of Anglo-American and Latin-American Law* (Littleton, Colo., 1981); Clarence J. Morrow, "Louisiana," and Marc Anal, "France," in *Matrimonial Property Law*, ed. W. Friedman (Toronto, 1955), 29–88, 3–28; Morton Horwitz, *The Transformation of American Law, 1780– 1860* (New York, 1992); and Richard B. Morris, *Studies in the History of American Law* (Philadelphia, 1959). See also Higginbotham and Kopytoff, "Racial Purity in Colonial and Antebellum Virginia."

tarial act his mixed-blood children; there were certain portions of his property that he was entitled to bequeath to those children; and the capacity of other family members to dispute the bequests was limited. In *The Grandissimes*, there is much resentment among the white members of the Grandissime family of Honoré's octoroon brother, also named Honoré, who has inherited the bulk of his white father's estate. On the other hand, in the United States, where the status of a child as slave or free always followed that of the mother, there were both stricter limits to the capacity of any white father to legally acknowledge those children for purposes of inheritance and a greater likelihood that the white father's "white" children could dispute any bequest. In light of these very different systems for placing people along the color line, Creoles had some reason to be concerned about the possible impact of the United States in the arena of family law.

Within this context, the creole anxiety about points of maternal genealogy in the novel may be understandable. It was of real significance that one be able to prove that one's maternal origins were "all pu'e wite." The narrator, genial as he is, seems to relish exposing the clay feet beneath creole genealogical pretension with respect to "maternal origins." In this work, creole records and relics, the means through which one might prove title (and sometimes the "title" one wants to prove is sentimental or moral rather than legal) through a female line, always turn out to be lost. The letter that supposedly accompanied the white Honoré's "great ancestress" to Louisiana and attested to her noble blood, is lost. The portrait that would establish Clotilde Nancanou's resemblance to her ancestress, the heroic *Fille à la Cassette* who would marry only for love (that fact constitutes her heroism), is "hopelessly lost in some garret." [21] And at times there is altogether too much insistence on the racial purity of Clotilde and Aurora Nancanou. It may well be here that one can see most clearly Cable's understanding of the threat nationalist assumptions about race and cultural legitimacy represented for Creoles.

The relevance of all of this preoccupation with the lostness of titles (be they titles to property or the more general entitlements to cultural preeminence) to the Reconstruction and Redemption eras is too obvious to belabor. Suffice it to say that for former Confederates in the

21. Cable, *The Grandissimes*, 22, 30.

United States as for Creoles in *The Grandissimes*, it was no simple matter to prove legitimate descent from antebellum origins.

The predictability of the reconciliation plot notwithstanding, the novel as Cable initially conceived it was significantly less focused on the development of the romance between the two major white characters. All of the evidence points to the fact that the work Cable first envisioned was more chronological, more discursive, and more "historical" in many ways. The original version began, for example, not with the masked ball where Aurora meets the white Honoré but with the story of Lukfi-Humma, an Indian princess who married one of the Grandissimes, and her genealogical legacy to the creole family. This story presents the narrator of the novel some opportunities for light satirizing of the pretensions of Creoles to racial purity. But between the writing of the manuscript of *The Grandissimes* and its publication in serial form in *Scribner's*, a battle of sorts took place between Cable and the *Scribner's* editors: whether the romance plot dealing chiefly with the white characters would be foregrounded, or the historical context dealing with issues of race and genealogy stemming from the legacies of colonialism and slavery; how prominent a role black and mulatto characters would play; and how much discursive editorializing about race and slavery could be permitted. As has already been suggested, Gilder and Johnson seldom addressed in any direct way the issue of race and slavery when articulating the general principles according to which the novel ought to be revised. Instead, they urged Cable to make the work as dramatic as possible and to avoid whenever possible the "terrible suggestion," which seems to have meant in this instance any hint of serious moral weakness in major characters or any reference to the continuing impact of slavery upon the novel's time present, the implication being that such references were in fact comments about the continuing impact of slavery upon the writer's and editors' time present.

Most of the specific changes readers suggested did have to do with race. The consequence was that Cable was repeatedly advised to eliminate or shorten the scenes with black characters. All of the most important black characters came in, one by one, for criticism. For example, the quadroon Palmyre was entirely unbelievable—her mere presence was a coarsening of the novel, while the free man of color was the weakest link in the narrative.[22] Robert Underwood Johnson also skirmished with Cable for quite some time over the turn of events that "elevated" the philosophical slavewoman Clemence above the rank of minor character. "It is inartistic for [Clemence] to *reason* so about slavery," he wrote on March 13, 1880. "The slave mind is not subjective or ratiocinative, it seems to me, but rather objective." Earlier he had elaborated the principle in more general terms: "The story must not lag a moment [after the June installment] for the secret is out and readers have four more installments in which to recede from the true climax of the story, which I take to be Honoré's restitution. This of itself is a great strain upon them and to stop for purely side-issue discussion is too much to ask of them" (February 11, 1880). To Cable's credit, he argued with Johnson over the characterization of Palmyre and the free man of color, and he categorically refused to alter the episodes with Clemence, her "subjective" speeches on slavery, and her murder at the hands of one of the Grandissimes. The reason he gave was that the character of Clemence was based on a real woman. Nevertheless, Cable did delete several long dialogues concerning the race issue in an attempt to make the novel dramatic. Cable appears not to have been comfortable with the bargain he struck with genteel realism on this point, for the historical, the coarse, the "terrible suggestion" remain—albeit displaced— within the reconciliation romance.[23]

In 1873, when Edward King first met him, Cable had been researching the city archives for information about the history of New Orleans and

22. In a letter of March 26, 1879, Robert Underwood Johnson criticizes the manuscript, suggesting that two readers find "the Bras-Coupé matter not a vital part of the plot and perhaps capable of condensation"; that Cable should move the "Masked Ball" to the first chapter; that "the Lukfi–Humma episode is devoid of interest"; and that none of the readers "see the necessity for making so much of 'La Fille à la Cassette.' " In addition, he reports that Palmyre and Bras-Coupé "are thought to be impossible." On April 2, 1879, Johnson remarks to Cable on his tendency to "go pamphleteering" and says that the scene between Palmyre and Joseph at the shop is melodramatic. On August 18, 1879, Johnson sends a postcard reminding Cable to "be dramatic, too much purpose!" And on December 2, 1879, Johnson writes that "the f.m.c. is the least interesting part of your story." All of these letters are in the George Washington Cable Collection.

23. Robert Underwood Johnson to George W. Cable, March 13, 1880, and February 11, 1880, in the George Washington Cable Collection.

had read, perhaps earlier, the Code Noir, the infamous Black Code that governed the treatment of slaves and persons of color under the colonialist governments. It was in outrage, he later reported, that he wrote the story "Bibi," now lost. Edward King was so impressed by the story that he sent it off to *Scribner's* for consideration, writing to Cable to "fear not . . . for your fame is sure if you continue to make Bibis." [24]

As it turned out, Gilder did not like the story. Neither did other editors. Arlin Turner suggests that the reason given by the editor of the *Atlantic Monthly,* George Parsons Lathrop, for its rejection may be representative: "Bibi" was unacceptable "on account of the unmitigatedly distressful effect of the story." There is little doubt that the story in this first version was indeed distressful. More than a month after leaving New Orleans, Edward King had written to Cable that "'Bibi' rode me as a nightmare last night." [25]

The story in this original version may have been considerably more distressful than it became after its revision and incorporation into *The Grandissimes.* "Bibi" was probably a very different story altogether, with more overt connections with the history of slave resistance in the West Indies and in colonialist Louisiana than "The Story of Bras-Coupé." Arlin Turner acknowledges that "Bibi" was "in broad outline a true story"—by which he means that it was drawn from history and legend, as was the case with so much of Cable's work. Edward King's first letter to Cable about the story would appear to corroborate Turner's conjecture. In this letter King writes that "'Bibi' has waltzed off to New York, along with Bienville and all the other heroes of that time." In that remark he reveals that "Bibi" could not have been the same story that was later "incorporated" into *The Grandissimes* as "The Story of Bras-Coupé," where there is no "Bienville" or any other "hero of that time," where the characters who populate the story are the fictional Grandissimes and the de Grapions, and the time is much later than the era of Bienville. [26] Although Cable later claimed that "The Story of Bras-Coupé" was written "much as it stands" before the novel was begun, it is clear that in Cable's revision of the tale for *The Grandissimes,* he altered the context of the story, with "Bienville and the other heroes of

24. Turner, *George W. Cable,* 54.
25. Biklé, *George W. Cable,* 48; Turner, *George W. Cable,* 54.
26. Turner, *George W. Cable,* 54.

that time," figures straight from Louisiana history, being replaced with the representative characters of the Grandissimes, the Fusiliers, and the other prominent Creoles of the novel. That change itself is significant because it recapitulates the principle of "universalization" and "transcendence of the historical" that governed Cable's editors in their suggestions for other revisions in the novel. It is here—in the relationship between the local or the historical and the universal and transcendent—that one finds delineated the aesthetic strategy, the principle of exchange and substitution, denial and displacement, that governs *The Grandissimes.*

Briefly, the story is of an African *candio* who is sold into slavery when he is defeated in battle by an enemy. When he arrives in New Orleans he is purchased by Agricola Fusilier, who admires his "physical beauties," and sells him again to his friend (and a remote relative of the de Grapions) Don José Martinez. Bras-Coupé—remarkably like his creole purchasers—has an aversion to work based on his aristocratic status but is finally persuaded to take a job as driver by the promise of the quadroon Palmyre Philosophe as a bride. That Palmyre does not love Bras-Coupé is of no concern to anyone except Palmyre and her mistress, the white Honoré Grandissime's younger sister and the betrothed of Martinez—until M. de Grapion, who has sent Palmyre to Mlle. Grandissime "on loan," so to speak, learns that she is to marry Bras-Coupé. Outraged that Agricola Fusilier would dare to "dishonor one who shared the blood of the De Grapions" (*i.e.,* Palmyre), M. de Grapion promises "to have the life of the man."[27]

Pride is pride. The wedding takes place, but the new Señora Martinez and Palmyre conspire to keep Palmyre from Bras-Coupé, who begins to suspect that something is afoot and who, drinking more and more and ridiculously got up in French regimentals, demands his bride. When she doesn't come, he loses his temper, knocks Señor Martinez to the ground, and curses him, the plantation, and everyone on it "who is not a woman." Then, amid the hysteria of the wedding guests who fear that they are about to witness an insurrection, Bras-Coupé flees into the swamp.

Señor Martinez is taken ill, the slaves on the plantation believe themselves to have been bewitched and cannot work, the worm is upon the

---

27. Cable, *The Grandissimes,* 170, 176.

crops, the plantation is ruined. Meanwhile, Bras-Coupé waits in the swamp until one day he joins the dance in Place Congo and is caught through the treachery of another slave. The provisos of the Code Noir are honored. Bras-Coupé has his ears shorn and his hamstrings severed and is brought back to the plantation where Palmyre attends him faithfully. Upon his deathbed, he is beseeched by the young mistress to bless her newborn son and lift the curse:

> The lady . . . knelt down beside the bed of sweet grass and set the child within the hollow of the African's arm. Bras-Coupé turned his gaze upon it; it smiled, its mother's smile, and put its hand upon the runaway's face, and the first tears of Bras-Coupé's life, the dying testimony of his humanity, gushed from his eyes and rolled down his cheek upon the infant's hand. He laid his own tenderly upon the babe's forehead, then removing it, waved it abroad, inaudibly moved his lips, dropped his arm, and closed his eyes. The curse was lifted.

The lifting of the curse is immediately followed by a scene devoted to the death of Bras-Coupé, who answers a priest's inquiry about where he is going after death, by "lift[ing] his hand" and whispering "with an ecstatic, upward smile . . . 'to—Africa.'" [28]

The story of Bras-Coupé is not an original one. Legends about a one-armed runaway known by that name had been numerous in New Orleans since antebellum days. Other postbellum versions of the story of Bras-Coupé appear in Marion Baker's *Historical Sketchbook and Guide to New Orleans*, compiled for the New Orleans Exposition in 1885, and Grace King's *New Orleans: The Place and the People*, which appeared in 1895, as well as in many later works, including William Faulkner's "Red Leaves." [29] That this story and others like it were so popular in Exposition and tourist publications may have to do with the need of the postbellum United States to contain—or rather to represent itself as transcending—history, most importantly the history of slavery in the United States.

Some of these readers of the Redemption era (and later) tell us that

28. *Ibid.*, 193.

29. Marion Baker, *Historical Sketchbook and Guide to New Orleans* (New York, 1885); Grace King, *New Orleans: The Place and the People* (New York, 1895), 80. See also John W. Blassingame, *Black New Orleans, 1860–1880* (Chicago, 1973), and Edward Larocque Tinker and Frances Tinker, *Old New Orleans* (New York, 1931).

Cable's story is based on the account of a real runaway slave by the name of Squire. According to Lafcadio Hearn, a well-known purveyor of the exotic to American audiences, the story of Squire was told to Cable by Alexander Dimitry, an author and bookstore proprietor in New Orleans. (This was the Dimitry whose son-in-law, George Pandely, was removed from office for a supposed trace of African ancestry; see Chapter 1.)

In a short report written for the New Orleans *Item* (October 27, 1880) Hearn recounts Dimitry's story.[30] The man known as Bras-Coupé was originally a slave living in New Orleans in the late 1850s. He was owned by an auctioneer, Joseph Le Carpentier. Le Carpentier, suffering from financial problems, was driven to sell his industrious and docile slave to John Freret, who owned a cotton press. Freret was not the kind master Squire was used to, and one day the two men got into an argument. When Squire lifted his arm to strike Freret, he found his own arm shattered by an iron bar. In that way he became known as Bras-Coupé. Understanding what his punishment for striking Freret would be, Squire fled to the woods, where he lived "for a long while" with the help of a Spaniard who supplied him with the clothes and the weapons necessary to his survival.[31]

After a time city officials began to receive complaints that a dangerous robber was working the Gentilly Road area. Men and women were robbed en route to the market in New Orleans; some women were raped on the road. They described the attacker as Bras-Coupé. Legends grew, but this man evaded authorities. Only when police offered a one-thousand-dollar reward was he finally caught, as it turns out through betrayal. The Spaniard who had befriended Bras-Coupé for so long crushed his skull with an iron bar as he slept beneath a tree in the woods. When the body was carried into New Orleans, people were astonished to discover that the fearsome Bras-Coupé was "only" old Squire, who had fled so long ago in order to save his own life. Cable's

---

30. Robert O. Stephens, in his "Cable's Bras-Coupé and Merimee's Tamango: The Case of the Missing Arm" (*Mississippi Quarterly*, XXXV [Fall, 1982], 387–405), details much of the newspaper coverage of the fugitive slave Squire, who is most likely the source figure for stories told by Dimitry to Hearn and by an anonymous black porter to Cable himself.

31. Lafcadio Hearn, "The Original Bras-Coupé," in *Essays on American Literature* (Tokyo, 1929), 60. The full account is reprinted in this collection.

Bras-Coupé is, to some extent, comparably sentimentalized as a proud but ultimately harmless primitive, inspired more by alcohol and love than by passion for any "subjective" ideal (since the slave mind, remember, was not supposed to be ratiocinative), but only to some extent.

If we return to accounts of the runaway written in the antebellum period (accounts that would have been very familiar to the historian Cable, if not to Lafcadio Hearn), the story is very different.[32] On July 19, 1837, the New Orleans *Picayune* reported the death of Squire at great length. This antebellum account connects the runaway with slave insurrections in a way that Hearn never does. The *Picayune* writer describes Squire as "Brigand of the Swamp," a "notorious black scoundrel" who ruled an "encampment of outlaw negroes" and lured slaves away from their masters to join his camp. The report concludes with the hope that Squire's murder will "lead to the scouring of the swamp round about the city. . . . While they can support a gang and have a camp, we may expect our slaves to run away and harrowing depredations to be committed upon society."

> This notorious black scoundrel was yesterday killed by a Spaniard in the swamp near the Bayou road. It will be remembered by all our citizens that Squire was the negro who has so long prowled about the marshes in the rear of the city, a terror to the community, and for whose head a reward of two thousand dollars was offered some years ago.
>
> The life of this negro has been one of crime and total depravity. The annals of the city furnish records of his cruelty, crime and murder.
>
> He had killed several white men in this place before he fled to the swamp and has up to the time of his death, eluded, with a dexterity worthy of a more educated villain, all the searching efforts of justice to capture him. He has lived for the last three years an outlaw in the marshes in the rear of the city. Many years since he had his right arm shot off; he is said, nonetheless, to have been an excellent marksman,

---

32. The Louisiana *Advertiser* for June, 1836, provides a brief account that was picked up by the Boston-based abolitionist newspaper *The Liberator* for July 2, 1836. In this version Squire is no solitary runaway but is a member of "a band of negroes" attributed with organized criminal activity: "The Louisiana *Advertiser* of the 8th, mentions that a band of runaway negroes in the Cypress Swamp in the rear of the city, had been committing depredations. On the morning of the 7th, they attacked and plundered the house of a widow named Shea, on the new Canal, and wounded a negro girl left in charge of the house who attempted to run for assistance. The laborers on the new canal volunteered to ferret them out, but being without arms, they had to desist."

with but the use of his left arm. Inured by hardships and exposure to the climate, he has subsisted in the woods and carried on, until this time, his deeds of robbery and murder with the most perfect impunity—the marshes surrounding the city being almost impenetrabl[e] to our citizens.

This demi-devil has for a long time ruled as the "Brigand of the Swamp." A supposition has always found believers that there was an encampment of outlaw negroes near the city and that Squire was their leader. He was a fiend in human shape and has done much mischief in the way of decoying slaves to his camp, and committing depredations upon the premises of those who live on the outskirts of the city. His destruction is hailed, by old and young, as a benefit to society.

A Spaniard was yesterday morning in the swamp, and proved the successful foe of this enemy to society. Squire raised his gun to shoot him; but failed, the gun having snapped. Immediately the Spaniard rushed upon him with a big stick—he gave him a blow which brought him to the ground, when his brains were literally beat out by the infuriated man. Proud of his victory, the conqueror came into the city and reported what he had done. On hearing that Squire was dead the authorities determined to have his body hauled to the city and forthwith appointed a guard of men to repair to the swamp and bring it.

About two o'clock yesterday his body was exhibited on the public square of the First Municipality. For the sake of example, two or three thousand slaves were encouraged to go and see it. Squire was so well known to the negroes of the city. It was thought it would have a salutary effect to let them gaze upon the outlaw and murderer as he lay bleeding and weltering in his gore. So enormous have been the crimes of this negro that the large multitude of slaves assembled to see the last of him, shuddered at the bare recital of his bloody and murderous deeds.

It is to be hoped that the death of this leader of the outlaw negroes supposed to be in the swamp will lead to the scouring of the swamp round about the city. This nest of desperadoes should be broken up. While they can support a gang and have a camp, we may expect our slaves to run away and harrowing depredations to be committed upon society.[33]

This account is interesting for what it reveals about the significance of Squire for the white community. Clearly this reporter (as well as the townspeople who recommended it) finds it useful to display Squire's

33. New Orleans *Daily Picayune*, July 19, 1837.

body to serve as a warning to slaves not to imitate the example of the fugitive. This was by no means the first such exemplary display. White Louisianians had long used this method of discouraging slave rebellions. A rebellion in 1794 at Julian Poydras' plantation was one such occasion; insurrectionists were hanged all along the route of insurrection to serve as a warning to other blacks. It is also interesting that the threat of rebellion is so effectively muted in this account—the reporter preferring to represent the deeds of Squire as individual criminal activity, while at the same time acknowledging him as the leader of a band of runaways and the source of temptation to other slaves to run away. It is a willful blindness to the political significance of *marronage* and to the possibility of widespread slave rebellion. Such blindness on the part of whites is mirrored in *The Grandissimes*, where the white protagonists move blithely about their business of love and adjustment to the new American government, oblivious to the evidence of any particularly widespread discontent among the black characters.

That Squire's role as a leader of other black fugitives, so prominent in the original newspaper account, is effaced in Hearn's post–Civil War version, where Bras-Coupé lives alone except for the assistance of (and subsequent betrayal by) a Spaniard, is evidence of the way stories are rewritten by different eras for their own purposes. Although the antebellum journalist makes no bones about the very real economic and social threat represented by runaways and implicitly acknowledges the effectiveness of such *marronage* even in the Deep South (whose [white] historians are more likely to be found uncovering or inventing reasons why slave insurrections there never functioned as they did in Haiti), the "moral" of Hearn's tale appears to be that the terrifying maroon turns out to be "only" old Squire, a solitary runaway, victim of two evils—the slave system and the Spaniard. In other words, he is a kind of Uncle Tom whose claims upon the reader are consistent with the sentimental ethos of domestic realism and with ethnocentric nationalism.[34] There could be any number of reasons for the transformation of the dangerous leader of a band of fugitives into a familiar old "darky," chief among them the conciliatory temper of the Redemption-era United States. In any case, such a rewriting of history can tell us a great

34. For a discussion of the rebel societies, see Richard Price, ed., *Maroon Societies: Rebel Slave Communities in the Americas* (New York, 1973).

deal about the kind of stories white Americans of Cable's day were most (and least) interested in hearing. Such information can enlighten us as to the conditions under which Cable wrote his best work and the import of its dialogism, for there are speakers in Cable's text—Raoul Innerarity, for example—whose understanding of Bras-Coupé is no different from Dimitry's understanding of Squire.

With some irony the narrator calls Raoul "that master of narrative and melody." At the "fête de Grandpère," Raoul entertains the Grandissime children with songs, dances, and stories, making his selections on criteria that remind us of Gilder's and Johnson's genteel aesthetic. He refuses, for example, to honor a girl's request that he sing "Yé tolé dancé la doung y doung doung" because it contains "too many objectionable phrases." "Oh, just hum the objectionable phrases and go right on," the girl demands, echoing the editorial advice Cable so often received from his editors. But Raoul sings another song, a love song, that he claims to have heard Bras-Coupé himself sing after a hunting trip during the days when he and José Martinez would hunt together. He also sings for the children "that song the negroes sing when they go out in the bayous at night, stealing pigs and chickens!" We are not lucky enough to hear much of the story of Bras-Coupé from Raoul's lips, only one or two references that suggest, obliquely to be sure, the gist of the tale à la Raoul. We do know that the story, as he conceives it, is the proper finale for an evening of song; its purpose is to elicit a sentimental reaction from the Grandissime girls, who "agreed, at the close that it was pitiful. Specially, that it was a great pity to have hamstrung Bras-Coupé, a man who even in his cursing had made an exception of the ladies." Yet these listeners do not argue that Bras-Coupé "had deserved his fate" and the party breaks up, with the girls "confirmed in this sentiment."

As if to comment upon the limitations of the sentimental domestication of Bras-Coupé, Cable places those portions of Raoul's story of Bras-Coupé within the context of the birthday celebration of the Grandissime patriarch. He makes it very clear that Raoul's story is simply the one most acceptable for the youngest members of the Grandissime clan. Raoul's Bras-Coupé is a singer and dancer whose songs and dances are entirely opaque; the words Raoul repeats—"Dé zabs, dé zabs, dé counou ouaie ouaie"—neither the reader nor Raoul understands. But this is acceptable; the point of Raoul's story—like the point of those expositions so associated with postbellum U.S. nationalism and like tourism—is to celebrate the present, not to analyze or critique the past.[35]

This particular version of the Bras-Coupé story had a powerful appeal for reading audiences in Victorian America. Other, comparable accounts of Bras-Coupé from this period still exist. According to the creole musician Louis Gottschalk (writing in 1881), stories of a superhuman black slave were current in his home in the late 1830s. Gottschalk's grandmother would tell him the story of a famous African whose huge voice used to shout "Dansez bamboula" in Place Congo on Saturday afternoons. The man was called "jean bras-coupé." (The lowercase spelling is from Gottschalk's own account.) According to this version, jean bras-coupé was originally the property of a doctor and cost two thousand dollars in the St. Louis slave market. One afternoon after dancing in Place Congo, bras-coupé escaped to the swamps where he still lived, dining well on his would-be captors. He protected himself by rubbing his skin with a special herb that ensured no bullet could penetrate him. Supposedly rifle balls would flatten on impact and drop right off. He could kill people by looking at them. A whole detachment of soldiers went into the swamp after him and not one of them ever came back; bras-coupé ate them, bones and all. And, of course, the redoubtable fugitive was still evading the noose at the time of the telling.

In all three accounts, the runaway is reduced (or elevated, if one prefers) to a figure of legend, either sentimental victim or bugaboo for children and tourists. Even by scholars of our own era, Bras-Coupé is most often represented as a sentimentalized victim of the old regime, a testament to the truth that "all Slavery is maiming," and a man whose defiance is ultimately traceable to his love for a woman. For all this "universalizing," however, which appears to suggest that the real problem with slavery was that it violated the slave's right to love where he or she chose to love, there are intriguing remnants, or a "counter-memory," of the old documentary historical reality in Cable's revision. They constitute a subtext of defiance and insurrection, a subtext that implicates not only the title character, Bras-Coupé, but all of the black characters in a pattern of defiance that many of the major white speak-

35. Cable, *The Grandissimes,* 216–17, 253.

ers seem curiously determined to ignore. It is interesting that the white Honoré responds to the story as told by Raoul by "feeling a kind of suffocation" and leaving the celebration to hunt up Frowenfeld, to whom he apparently tells his own version of "The Story of Bras-Coupé." And later, the dark Honoré also tells his own version of the story to Frowenfeld.[36] It is presumably from all three versions that the genial narrator constructs his tale for his readers.

Despite Raoul's "suffocating" manipulation of history in the interest of convention, there remains in his songs, as in the legends and other Redemption-era accounts of Bras-Coupé, a contextual richness that he does not seem to understand but that links the hero to some very real eighteenth-century slaves whose stories are recorded in the histories of Louisiana and the Caribbean that Cable would have read. Among those details are the use of song to signal to accomplices, the ritualistic dance, the protecting herb or fetish, the mesmerizing gaze, and cannibalism. This context, clearly no more than superstition, or "color," for many of the white storytellers of Cable's day, had a more powerful political role in African and Afro-Caribbean cultures. There the rites associated with voodoo ceremonies were, more often than not, connected with self-government and organized resistance among enslaved people.

As a result of the kind of reading he did during the years when he was writing his first stories and *The Grandissimes,* and as a result of his own interest in what Arlin Turner terms "true stories," Cable would have been more familiar with this context than his editors and many of his readers and interpreters (including Lafcadio Hearn, whose interests were more often directed toward song and legend than toward history). In particular, Cable seems to have known that the leaders of slave insurrections in the Caribbean were often voodoo priests who used their considerable authority to communicate with, organize, and direct their followers in insurrectionary acts. The renowned Boukman (the name is sometimes spelled "Bouqueman"), who led uprisings during the early years of the revolution, is a case in point:

> In order to wash away all hesitation [to revolt] and to secure absolute devotion [Boukman] brought together on the night of 14 August 1791 a great number of slaves in a glade in Bois Caïman [Alligator Woods] near

36. Louis Moreau Gottschalk, *Notes of a Pianist,* ed. Clara Gottschalk (Philadelphia, 1881), 104–105; Cable, *The Grandissimes,* 221, 257.

Morne-Rouge. They were all assembled when a storm broke. Jagged lightning in blinding flashes illuminated a sky of low and somber clouds. In seconds a torrential rain floods the soil while under repeated assaults by a furious wind the forest trees twist and weep and their largest branches, violently ripped off, fall noisily away. In the center of this impressive setting those present, transfixed, gripped by an inspired dread see an old dark woman arise. Her body quivers in lengthy spasms; she sings, pirouettes, and brandishes a large cutlass overhead. An even greater immobility, the shallow scarcely audible breathing, the burning eyes fixed on the black woman soon indicate that the spectators are spellbound. Then a black pig is brought forward, its squalls lost in the raging of the storm. With a swift stroke the inspired priestess plunges her cutlass into the animal's throat. . . . The hot, spurting blood is caught and passed round among the slaves; they all sip of it, all swearing to carry out Boukman's orders. The old woman of the strange eyes and shaggy hair invokes the gods of the ancestors while chanting mysterious words in African dialect. Suddenly Boukman stands up and in an inspired voice cries out, "God who made the sun that shines on us from above, who makes the sea to rage and the thunder roll, this same great God from his hiding place on a cloud, hear me, all of you, is looking down upon us. He sees what the whites are doing. The God of the whites asks for crime; ours desires only blessings. But this God who is so good directs you to vengeance! He will direct our arms, he will help us. Cast aside the image of the God of the whites who thirsts for our tears and pay heed to the voice of liberty speaking to our hearts."[37]

A couple of nights later, an uprising occurred, resulting in the burning of several plantations and the deaths of a number of whites.

On the surface, the real Boukman seems to have little in common with the fictional Bras-Coupé of *The Grandissimes*, whose cooperation as a slave is purchased with the promise of Palmyre as a bride and who is motivated in his defiance less by a desire for freedom than by a desire for a drink. Under such circumstances, it is easy to overlook the fact that Cable not only attributes his Bras-Coupé with voodoo powers comparable to those of Boukman but also connects these powers, albeit subtly, with political defiance and the threat of insurrection. Perhaps the most overt example occurs during his wedding celebration, when Bras-Coupé is refused his request for more wine. In order to defend

37. Turner, *George W. Cable*, 68; Jean Fouchard, *The Haitian Maroons: Liberty or Death*, trans. A. Faulkner Watts (New York, 1981), 340–41.

himself from his master's blow, he strikes back, knocking Señor Martinez to the ground. "Single-handed and naked-fisted in a room full of swords, the giant stood over his master, making strange signs and passes and rolling out in wrathful words of his mother tongue what it needed no interpreter to tell his swarming enemies was a voudou malediction." During this altercation, the white wedding guests stand "as if frozen, smitten stiff with the instant expectation of insurrection, conflagration, and rapine."[38]

Cable's account of Bras-Coupé in this scene is certainly as melodramatic as Sannon's description of Boukman. After he strikes Martinez, "the storm fell like a burst of infernal applause," followed by "a whiff like fifty witches" and a cloud, cloaked like the conventional villain of melodrama, "fierce" and "black," which "belches" lightning.[39] What is especially interesting is that the appeal to melodrama seems to be at odds with the rhetorical strategies the narrator has resorted to thus far in his account of Bras-Coupé. That narrator's tone throughout the first half of the story has been light, conversational, full of allusions to nineteenth-century Victorian Christianity and to popular literary figures like Tennyson, but the switch to melodrama is surprising in this narrator so remarkable for his lightness and geniality. If the switch to melodrama is surprising, it is also strategic, another of those tonal digressions that disguise the harsh—Cable's narrator uses the term "coarse"—reality of the slavery ethos that would in this scene make of marriage a "by-play" and a groom's hand a "paw." But it also introduces a heavier, more symbolic use of language reminiscent of Herard Delisle's account of Boukman.

It is such language that transfers the reader's attention from the conflicts among the characters stemming from their involvement in the love story to the conflicts that stem from the characters' involvement in the political and economic systems they represent, or enact. Bras-Coupé, in this portion of the story, is only incidentally a lover deprived of his beloved. From the perspective of the reader the flight of Bras-Coupé has resulted not only, nor even chiefly, in the loss of the beloved, but in the transformation of a love story into a story of economic, political, and moral disaster. We hear little more of Bras-Coupé until his

38. Cable, *The Grandissimes*, 235–36.
39. *Ibid.*, 234.

capture but are much more focused on the plantation in ruins, the masters without authority, the slaves ill or mutinous, and the white Mademoiselle, now Madame, quietly disapproving of her husband's betrayal of Bras-Coupé and Palmyre.

Despite the melodramatic style of the telling, that the effect of the runaway on the economy and politics of the plantation is so great is entirely realistic. The actual threat of fugitive slaves was always economic and political. Antebellum journalists (like the reporter quoted above) stress the theft and destruction to plantations and homes caused by maroons. Colonialist historians detail the connection between *marronage*, political defiance, and economic ruin. Within such a context, those Redemption-era stories of solitary fugitives whose motivations are entirely individual and whose depredations are sporadic and economically insignificant, like Hearn's "Squire" and Raoul's Bras-Coupé, do as much to obscure "The Story of Bras-Coupé" as to elucidate it.

It may be even more telling that Cable also went to some trouble to embed the story of Bras-Coupé in the narrative in such a way as to cast some doubt upon its authenticity as presented to the reader and to call attention to the act of storytelling itself (in a manner which seems at times Faulknerian). The narrator tells us that the story was told three times on one day: once by Raoul; once by the white Honoré, who is concerned that the mistreatment of Bras-Coupé "revived a war" after peace had been struck between the Grandissimes and the de Grapions; and yet once again by the dark Honoré, for whom the story constitutes a comment upon his own failures to champion the people U.S. law and tradition would associate him with. The narrator, after informing us of the three tellings, also informs us that "we shall not follow the words of any one of these"; so, in effect, we have a fourth teller as well, the genial and digressive narrator himself.[40] There is hardly a better record of the dialogic nature of *The Grandissimes* than "The Story of Bras-Coupé," for the narrator's voice embodies no more authority than the voices it purports to override by diverging from the "words of any of these." In fact, its function seems not to be to present anything resembling an "authorized" version of events but to signal for the astute reader the "constructedness" of the story. Finally, the narrator seems as

40. *Ibid.*, 259, 219.

interested in satirizing the claims of truth telling in fiction as in uncovering any particular truth about Bras-Coupé.

Despite the delusive familiarity of a sentimentalized Bras-Coupé, in creating his fugitive Cable drew upon very different kinds of stories of Louisiana rebels that have their origin in stories from the West Indies (like the story of Boukman recounted above), where *marronage* had not only a role to play in isolated insurrections but also finally in the Haitian revolution under the leadership of Toussaint L'Ouverture.

In a letter to his daughter Lucy, written in 1899, Cable reports having heard a porter talk of Bras-Coupé at about the same time that he, Cable, "was first enjoying the impulse to write stories and had been reading in the colonial [French and Spanish] history of Louisiana some account of the characteristic traits of various tribes of negroes from which slaves were imported into this country." [41] According to the anonymous porter, the "real" Bras-Coupé was an Arada prince whose pride forbade him from working and who took a hatchet to his right hand to ensure that work would not be required of him. In another letter, Cable recalls having read "many of the old Relations of the priest explorers and much other French matter of early historical value." [42]

One likely source of such relations is *Historical Collections of Louisiana*, published in 1851 by Benjamin Franklin French. As mentioned earlier, Cable had requested a copy of French's collection from his editors in 1876 when he began his research for *The Grandissimes*, but he was probably already familiar with the work, having begun his readings in Louisiana history in the late 1860s. According to French, when in the mideighteenth century Louisiana colonists had to choose a hangman, they offered the position to a slave named Johnny, promising to give him his freedom in return. The slave was unwilling and when he discovered that he would be forced to accept the position, mutilated himself:

> He took an axe, and laying his arm on a block cut off his hand, and returning to the meeting showed his maimed limb, and his consequent inability to exercise the office with which they would have honored him. It is easy to imagine the effect produced by this . . . action; the first

41. Biklé, *George W. Cable*, 179–80n. In an unpublished portion of this letter, Cable refers to the porter as confusing Bras-Coupé with the famous rebel St. Malo. George W. Cable to Lucy Leffingwell Cable Biklé, February 12, 1899, in the George Washington Cable Collection.

42. Biklé, *George W. Cable*, 180, 47.

thought was to save his life; he was put in the hands of surgeons, cured and made commander of the company's negroes. As for the office, another less delicate was found, who accepted it at the price of his freedom, so that the hangman in the colony is a negro.[43]

Cable must have encountered a similar story in Charles Gayarré's *History of Louisiana*, which he may have read even earlier (using it in his final column for the *Daily Picayune*, written in 1872, the same year that "Bibi" was first circulated). Gayarré's version of "the negro Jeannot" differs in respect to the character of Jeannot and supplements French's somewhat restrained account with some interesting modifications. According to Gayarré, "Jeannot [offered the honorable position of colony hangman] was a high-spirited black and peremptorily refused the favor." As a result of Jeannot's act of self-mutilation, "The French were struck with admiration, and Jeannot was appointed overseer of all the negroes belonging to the company."[44] Although these stories do not portray Jeannot as a fugitive, many of the elements to be found in accounts of Haitian maroons are present: defiance, mutilation, and consequent leadership of other slaves.

There is, however, a more intriguing source for Bras-Coupé than French or Gayarré. Cable often relied upon a history, *Description topographique, physique, civile, politique, et historique de la partie française de l'Isle Saint Domingue*, written by a Haitian Creole, Médéric-Louis-Élie Moreau de Saint-Méry, which details the activities of certain black rebel leaders in eighteenth-century St. Domingue. That Cable did use this quite reliable and extensive work is proved by a small notebook held at Tulane University in which he kept meticulous records of facts that struck him as useful. In that notebook, there are numerous references to this source (as well as to many others), and Cable must have found in Moreau de Saint-Méry the account of a Haitian slave named Jean Baptiste who could have been an Arada warrior. This man, who hated the agricultural work he was required to do on his master's Haitian plantation, dreamed that if he carved for himself a wooden arm identical to his own right arm he would become free. He did so and then amputated his right arm, although it took him four strokes to do so. It

43. Benjamin Franklin French, comp., *Historical Collections of Louisiana* (New York, 1851), Vol. V, 121.
44. Gayarré, *History of Louisiana*, 341–42.

is unlikely to be a coincidence that, in *The Grandissimes*, it is a small right arm—the hand of which grasps a dirk, not wooden but molded of myrtle wax and hidden in a "small black coffin"—that links Clemence and Palmyre to attempts to "voodoo" Agricola Fusilier (the Creole responsible for the mutilation and death of Bras-Coupé) and, finally, associates both of these women with insurrectionary activities.[45]

But the account most strikingly similar to that of Cable's Bras-Coupé is Moreau de Saint-Méry's story of the great rebel leader François Macandal, executed in 1758. Bras-Coupé—first a gamekeeper for his Spanish master, then fugitive and voodoo priest—causes a plague of worms to infest Señor Martinez's plantation and a fever to come upon Martinez and his slaves: "Those to whom life was spared—but to whom strength did not return—wandered about the place like scarecrows, looking for shelter and made the very air dismal with the reiteration, '*No' ouanga*' (we are bewitched). *Bras-Coupé fe moi des grigris* (the voudoo's spells are on me)."[46]

Bras-Coupé is finally caught when he comes to join the *calinda* dance in Place Congo and drinks too much. The story of François Macandal is similar. Born in Africa, this man was enslaved on a plantation in Limbé. When he caught his hand in a mill, the hand had to be cut off, and Macandal was made into an animal keeper. He became a fugitive in the mountains and claimed to be sent by the Creator to liberate his people. This Macandal, one of the most effective rebels in the history of Haitian slave resistance, was famous for his use of poisons against his enemies. Other blacks were so afraid of him, according to Moreau de Saint-Méry, that they submitted to him in everything. He taught the use of poisons to others and positioned agents in all parts of the colony so that death sentences could be carried out with ease. Part of his scheme was to murder all the whites on St. Domingue, and he had such great success in his use of poisons that the white populace was in great fear of him and his accomplices. One day the slaves on the plantation were having a *calinda* and Macandal, accustomed to going where he

45. Cable, Ledger-Book, in George Washington Cable Collection, Manuscripts Department, Howard-Tilton Memorial Library, Tulane University, New Orleans, La.; Médéric-Louis-Élie Moreau de Saint-Méry, *Description topographique, physique, civile, politique, et historique de la partie française de L'Isle Saint-Domingue* (Paris, 1958) I, 61–62; Cable, *The Grandissimes*, 414.

46. *Ibid.*, 240.

liked without fear of capture, showed up. A young black man informed the owner, who distributed a great amount of *tafia* among the revelers. Macandal was captured when he became drunk. At his execution he struggled so hard in the flames that he broke the chain holding him to the wooden stake and fell beneath the platform. A cry went up—"Macandal sauvé"—and although he did apparently die in the flames, many continued to believe that Macandal lived.[47]

Moreau de Saint-Méry is not the only source for information about this renowned rebel leader. We know from other sources that he was a fugitive for eighteen years, that he resided in the mountains and came down at night to meet with his followers around low-lying plantations. During his lifetime (and for a long time afterward) poisonings of both blacks and whites were frequent. Most blacks who employed poisons against their white masters and their families were house servants, well trusted, and this fact astounded and terrified many white commentators. Macandal, like Bras-Coupé, is attributed with many powers, among them prophecy, eloquence, and courage. Some even believed that he was immortal, and he himself contributed to this belief. According to legend, he promised that he could not be killed by whites but that God would change him into a mosquito that would wreak destruction everywhere. After his execution, instances of poisonings continued until, in March of 1758, the local government made it illegal to create "Macandals," which were defined not only as poisons but as fetishes, or *gris-gris*, for casting spells. Of course, these prohibitions were ineffective.[48]

47. Moreau de Saint-Méry, *Description topographique*, II, 629–31.

48. For accounts of West Indian insurrectionary and revolutionary activity in the mountains of Haiti, see Fouchard, *The Haitian Maroons;* Robert Debs Heinl, Jr., and Nancy Gordon Heinl, *Written in Blood: The Story of the Haitian People, 1492–1971* (Boston, 1978); Price, ed., *Maroon Societies;* Thomas O. Ott, *The Haitian Revolution, 1789–1804* (Knoxville, 1973). Toussaint L'Ouverture's revolution had begun in 1791, under the leadership of a fugitive slave named Boukman, a driver, and his fellow rebels Fatras Baton (Broomstick), Jean-François Papillon, Georges Biassou (the man who promised that every slave who died in battle would reawaken in Africa), and a man known simply as Jeannot. Jeannot was remarkable for the horrible tortures he devised for his white captives; they were, in fact, so horrible that Papillon and Biassou finally shot Jeannot to put a stop to the horror. There is also an account, in Fouchard's *The Haitian Maroons*, of a maroon leader called "Colas Jambes Coupées" (in full possession of both legs, as Cable's Bras-Coupé is in full possession of both arms) who was executed in June, 1724, in Haiti. In 1780, a notice

That Cable would not have distinguished between accounts of the West Indies and accounts of Louisiana makes perfect sense. Louisiana in the last decade of the eighteenth century and the first few years of the nineteenth was still very much a Caribbean culture. No firm distinction between West Indian rebels and Louisiana fugitives would have been drawn during these years, particularly during the Haitian revolution of 1791–1804 (approximately the time spanned in *The Grandissimes*) when fugitives, black and white, sought asylum in New Orleans. Among Louisianians there was, of course, a perception that revolt could be "imported" from Haiti, a perception that led the colonial government to attempt to stop the flight of refugees from Haiti into Louisiana. Such attempts were ineffective. At the time, Louisiana was, like Haiti, a part of France's holdings in the Caribbean. Despite the determination of later nineteenth-century historians like French (and even Gayarré, to some extent) to write of colonial Louisiana less as if it were a French colony than a relatively undeveloped territory of the United States, there are too many striking parallels between the accounts of West Indian maroons and the account of the fictional Bras-Coupé to permit such a misconception to influence our reading of the story of Bras-Coupé. For example, a West Indian rebel leader named Georges Biassou, who died in 1791 and who was an early associate of Boukman, would promise, at the height of the voodoo ceremonies of Bois Caïman, that every slave killed in battle would reawaken in Africa. In *The Grandissimes*, the dying Bras-Coupé, when asked by a priest if he knows where he is going, smiles and answers, "To—Africa." [49]

It is interesting that the Bras-Coupé of *The Grandissimes* should be

---

appears calling for the capture of Colas Jambes-Coupés, who had several conspirators with him. Fouchard also tells of the capture of a slave called Pompey in 1747; Pompey had found refuge on a mountain called Morne Bleu (316).

Poisonings began in the early seventeenth century; in 1738, the government issued a decree against poisoning. In 1746, slaves were forbidden to attempt to make any medicines in an attempt to cure any illness other than snakebite. François Macandal was the first rebel leader to use poisons as part of organized rebellion. Boukman and Biassou were linked with voodoo ceremonies, which were inextricably bound with insurrectionary activities. One band of rebels was led by a man who claimed to be invulnerable to cannon fire (echoing the detail of the "special herb" used by jean bras-coupé in Gottschalk's account). See Fouchard, *The Haitian Maroons*, 289–367.

49. Heinl and Heinl, *Written in Blood*, 45; Fouchard, *The Haitian Maroons*, 346; Cable, *The Grandissimes*, 193.

so silent, remaining in the background, relying on the language of riddle and gesture, prayer and curse (all bound up, albeit subtly, with voodoo rituals and ceremonies of resistance) for the Bras-Coupé of history is eloquent. Clearly, for Cable, history can be spoken only at great aesthetic risk.

The relevance or lack of relevance of the Bras-Coupé episode to the progress of the plot was the subject of some discussion among readers and reviewers of Cable's own day. At least one reviewer found it necessary to assert that the story of the victimized runaway is indeed central, "an integral part of the structure of the novel." Cable's own accounts of how the story of Bras-Coupé came to occupy the center of *The Grandissimes* are somewhat contradictory. In an 1899 account he wrote that he "was moved to write [*The Grandissimes*] as an expansion of the Bras-Coupé story." And in an article written five years earlier, in 1894, for the *North American Review,* Cable writes:

> In *The Grandissimes*—three syllables, yes, not four—there is a short story, to and around which the whole larger work is built. It is the episode of Bras-Coupé, which was written much as it stands before the novel was begun. I do not know that anyone has ever resented this piece of incorporation, yet I mention it to disclaim all present approval of such methods. The only method I know by experience to be worse is the expanding of a true story into a novel, which I did in *Doctor Sevier*.

Earlier in the same article, Cable writes that he had a purpose from the very beginning of the project:

> One of the first things decided was how the tale should end. For the rest it consisted mainly in a choice and correlation of the characters I designed to put upon my stage. The plot was not laboriously planned. It was to be little more than the very old and familiar one of a feud between two families, the course of true love fretting its way through, and the titles of hero and heroine open to competition between a man and his friend for the one and a mother and daughter for the other. Upon this well-used skeleton I essayed to put the flesh and blood, the form and bloom, of personalities new to the world of fiction. To do this and to contrive a plausible variety of scenes and incidents that should secure to these children of the fancy the smiling acquaintance of the reading world, were far more than a sufficient tax on the supposed redundancy of my powers of invention.[50]

50. *Atlantic Monthly,* XLVI (December, 1880), 830; Kjell Ekström, *George Washington*

On the one hand, then, the novel grew up around the story of Bras-Coupé; on the other, its plot, "not laboriously planned," centered on a family feud and the progress of love among the white characters, with the story of Bras-Coupé a piece of incorporation, the character himself one of those personalities new to the world of fiction. Furthermore, the story of Bras-Coupé was written long before the novel was conceived, and the action of the novel takes place a full eight years after the death of the proud African *candio.*

At first sight, the story of Bras-Coupé and the story of family-crossed lovers appear to share little more than a cast of characters, all of whom have some knowledge of and some of whom bear responsibility for the memorable atrocity. The progress of the love story, the chief plot interest, is not seriously affected by the Bras-Coupé episode. And although Honoré Grandissime, the turncoat who loves a de Grapion, clearly feels that the mistreatment of Bras-Coupé at the hands of the Grandissimes is a serious tragedy that started a war where peace had reigned before (between the Grandissimes and the de Grapions), he is less interested in the wars between slave and slaveholder.

Never trust the teller, trust the tale. I find it hard to believe that the historical context, so familiar to the author and so much more relevant to the original "Bibi" from which "The Story of Bras-Coupé" evolved, is irrelevant to the function of the runaway slave in *The Grandissimes.* It may well be that Gilder and Johnson's aesthetic of genteel realism forced the context "underground," so to speak, but that context does remain to influence the story in subtle but powerful ways.

Richard Chase has written that Bras-Coupé functions "as a kind of archetypal image which gives meaning and resonance to the book." Certainly, Bras-Coupé can be read as archetype. But he might also be read in other ways—as the catalyst for Cable's double-edged satire on white complacency or as a locus for a stream of black disaffection and defiance that runs throughout the text. The figure of the Noble Savage is often used in satirical writing "not to dignify the native, but rather to undermine the idea of nobility itself." Given the existence of classes in Western Europe that result in a system of inherited status and inherited privilege, "Noble Savage" is a kind of oxymoron, "since the

---

Cable: A Study of His Early Life and Work (Cambridge, Mass., 1950), 101; George W. Cable, "After-Thoughts of a Storyteller," *North American Review,* CLVIII (1894), 18, 17.

idea of nobility (or aristocracy) stands opposed to . . . savagery . . . as 'civility' stands to 'barbarism.' " [51]

Creole Louisiana was one of the few places in the United States where European ideas of nobility and aristocratic privilege had any real currency after the early nineteenth century; that was the case only because Louisiana remained a European colony until 1803 and maintained cultural ties with France, Spain, and the West Indies even after the cession. If we read the story of Bras-Coupé within this context, it does seem to operate as a means to anatomize ideas of nobility or entitlement still operating vestigially in the Louisiana of Cable's generation. Bras-Coupé is configured as a type of the royal slave who both represents and anatomizes his masters. The most striking characteristics that Bras-Coupé is given by the Creoles who own him are his concept of himself as king and warrior taken in battle (a man who might be killed sooner than he would be shamed), a royal disinclination to work, and a preoccupation with ceremony. In short, he is very much like his French and Spanish creole owners. The admiration that José Martinez feels for Bras-Coupé is based on their likenesses, for—slave that he is—Bras-Coupé is a king. For Martinez, Bras-Coupé is an emblem of royalty, himself his owner's fetish or, rather, himself a fetishistic representation of his owner's aristocratic status. [52]

No doubt many U.S. readers in 1880 would have noted Cable's satirizing of creole aristocracy. Creoles themselves certainly noted it, and they let Cable know that they noted it. It is not so certain that U.S. readers in 1880 would have noted Cable's critique of *U.S.* cultural complacency. But Cable's satire is double-edged. The scene devoted to Bras-Coupé's death is sentimental and melodramatic, but it is a moment of central importance for the question of what the Bras-Coupé episode signifies and how it signifies in *The Grandissimes*. I have discussed briefly the aesthetic of genteel realism that informed the editorial advice Cable was given by Richard Watson Gilder and Robert Underwood

51. Richard Chase, *The American Novel and Its Tradition* (New York, 1957), 168; Hayden White, *Tropics of Discourse: Essays in Cultural Criticism* (Baltimore, 1978), 191.

52. One might see the same tendency to represent the slave as fetish for aristocratic power in John Pendleton Kennedy's *Swallow Barn; or, A Sojourn in the Old Dominion,* particularly in Chap. 46, "The Quarter" (1851; rpr. Baton Rouge, 1986), 449–60. See also Hayden White's discussion in "The Noble Savage Theme as Fetish," in *Tropics of Discourse,* 183–96.

Johnson, but realism itself has a complicated history. Efforts to define it and to illustrate it with reference to particular authors—Howells, James, Norris, and so on—have never been entirely successful. There were a number of "realisms" in the period. The "genteel realism" advocated for family magazines like *Scribner's* and *The Century* have a clearer connection than some others (*e.g.,* the critical realism of the late Howells and the naturalists) to the sentimental tradition of domestic realism.

Nina Baym has observed that in midcentury "woman's fiction," "domesticity is set forth as a value scheme for ordering all of life, in competition with the ethos of money and exploitation that is perceived to prevail in American society." The genteel aesthetic of the postwar era grew out of the conventions of woman's fiction to some extent, even though the element of feminist or prefeminist protest that so informed the novels Baym discusses was largely eradicated by the genteel aesthetic.[53] In revising "Bibi" for his Victorian family audience, Cable (and his editors) chose to follow in that pathway. In one sense, "The Story of Bras-Coupé" is ostensibly the story of the salvation of the savage through "feeling," understood as one of the most fundamental of civilizing emotions and one often produced through the ministrations of women, in this case Señora Martinez and Palmyre Philosophe.[54]

Consistent with the tradition, Cable seems to have envisioned the development of the Bras-Coupé story within *The Grandissimes* in terms of the progress of his domestication. Initially, Bras-Coupé is constructed as a wild man—defined in terms of his rebelliousness and his physical size. He has no interiority to speak of (or from). In fact, the Creole Agricola Fusilier finds it somewhat amusing that Bras-Coupé's "owner," Don José Martinez, is looking for someone to "interpret" Bras-Coupé's language. "Where," the narrator asks, mimicking Agricola, but with some lightly satirical intonation, "might one find an interpreter— one not merely able to render a Jaloff's meaning into creole French, or

---

53. Nina Baym, *Women's Fiction: A Guide to Novels by and About Women in America, 1820–1870* (2nd ed.; Urbana, 1993), 27.

54. Certainly by the time Cable began to write, the sentimental appropriation of the *slave*—i.e., of a person defined exclusively according to his market value—by the ideology of domesticity had already been accomplished by Harriet Beecher Stowe in *Uncle Tom's Cabin* (one of the few works of fiction, if you will recall, that Cable read before he began to pursue authorship under the direction of his editors) and other writers.

Spanish, but with such a turn for diplomatic correspondence as would bring about an 'understanding' with this African buffalo?"[55] The interpreter turns out to be a woman, and the subsequent development of the prince's life story in the novel is the story of his moral progress according to sentimental narrative. In fact, the pose of Bras-Coupé in his final moment—hand and eyes lifted to heaven—is the pose most often associated with the death scene in sentimental narrative. (Mark Twain would have some fun with it in *The Adventures of Huckleberry Finn* in describing the funeral art of Emmeline Grangerford.)

It is not impossible to read the deathbed scene "straight." Anyone who is not acquainted with the history behind the figure of Bras-Coupé might read it so. Readers who remain uncomfortable with the quality of the scene might attribute its sentimentality to Cable's failure of imagination or art. Cable would certainly show himself to be capable of failures of imagination and art—even of artistic dishonesty—as his career went on; but *The Grandissimes* is his masterpiece, and honest. In this work, the two strains of narrative—the strain of sentimentality associated with genteel realism within which Bras-Coupé is a domesticated "man of feeling" and the strain of New World historiography—coexist in some creative tension. The displacement of the history of slave insurrection by a conversion narrative suggests the possibility of the displacement of the conversion narrative by insurrection, and this is exactly what happens in *The Grandissimes*. The death/conversion of Bras-Coupé is *not* followed by peaceful coexistence between black and white, despite the symbolic "lifting of the curse." It is followed by the carving of a wooden fetish that continues to function as the rebel's "strong right arm" among slaves and free people of color.

The significance of "The Story of Bras-Coupé" is not solely for the white characters or white readers. *The Grandissimes* is full of black characters. They appear on every page: the naked black boy, the "pathetically ugly black woman," the dwarf, the gigantic cartsman, the little yellow maid, the somber free man of color, the cold and beautiful quadroon, the satiric *marchande de calas*. Some of these characters are little more than extras on the set; others are of more importance to the development of the story. But even the extras are interesting in their supposed insignificance: characters like Alphonsima the cook, who despite

55. Cable, *The Grandissimes*, 173.

her reputed ugliness remains oddly faceless, although she seems always to be passing quietly through the house or accompanying her white mistress on an errand; the "little yellow maid," never given a name, face, or voice, borrowed by Clotilde so that she can visit Frowenfeld's shop with some propriety; the "naked black boy," also silent, unnamed, and relatively faceless, who runs errands, sleeps in hallways, and hovers in doorways; the "dwarf Congo woman," little more than an "odd black shape" who wheels out of Frowenfeld's way as he ducks into Palmyre's house, delivers a "stunning blow" to the back of Frowenfeld's head when she suspects that he might have less than honorable intentions, and is then "hurled . . . snarling and gnashing like an ape, against the farther wall." [56]

Others are more significant. There is Palmyre, whose need for vengeance results in the death of Agricola Fusilier. There is Clemence, a thinker, whose satirical wit implicates her in attempts to terrorize Agricola. And there is Honoré Grandissime, free man of color, whose money saves the Grandissime family but who commits suicide when he learns that Palmyre cannot return his love. Yet in this novel, which is so full of sound and color, lightness and motion, all of these characters (with one exception) share two very significant qualities: silence (a refusal to speak or difficulty in speaking) and an oppressive physical presence—qualities that seem to have been bequeathed to them through the Bras-Coupé story. If "The Story of Bras-Coupé" provides the author with a catalyst for the satirizing of white Creoles and white readers, the Bras-Coupé of history provides a means through which the black characters create a history for themselves and a strong subversive presence in the text.

This becomes apparent when we look closely at the events surrounding the murder of the satirical slavewoman Clemence. Cable has been greatly praised for his depiction of the *marchande de calas*, whose character defies easy explanations. Clemence turns out to be the only black character in the text who speaks with any degree of freedom about herself or about the Creoles who surround her. If what she has to say about the Creoles is scathing, what she has to say for herself is revolutionary. Of course, she speaks from behind the mask of black trickster, through song and mimicry, finally counting too much on the efficacy

56. *Ibid.,* 201.

of that mask to provide safety but speaking nonetheless. It is through Clemence that Frowenfeld comes to understand that the "something wrong" in New Orleans has to do with slavery and its legacies, but her speech strategies are also designed to enable her to function as an insurrectionist, to be both visible and invisible: "Oh! yass, sah; Mawse Honoré knows me, yass. All de gen'lemens knows me," she insists. "I sell de *calas;* mawnin's sell calas, evenin's sell zinzer cake. *You* know me. . . . Dat me w'at pass in rue Royale ev'y mawnin' holl'in' *'Be calas touts chauds,'* an' singin'; don't you know?"[57] The truth is that none of the white characters know Clemence. Her speech strategies enable her to signify on her own invisibility and visibility as well as on the visibility and invisibility of "bras-coupé" (as a figure of speech for slave resistance) in various contexts.

It is likely that Cable worked deliberately with the original "Bibi" and the rich historical context of the Bras-Coupé figure in an attempt to communicate to his readers that black rebellion was still very much a possibility in the postbellum United States if whites would not or could not deal honorably with former slaves. In "The Freedman's Case in Equity," published five years after *The Grandissimes,* Cable protests the return of jurisdiction over the freedman to the former slave states and predicts that the question of equity for black citizens will be returned "to the silence and concealment of the covered furrow. Beyond that incubative retirement no suppressed moral question can be pushed; but all such questions, ignored in the domain of private morals, spring up and expand once more into questions of public equity; neglected as matters of public equity, they blossom into questions of national interest; and, despised in that guise, presently yield the red fruits of revolution."

Cable could hardly have made a clearer statement of the significance of the Bras-Coupé story to *The Grandissimes* without direct reference to that novel. Elsewhere in the same essay he refers to "a system of vicious evasions" as one possible outcome of the return to the South of responsibility for the freedman; he advises his readers "to go back to the roots of things and study closely, analytically, the origin, the present foundation, the rationality, the rightness of those sentiments surviving in us which prompt an attitude qualifying in any way peculiarly the

57. *Ibid.,* 105.

black man's liberty among us. Such a treatment will be less abundant in incident, less picturesque; but it will be more thorough."[58] He might, in 1885, still have been arguing with Robert Underwood Johnson over the revisions of *The Grandissimes*.

In the exchanges it negotiates among competing discourses (historiography, satire, sentimental narrative), *The Grandissimes* reveals a great deal about the shape and scope of white hope and anxiety in the late nineteenth-century United States and the specific anxieties of the white South and of the white writer with respect to the ideology of nationalism and moral uplift. *The Grandissimes*, like *Pudd'nhead Wilson and Those Extraordinary Twins, Light in August,* and *Absalom, Absalom!,* turns out to be an anatomy of the ideology of white entitlement, of reunification and new beginnings, an anatomy of the official optimism of the postbellum United States as it is constructed upon the foundation of the tragic history of slavery and colonialism in the New World. It is an anatomy that takes its shape from the author's own situation, as white and southern and reconstructed, with respect to the ideology of the United States as the place where the past was to be transcended and history was to be culminated, or "finaled," by what Lewis P. Simpson has identified as the defining characteristic of modernity, the conjunction of individual will and memory.[59] It is my contention that Cable's literary work is less dialectical than dialogic in its engagement with history and the ideology of American romantic nationalism, that in no sense does the political agenda articulated in so many of his essays exhaust the resources of his fiction, that the sense of history and the movement of history in *The Grandissimes* are much more complex than critics have yet given them credit for being, and that in revising the manuscript Cable managed more to construct a dialogue with his editors about the relevance of history in the United States than to enact their reconciliationist agenda.

Cable's reputation as a reformer as well as the literary historian's tendency (derived from Parrington) to read literary texts as more or less dramatically rendered "statements" or "positions" means that *The*

58. Cable, "The Freedman's Case," 52, 53–54.

59. Lewis P. Simpson, "The Fable of the Writer in Southern Fiction," *Prospects*, VII (1982), 250.

Grandissimes has been assessed chiefly in terms of its value as a coherent (and realistic) statement about race and caste in the postbellum South. But recently, narrative theories have taught us to look at texts not only as coherent representations of experience but also as battlegrounds, or carnivals if you prefer, of competing discourses. Cable himself tells us that when he wrote the novel he "was still very slowly and painfully guessing out the riddle of our Southern question," and *The Grandissimes*, with its genial and digressive narrator, its intriguing postponements and deflections, its usurpation of narrative authority by various speakers, embodies riddle better than it solves riddle.[60] In this sense, *The Grandissimes* is the terrain upon which the most liberal white southerner of his day argued with himself, with the South, and with the newly unified and increasingly nationalistic United States over the meaning of the past and the possibility of a future for the southerner (and, through implication, for the American, northerner or southerner).

The unfolding of *The Grandissimes* around "The Story of Bras-Coupé" makes it clear that in the United States of 1803 (as in 1865), the possession of the past was of much less use than the loss of a past, chiefly for reasons having to do with the ideological relationship of the United States to the idea of history. The concept of America as "an emancipation from history" is a common one, as Lewis Simpson observes, and—true to the principle—in *The Grandissimes* the possession by the slavewoman Clemence of the "bras-coupé," a reminder of slave resistance, results in her murder and—indirectly—in the exile of the quadroon Palmyre Philosophe and Honore's octoroon brother of the same name, Honoré Grandissime f.m.c. In both instances this is a symbolic but heavily ironic "emancipation" of the white culture from its historical foundations in slavery, despite the abhorrence of all such doings that constitutes the narrator's response to the murder and the exile of the man and woman of color.[61]

The aesthetic logic that governs the displacement of history in the story of Bras-Coupé is recapitulated throughout the text whenever the relationship of black and white, Creole and American, is at issue. In this sense *The Grandissimes* is something of an arena within which these identities are contested. If the text coheres, it coheres, paradoxically,

60. Rubin, *George W. Cable,* 78.
61. Simpson, *Mind and the American Civil War,* 90.

around this contested issue of one's identity as black or white, Creole or American. "The Story of Bras-Coupé" as it is told (and not told) in the text, provides, ironically, an occasion for the articulation of stories of white inheritance and entitlement; it is indeed curious that so often conversations among the white characters about titles and property precede or follow very close upon the heels of some reference to Bras-Coupé. Bras-Coupé also provides a discursive site wherein the author can construct for his black characters a strong subversive presence founded on historical actuality. Although its most direct influence is upon Clemence, whose murder by members of the Grandissime family is directly related to her connection with a "bras-coupé," it also provides an intriguing, albeit circuitous, context for the political estrangement of the free man of color as well as for his return as the murderer of Agricola Fusilier, the chief spokesman for white supremacy in the novel.

In the United States during the Reconstruction years, the rhetorical situation of the white southerner was complex. Old methods of self-definition had been overturned with the assimilation of former slaves into the political body of the United States. No longer was it as easy to define one's own legitimacy by negation of the legitimacy of others, although with the help of scientific racism the very determined managed to do so. Consequently, one sees in postbellum southern literature an appropriation of black character types that had appeared frequently in abolitionist literature prior to the Civil War and almost never appeared in antebellum southern literature. The runaway slave, or insurrectionist, is one of those characters; the mixed-blood is another.

If one examines some of the rhetoric of race as it was used by many whites during the era, one cannot help but notice the way that the "threat" represented by socially and politically enfranchised freedmen is so often represented in terms of "amalgamation," another term for "social equality." The almost hysterical response of the white southerner to that bugaboo, his apparent inability to imagine that political and civil rights for former slaves could fail to lead to anything but "mulatto rule," combined with the popularity of the "Creole" as a representation of the unreconstructed white southerner, may help to explain the not infrequent appearance of the creole man of color as both representative of the white southerner under the new dispensation and his greatest fear.

Of course, the white southerner's construction of black and mulatto characters for purposes of self-definition was still racist. There was never any sense in which the white southerner—even a Cable, as reconstructed as he was—would have depicted himself directly and without anxiety in the guise of a black or mulatto character. The construction is more complex, and more insidious. For all of the similarities that might appear to exist between a mulatto and a white character in this literature, by the end of the story the mulatto will have been defined as different and will have been eliminated from the narrative in one way or another. And for all of the contrasts that might appear to exist between a black insurrectionist and white southerners in this literature, by the end of the story the insurrectionist will have been transfigured into a representation of the white southerner himself. In both instances, however, the black or mulatto character ends up carrying those qualities and characteristics that the white southerner found most troublesome in himself. In most cases, these black and mulatto characters are the post–Civil War white southerner's best tools for exploring the pressing issue of his or her own capacity for, and resistance to, assimilation to a national ideal.

In *The Grandissimes* there is initially some confusion in the mind of the German-American Frowenfeld over the identity of Honoré Grandissime, who is represented as the finest flower of the family, a progressive merchant among land-poor planters, both capable of working with the new government and willing to do so. Frowenfeld, when he first meets the dark and languid *rentier* who signs his name as "Honoré Grandissime," is unprepared to see this particular man, so French and so aristocratic, write that name, the name the "universal" (*i.e.*, the American) mind takes to be synonymous with an enterprising activity inconsistent with "Parisian airs." Is the Honoré whom the immigrant Frowenfeld has heard so much of really the dark and aristocratic *rentier*, Frowenfeld's landlord, a man who "lives off of the droppings of coupons, rents, and like receivables" and can hardly speak English? It is not until over a hundred pages into the text that the exotic *rentier* is identified as "nod whide" and an unnamed Creole who has been such a friend to Frowenfeld is identified as the "real" Honoré.[62] Prior to that

62. Cable, *The Grandissimes*, 42, 107.

revelation, there are only hints that the "real Honoré" is anything other than a European, French-speaking aristocratic colonist characterized, as so many of the Creoles are characterized in this book, by a touchy pride, by superstitiousness, by fatalism, and more importantly, by economic and political superfluity.

That the real Honoré turns out not to be the languid *rentier* is a relief for Frowenfeld. For the white southerner, however, the revelation of the French-speaking aristocratic Creole as "black" may have had a different significance. For the white southern reader at this time, the fact that a black man could be taken for a white man could not fail to suggest the possibility that the white man might be identified as black. As counterintuitive as this inversion might seem—and it may seem counterintuitive only to white persons reading these lines—this is exactly what happens in the novel. The dark Honoré possesses *no* physical or behavioral indications of slave descent. On the other hand, he possesses every physical and behavioral indication of creole origin and self-definition except one: he is wealthy, a landholder, a slaveowner, well dressed, well groomed, possessed of a European education, superstitious, fatalistic, proud. The one thing he isn't is talkative, as most of Cable's Creoles are. In effect, the dark Honoré is defined as a Creole; he is stipulated as black.

That the free man of color is hardly the man that the U.S. immigrant envisioned when he imagined the finest flower of Grandissime stock is precisely the point of the dark Honoré's role in the novel. He is never the man the U.S. reader envisions, not as son or friend or husband or citizen. In these texts the free man of color is the repository for whatever is "not American." Nevertheless, if he is not the man one envisions, he may in fact be the man one *is*. Much is made of Frowenfeld's initial (and rather long-lasting) assumption that the free man of color *is* the Honoré Grandissime he has heard so much of. This tight pairing of the Europeanized man of color and the Americanized Creole, of black and white, would seem to suggest that they are alternative visions of a cultural self and would undermine the nationalistic optimism that seems to govern *The Grandissimes*, at least on the level of plot.

The attractiveness of the vision of white emancipation from history for white Americans both north and south can be seen in the responses of white readers to Cable's creole heroines, Aurora and Clotilde:

> It is not strange that the dwellers round about dispute as to which is the
> fairer, nor that in the six months during which the two have occupied

No. 19 the neighbors have reached no conclusion on this subject. If some young enthusiast compares the daughter—in her eighteenth year—to a bursting blush rosebud full of promise, some older one immediately retorts that the other—in her thirty-fifth—is the red, red, full-blown faultless joy of the garden. If one says the maiden has the dew of youth,— 'But!' cry two or three mothers in a breath, 'that other one, child, will never grow old. With her it will always be morning. That woman is going to last forever; ha-a-a-a!—even longer!'[63]

A reviewer in the *Democrat* wrote, "As for the ladies Nancanou [Aurora and her daughter Clotilde], there can be but one verdict—they are perfectly *delightful!*" William Dean Howells, devotee of "the smiling aspects of life," found the creole ladies irresistible, especially Aurora, whom he calls the "supreme grace" of the novel, and he admired her precisely for her perennial youth and freshness. "She is," he writes, "always the wild, wilful heart of girlhood, which the experiences of wifehood, motherhood, and widowhood have left unchanged. She is a woman with a grown-up daughter, but essentially she is her daughter's junior, and, adorable as Clotilde is in her way, she pales and dulls into commonplace when Aurora is by."[64] Her nature is to be always young, always beautiful, and importantly for its implicit commentary on the relationship between America and its history, always innocent.

At the end of the story, Palmyre and the dark Honoré, aboard a ship bound for France, excite the interest of the ship's captain, who conjectures that the two "very elegant-looking people and evidently rich . . . had much the look of some of the Mississippi River 'Lower Coast' aristocracy," one of those pointed suggestions of race mixing among the elite that galled some creole readers.

The rents of No. 19 rue Bienville and of numerous other places, including the new drug-store in the rue Royale, were collected regularly by H. Grandissime, successor to Grandissime Freres. Rumor said, and tradition repeats, that neither for the advancement of a friendless people, nor even for the repair of the properties' wear and tear, did one dollar of it ever remain in New Orleans; but that once a year Honoré, "as instructed,"

63. *Ibid.*, 79.

64. Turner, *George W. Cable,* 101; W. D. Howells, "From Mr. G. W. Cable's Aurora and Clotilde Nancanou," *Critical Essays on George Washington Cable,* ed. Arlin Turner (Boston, 1980), 125.

remitted to Madame—say Madame Inconnue—of Bordeaux, the equivalent, in francs, of fifty thousand dollars. 'Let us see: fifty times twenty—one million dollars.' But that is only a *part* of the *pecuniary* loss which this sort of thing costs Louisiana.

But we have wandered.[65]

Regardless of the fair prospects embodied in the white heroines (who are otherwise none too compelling as characters), the story told and retold throughout the novel is the story of the debt of the southerner to history. That it should be black and mulatto figures who represent that debt is not surprising. As already discussed, intellectuals as different as Thomas Jefferson and Ralph Waldo Emerson had agreed— with the typical self-centeredness of the culturally centered—that the real tragedy of slavery was its effect on the slaveholder, whose own fitness for Republican self-government was compromised by his involvement with the slave as well as with the colonialist system of slavery. "But we have wandered." Cable's resistance to this typical white ethnocentrism is apparent in the satirical tone with which the narrator stresses the "pecuniary loss" to Louisiana represented by the dark Honoré's expatriation and suicide.

Gilder's and Johnson's fostering of a literature characterized by dialect, by warmth and "color," by "charm" and "vivacity," does constrict, to some extent, the author whose fiction is based so firmly in the "annals of colonization." But the shift of import in *The Grandissimes* between political resistance and romantic reconciliation reveals Cable's discomfort with the aesthetic ideology that would govern the work of southern authors during the Redemption era. Under the guise of the "artistic," which suggested the "universal" as opposed to the particular and was placed in opposition to what Gilder called the "historical tendency" of "local color," it functioned chiefly as an attempt to return to a comfortable version of the racial status quo on all fronts. That the racial status quo would be expressed in terms of "whiteness," which suggested integrity, unity, reassuring homogeneity, should not be surprising; it is no coincidence that "white" has been associated, since the revolutions of the eighteenth century, with reactionary or royalist political causes. I cannot believe that Cable, so steeped in historical writ-

65. Cable, *The Grandissimes*, 436, 438.

ings, was not on some level aware of this, nor should it be surprising that "color," in just about all of its manifestations—racial, local, or historical—was a disturbing concept during the period.[66] Should a story involve characters who were not "universal," which more often than not meant characters who were not white and middle-class Americans or did not aspire to be, those characters must be subordinated or transcended as part of the "atmosphere" or "color" of the work, by the discourse of "whiteness," with all its suggestions of national unity and personal integrity.

This is a pattern that is to be recapitulated, with greater intricacy and variation in import, in Mark Twain's *Pudd'nhead Wilson and Those Extraordinary Twins* and in William Faulkner's *Absalom, Absalom!* In both these texts, a troublesome character is defined with all of the qualities supposedly possessed by the unreconstructed white southerner—wealth, aristocratic origins, sophistication, associations with colonialist slave cultures, and so on—and is then later stipulated as "black" and noisily (but incompletely) purged from the narrative. This pattern of imaginative reconstruction of the white southerner is a record of the complex response of postbellum white southerners (even the vocal and committed Cable) to the ideal of southern assimilation to the reunified and increasingly nationalistic United States. If Lewis Simpson is correct in his observation that "the literary destiny of the American South has been to assimilate the West to the historical vision of America as an integral part of the Atlantic and Mediterranean worlds, or, in short, the historic European culture,"[67] then Cable's text, however optimistically nationalistic in some respects, might be said to contain undercurrents that lead in this direction—and indeed in other, more southerly and more dangerous directions—by qualifying the dream of ahistorical nationalism.

66. See Hayden White's discussions of "whiteness" and "color" in his discussions of the noble savage and the wild man in the eighteenth century. "The Forms of Wildness: Archaeology of an Idea," in *The Wild Man Within: An Image in Western Thought from the Renaissance to Romanticism,* ed. Edward Dudley and Maximillian E. Novak (Pittsburgh, 1972), 3–38; and "The Noble Savage Theme as Fetish," in *Tropics of Discourse,* 150–96. See also White's "The Politics of Historical Interpretation: Discipline and De-Sublimation," in *The Content of the Form: Narrative Discourse and Historical Representation* (Baltimore, 1987), 57–82.

67. Lewis P. Simpson, "Home by Way of California: The Southerner as the Last European," in *Southern Literature in Transition: Heritage and Promise,* ed. Philip Castille and William Osborne (Memphis, 1983), 63.

3

MARK TWAIN, AMERICAN NATIONALISM, AND THE COLOR LINE

"What is a White Man?"
> —title of Charles Chesnutt's essay in the New York *Independent*,
> 1889

In late 1884, Samuel Clemens and George W. Cable set out to travel through the northeastern and midwestern states (as far south as Missouri) and to present material from their published and forthcoming work. They were billed as "Twins of Genius and Versatility." The fact is that in many ways these twins could not have been any more "extraordinary" than Luigi and Angelo Cappello. The devout Cable, like Angelo, refused to travel on Sundays; Clemens—a Luigi—resented the piety and wrote to his wife: "I do not believe that any vileness, any shame, any dishonor is too base for Cable to do, provided by doing it he can save his despicable Sabbath from abrasion. In him this superstition is lunacy—no idiocy—pure & unadulterated. Apart from this & his colossal self-conceit & avarice, he is all great & fine: but *with* them as ballast, he averages as other men & floats upon an even keel with the rest."[1]

In his pique Clemens credited Cable with teaching him "to abhor and detest the Sabbath-day and hunt up new and troublesome ways to dishonor it."[2] Then there was Cable's reputation as a serious essayist and committed reformer, compared to which the unpretentious humor of "Mark Twain" seemed to some Victorian audiences (including Clem-

---

1. *Love Letters of Mark Twain*, 234.
2. Guy Cardwell, *Twins of Genius* (East Lansing, Mich., 1953), 55, 64.

ens himself at times) fairly light. He admitted as the tour ended that Cable's intellect was "greater and higher" than he had known, and Cable's influence on *Huckleberry Finn* has been duly acknowledged.[3]

But Sam Clemens was different—more social anatomist than social reformer. It is a commonplace of scholarship on Mark Twain and his work that he is, in Dreiser's words, "Mark the Double Twain"; that running through his work are the themes of twinning, doubling, impostures and impersonations, role playing, and role defying.[4] If Cable did his best work when he was immersed in southern politics, living in the South, Clemens' best work was often written from a distance. In fact, claiming that the "Mark Twain" persona is "southern" can provoke arguments. Samuel Clemens' childhood, I concede, was characterized by numerous displacements—geographical, economic, and social—but his parents were like any number of migrating Virginians of the 1820s and 1830s in their efforts to make their fortunes in the West.

There on the frontier of Clemens' youth, the memory of a southern ancestry coexists with the realities of migration, which included loss of place, the breaking up of social hierarchies, displacements of authority, and sometimes violent or fraudulent attempts to reconstitute order. Former entitlements (whether to vast tracts of Tennessee land or to an earldom in England) become the subject of legend and pretense on the American frontier. Dreams on the frontier are often dreams of reclamation and realization of past glory and past stability in the face of present social, economic, but also ethnic and racial metamorphoses. The fact remains that "Mark Twain" was the creation of a southerner, Samuel Langhorne Clemens, who had grown up in a slave state and served, very briefly, as a Confederate irregular during the Civil War. But in the autumn of 1862, just a few months prior to the first appearance of "Mark Twain," he had become a Union man. The first line of his first sketch under the pseudonym was, "I feel very much as if I had just awakened out of a long sleep."[5]

The world that he had awakened into would be very different from

---

3. *Mark Twain's Letters,* ed. Albert Bigelow Paine (New York, 1917), 450; see also Cardwell, *Twins of Genius,* 68–77.

4. Theodore Dreiser, "Mark the Double Twain," *English Journal,* XXIV (1935), 615.

5. *Mark Twain of the Enterprise: Newspaper Articles & Other Documents, 1862–1864,* ed. Henry Nash Smith (Berkeley, 1957), 49; James Cox, *Mark Twain: The Fate of Humor* (Princeton, 1966), 5.

the old one. Mark Twain's clearest advantage may have been his position on the threshold between old and new, a position that enabled him to observe both, and may be the source of his talent for representing the postbellum United States in terms of the antebellum South. Even though Sam Clemens had in some sense fled the South (as so many southern artists and intellectuals have done), Mark Twain would return again and again to that scene of slavery and loss in and around the Mississippi River, to the displaced slaveholders who dreamed of future wealth and past glories, and to the slaves who were among the victims of those dreams. In returning to that scene, Clemens found a voice that spoke of displacement, loss, and desire in frontier slave communities like Dawson's Landing and spoke often as a slave. More than any other writer of his generation, he was fascinated by the persistence of slavery in a United States supposedly devoted to freedom, by the presence of history in "the great nation of futurity," and by the disordered recapitulation and reproduction of old and broken social roles in a progressive United States.

Beginning in 1873 with *The Gilded Age*, he interested himself in the selling out of war ideals of freedom and equality. One has only to recall the "ruse" in that book of claiming some of the extensive Tennessee lands for a black school, although other instances abound. But it is with *The Adventures of Huckleberry Finn*, begun at the end of Reconstruction, that the national discourse about the reunification of North and South, "reconciliation," "redemption," and identity starts to figure in a major way in the fiction. Almost a decade older than his "twin," Mark Twain was almost fifty when his first real masterpiece—the text from which "all American literature descends"—appeared, during the year of the lecture tour. Not only was it the work of an older and very different man but, whereas Cable's best work was deeply rooted in the optimistic assimilationism of Reconstruction, Twain's was much more the product of his disappointment in the corruptions and failures of that project. If the ending of *The Grandissimes* (written in 1878 and 1879) gently warns its white readers about the possible consequences of trying to deprive former slaves of their political and economic rights as U.S. citizens, the ending of *Huckleberry Finn* (written in 1883 and 1884)—with its "game" of "setting a free nigger free"—is much harsher in its indictment of white enslavement to convention and provincial self-interest in dealing with freedmen.

The novel opens with Huck engaged in a debate with himself about his nature and capacities for reclamation, as well as the value and validity of conventional ideas of reclamation and respectability. Yet the events of the tale soon catapult him right into the middle of the debate over chattel slavery, like Brer Rabbit into the briarpatch. In his negotiations with himself and with the other characters in the book about the issue, he assumes various roles with respect to the runaway Jim (protector, tormenter, son, friend, even the role of the slaveholder himself) as the two "drift" ever so slowly "down the river," when they have every intention of going "up" to freedom.

Within the context of the political events of the decade in which the book was written, there is certainly a great deal of ironic import to the fact that what is supposed to be, for Jim and Huck, a journey northward to freedom turns out to take them south instead, deeper into the scene of slavery. Here both are forced to assume various disguises which, paradoxically, at once enslave them and permit them to maintain some degree of freedom within slavery. Figuratively speaking, this is exactly what Mark Twain may have seen happening in the United States in the late 1870s and early 1880s, when he was writing *The Adventures of Huckleberry Finn*. The return of the government of the South to the white man beginning in the mid-1870s was wholesale abandonment of the ideals that had turned the Civil War from a war to preserve the Union into a war to free the slaves and laid the foundation for a return to the old disguises and roles that ensured survival under the old system. The rise of Bourbon rule did little more than to set the stage for what some have called the "southernization" of the United States, when scientific racism and segregation replaced slavery as the means through which the freedoms of black persons would be circumscribed throughout the United States. Even the use of the 1830s and the 1850s as the temporal setting for the narrative is relevant, for national discourse about slavery in these decades was remarkably like the discourse of the post-Reconstruction years in the prevalence of talk of "reconciliation" and "redemption," the 1830s having been years of conscious efforts on the part of politicians and pundits to foster understanding between the white North and the white South as part of the defense of slavery. In John Pendleton Kennedy's *Swallow Barn*, for example, published first in 1832 and again in 1851, the preface announces the intention of helping the northerner to understand slavery as a paternalistic and protective institution.

The discourse associated with the Redemption era was similar in its appropriation of the rhetoric of reconciliation, mutual understanding among whites, and the ethos of white paternalism. *The Adventures of Huckleberry Finn* operates critically upon that discursive context: by the end of the book the reader understands slavery as anything but paternalistic and protective, and of no little interest is the capacity of slavery to enslave the master as well as the slave. Huck's decision to "light out for the Territories" to avoid the various slaveries associated with civilization is doubly ironic in its indictment of the "respectability" that sanctions legal servitude and in its futility. Should Huck really "light out," he would no doubt find exactly what Mark Twain found in the Nevada Territory—more civilization and more slavery. Freedom is forever receding in the work of Mark Twain.

"His Grandfather's Old Ram," a standard feature of Mark Twain's lectures in 1884, offers an instance of his preoccupation with the impossibility of escape in the figure of the old miner, who possesses "the sort of memory which is too good, which remembers everything and forgets nothing, which has no sense of proportion . . . and thus retards the progress of a narrative."[6]

The old miner starts out to tell a story of his grandfather's old ram but never gets to the point. Instead, he is distracted by what seem to the listeners to be irrelevant details:

Well, as I was a'sayin', he bought that old ram from a feller up in Siskiyou County and fetched him home and turned him loose in the medder, and next morning he went down to have a look at him, and accident'ly dropped a ten-cent piece in the grass and stooped down—so—and was a-fumblin' around in the grass to git it, and the ram he was a-standin' up the slope taking notice, because he had his back to the ram and was int'rested about the dime. Well, there he was, as I was a-sayin', down at the foot of the slope a-bendin' over—so—fumblin' in the grass, and the ram he was up there at the top of the slope, and Smith—Smith was a-standin' there—no, not jest there, a little further away—fifteen foot perhaps—well, my grandfather was a'stoopin' way down—so . . . Smith of Calaveras . . . no, no it couldn't ben Smith of Calaveras—I remember now that he—b'George it was Smith of Tulare County—'course it was, I remember it now perfectly plain.

6. *Mark Twain in Eruption: Hitherto Unpublished Pages About Men and Events*, ed. Bernard De Voto (1940; rpr. New York, 1969), 218.

Well, Smith he stood just there, and my grandfather he stood just here, you know, and he was a-bendin' down just so, fumblin' in the grass, and when the old ram see him in that attitude he took it fur an invitation—and here he come! down the slope thirty mile an hour and his eye full of business. You see my grandfather's back being to him, and him stooping down like that, of course he—why sho! it warn't Smith of Tulare at all, it was Smith of Sacramento—my goodness, how did I ever come to get them Smiths mixed like that—why Smith of Tulare was jest a nobody, but Smith of Sacramento—why the Smiths of Sacramento come of the best Southern blood in the United States; there warn't ever any better blood south of the line than the Sacramento Smiths.

The digressions are not irrelevant. What distracts the old miner, time and time again, is the identity of his characters, the necessity of keeping his Smiths straight and knowing who married whom, their subsequent history, and the overall meaning of that personal history in the larger scheme of national history in the service of providence: Sally Hogadorn marries a missionary and goes "carrying the good news to the cannibals out in one of them way-off islands . . . and they et her; et him too, which was irregular; it warn't the custom to eat the missionary, but only the family." The cannibals claim that the eating of the missionary was an accident. But the old miner doesn't believe in accidents: "There ain't nothing happens in the world but what's ordered just so by a wiser Power than us, and it's always fur a good purpose. . . . No, sir, there ain't no such thing as an accident. Whenever a thing happens that you think is an accident you make up your mind it ain't no accident at all— it's a special providence." The subject of family bloodlines and special providences leads the old miner to take up the issue of pedigree and who or what is or is not capable of carrying out a special providence. Dogs, for instance, can't be depended upon in those circumstances— even the finest of dogs, like Jasper:

[He was] a mighty good dog . . . no common dog . . . no mongrel; he was a composite. A composite dog is a dog that's made up of all the valuable qualities that's in the dog breed—kind of a syndicate; and a mongrel is made up of the riffraff that's left over. That Jasper was one of the most wonderful dogs you ever see. Uncle Lem got him of the Wheelers. I reckon you've heard of the Wheelers; ain't no better blood south of the line than the Wheelers.

Well, one day Wheeler was a-meditating and dreaming around in the carpet factory and the machinery made a snatch at him and first you know he was a-meandering all over that factory, from the garret to the cellar, and everywhere, at such another gait as—why, you couldn't even see him; you could only hear him whiz when he went by. Well, you know a person can't go through an experience like that and arrive back home the way he was when he went. No, Wheeler got wove up into thirty-nine yards of best three-ply carpeting. The widder was sorry, she was uncommon sorry, and loved him and done the best she could fur him in the circumstances, which was unusual. She took the whole piece— thirty-nine yards—and she wanted to give him proper and honorable burial, but she couldn't bear to roll him up; she took and spread him out full length, and said she wouldn't have it any other way. She wanted to buy a tunnel for him but there wasn't any tunnel for sale, so she boxed him in a beautiful box and stood it on the hill on a pedestal twenty-one foot high, and so it was monument and grave together, and economical—sixty foot high—you could see it from everywhere—and she painted on it 'To the loving memory of thirty-nine yards best three-ply carpeting containing the mortal remainders of Millington G. Wheeler go thou and do likewise.'[7]

"His Grandfather's Old Ram," for all of its lack of pretension, takes as its subject the weighty questions of U.S. historiography—who we are and what we are about. It deals irreverently with dreams of U.S. providential historiography and in the process reveals Mark Twain's preoccupations with the nightmare of ruined bodies, broken homes, and atrophied aspirations. It also reveals, in its careful drawing of distinctions between a "composite" dog and a "mongrel," the growing tension between the assimilationist spirit of Reconstruction and the fears of "amalgamation" that followed that era.

"Mark Twain" began, and remained, a voice animated by issues of cultural inheritance as they conflict with the ideology (a particularly American and nationalistic ideology) of freedom and self-making (an ideology entirely comfortable with the doctrines of scientific racism). His treatment of these issues after the late 1870s always involves, directly or indirectly, the context of his southern origins, albeit he often uses the England of the sixteenth and seventeenth centuries as analogue to the antebellum South.[8] If he is unlike Cable in his irreverence, he is

7. *Ibid.*, 218–19, 221, 222.
8. Louis D. Rubin, Jr., in his essay " 'The Begum of Bengal': Mark Twain and the

not unlike his twin in his preoccupation with the impact of "southernness" upon "Americanness," with the recalcitrance of the southerner
as a determining feature of the national character, and with the southern strain within the American nation, a strain that tied the United
States to its history and seems to undercut at every moment the ideology of self-making so dear to the hearts of northern/Puritan Americans. In Mark Twain, it is southernness (defined as history itself, as well
as the complicity of men and women with history) that finally defines
the United States, and defines humanity.

To the extent that the Civil War was fought to free the United States of
slavery, Mark Twain (experienced in the deceptions of the supposedly
fluid frontier) deemed it a failure. Slaveries of various kinds prolifer-
ated during and following Reconstruction: spoilsmanship, party politics, the return of the former slave to a semislave status throughout the
South. But the rhetoric of race, slavery, and Americanism was very
different in the years immediately before and after the Civil War. "We
are the Romans of the modern world, the great assimilating people,"
Oliver Wendell Holmes said in 1858.[9] After the war, John Stuart Mill
wrote confidently to E. L. Godkin that "the great concussion which has
taken place in the American mind must have loosened the foundations
of all prejudices, and secured a fair hearing for impartial reason on all
subjects such as it might not otherwise have had for many generations."[10] And with the rise of the Radical Republicans, assimilation became—for a very brief time and in defiance of the cultural legacies of
racism—an official policy. Elisha Mulford wrote, with typical Republican optimism, that the United States must be "inclusive of the whole

---

South," in *William Elliott Shoots a Bear: Essays on the Southern Literary Imagination* (Baton
Rouge, 1975), argues that one might read *A Connecticut Yankee in King Arthur's Court* as
a kind of "fable of the New South," with Hank Morgan operating upon feudal England
much as Henry Grady and others would operate upon the South in order to transform
it into "a replica of the industrial Northeast where the adult Samuel Clemens lived" (50).
But it is important to note as well that Hank Morgan fails, not only because of the depravity of the South, but also because of the incredible naïveté of the Yankee reformer.

9. Oliver Wendell Holmes, quoted in Merle Curti, *The Growth of American Thought*
(New York, 1943), 233.

10. See Robert Kelley, *The Transatlantic Persuasion: The Liberal-Democratic Mind in the
Age of Gladstone* (New York, 1969), 299.

people. . . . There is no difference of wealth, or race, or physical condition, that can be made the ground of exclusion from it." The Reverend
Henry Ward Beecher (who met and encouraged Mark Twain in 1868
and remained a neighbor) celebrated U.S. assimilationism in an Independence Day essay in 1876. William T. Harris argued in an 1874 essay
entitled "On the Relation of Education to the Individual, to Society, and
to the State" that a "new man" was developing in the United States.[11]
Interestingly, he situated the origins of this new man in the Mississippi
River valley, the locus of Mark Twain's art (as it was of Cable's and
Faulkner's), where French, Spanish, English, Native Americans, Africans, and later Germans, Italians, and Chinese met and mingled.

It might legitimately be objected at this point that the U.S. Negro
constituted in the mind of many whites a special category, excluded by
a rhetoric of "race" and "nation" that took Western Europe as the origin
of those populations to be assimilated in the United States. And such
an objection has merit. As Winthrop Jordan has shown, the origins of
white racism can be traced back to the early Renaissance, when northern Europeans began to travel southward and eastward and to encounter yellow, brown, and black peoples for the first time. And when
evolutionists like Herbert Spencer argued that American racial inter-
mixture would create in the United States a superior man out of the
races of immigrants, he meant immigrants from northern Europe.[12]

For all of his growing repugnance for the corruptions of the era,
Mark Twain embraced its optimistic assimilationism, at least rhetorically. On June 8, 1874, the "Bay," as Clara Clemens was called, "the
great American Giantess," was born at seven and three-quarter pounds,
dark-complected, and with a full head of hair:

> [She] could live on nothing but breast milk, and her mother could not
> furnish it. We got Mary Lewis, the colored wife of the colored lessee of

11. Elisha Mulford, *The Nation: The Foundations of Civil Order and Political Life in the
U.S.* (Boston, 1886), 397; Rev. Henry Ward Beecher, "The Advance of a Century," New
York *Tribune Extra*, July 5, 1876, p. 38; William T. Harris, *Wisconsin Journal of Education,*
IV (1874), 1–11.

12. See Allan Nevins, ed., *America Through British Eyes* (New York, 1948), 355. But
against any absolutist application of that principle, one might offer in evidence the history
of race mixing in Western European-held colonies—and especially in the West Indies
and Mississippi River valley regions—throughout the centuries, as well as the racial
philosophy that underlay Reconstruction.

Quarry Farm to supply it a couple of weeks, but the moment we tried to put her on prepared food she turned blue around her mouth and began to gasp. We thought she would not live 15 minutes. Then we got Maggie O'Day from Elmira, who brought her blind child with her and divided up her rations—not enough for the two; so we tried to eke out the Bay's supply with prepared food, and failed.—She turned blue again and came near perishing.

We never tried prepared food any more. Next we got Lizzie Botheker, and had to pay her worthless husband $60 to let her come, besides her wages of $5 per week.

Next we got Patrick's wife (our coachman) Mary McAleer, to furnish milk for the Bay.

Lastly we got Maria McLaughlin, wife of a worthless Irishman.

No. 1 was a mulatto, No. 2 was half-American, half Irish, No. 3 was half German, half Dutch, No. 4 was Irish, No. 5 was apparently Irish, with a powerful strain of Egyptian in her. This one ended the procession,—and in great style too.

It has always been held that mother's milk imparts to the child certain details of the mother's make-up in permanency—such as character, disposition, tastes, inclinations, traces of nationality and so on. Supposedly, then, Clara is a hybrid, a polyglot, a person of no particular country or breed, a General Member of the Human Race, a Cosmopolitan.

She got valuable details of construction out of those other contributors, no doubt . . . but it was the mighty Egyptian that did the final work and reared upon it the imposing superstructure. There was never any wet-nurse like that one—the unique, the sublime, the unapproachable! She stood six feet in her stockings, she was perfect in form and contour, raven-haired, dark as an Indian, stately, carrying her head like an empress. She had the martial port and stride of a grenadier, and the pluck and strength of a battalion of them. In professional capacity the cow was a poor thing compared to her, and not even the pump was qualified to take on airs where she was. She was as independent as the flag, she was indifferent to morals and principles, she disdained company, and marched in a procession by herself. She was as healthy as iron, she had the appetite of a crocodile, the stomach of a cellar, and the digestion of a quartz-mill. Scorning the adamantine law that a wet-nurse must partake of delicate things only, she devoured anything and everything she could get her hands on, shoveling into her person fiendish combinations of fresh pork, lemon pie, boiled cabbage, ice cream, green apples, pickled tripe, raw turnips, and washing the cargo down with freshets of coffee, tea, brandy, whiskey . . . anything that was liquid; she smoked pipes, cigars, cigarettes, she whooped like a Pawnee and swore like a demon; and then she would go up stairs loaded as described and perfectly delight the baby with a banquet which ought to have killed it at thirty yards, but which only made it happy and fat and contented and boozy. No child but this one ever had such grand and wholesome service. The giantess raided my tobacco and cigar department every day; no drinkable thing was safe from her if you turned your back a moment; and in addition to the great quantities of strong liquors which she bought down town every day and consumed, she drank 256 pint bottles of beer in our house in one month, and that month, the shortest one of the year. These things sound impossible, but they are facts. She was a wonder, a portent, that Egyptian.

The sketch itself is an instance of southwestern humor come to domestic life in Hartford, Connecticut, but it also exhibits the vibrant U.S. optimism of the postwar North and implicitly predicts a great future for Clara, the "American giantess," who for a time insisted upon using the names of her wet nurses—"Clara Lewis O'Day Botheker McAleer McLaughlin Clemens." Later on, Clemens chalked up Clara's spirit to the amalgam of races and nationalities by which she was nourished. Of the day Susy, Clara, and Daisy Warner fell into the oat bin in the stable and the coachman got them out, he writes: "It was not Susy that arranged that scrape, it was Clara; Susy was not an inventor of adventures, she was only an accommodating and persuadable follower of reckless inventors of such things, for in her gentle make-up were no nineteen second-hand nationalities and the evil energies of that Egyptian volcano. Susy took, in turn, each step of the series that led up to the scrape, but she originated none of them, it was mainly Clara's work, the outcome of her heredities." [13]

Clemens idealized his eldest daughter Susy, but it may have been Clara he most identified with himself, at least in this sketch. Like her father, she was outgoing, a show-off, mischievous when a child. Like her father, she grew up to be a performer. And like her father (but to her father's chagrin), she resisted the conventions and gentilities of polite society at times. [14] Most importantly for my argument, her

13. Quoted in Edith Salsbury, ed., *Susy and Mark Twain: Family Dialogues* (New York, 1965), 33–34, 19, 151, 21–24.

14. At one point, Clemens had to write to the adolescent Clara to berate her for "excluding herself with forty officers" at a party in Berlin. "Didn't it occur to you that

father identified her—at least during her childhood—with U.S. assimilationism.

A few years later, at the end of 1881, when Mark Twain spoke at the annual meeting of the New England Society of Philadelphia, his voice had changed. He began by playing more or less good-humored havoc with the pretensions that went into the making of such societies, denigrating the achievements of the Pilgrim ancestors of the members of that society, and claiming for himself and for his own frontier South a preeminence insofar as genealogy was concerned: "I am a border ruffian from the state of Missouri. I am a Connecticut Yankee by adoption. I have the morals of Missouri and the culture of Connecticut, and that's the combination that makes the perfect man." He claims ancestry from "an early Indian," his "first American ancestor," and later from the Quakers, particularly Elizabeth Hooten and Roger Williams. His comments had begun to take on a sharper edge. "All those Salem witches were ancestors of mine," he said.

> The first slave brought into New England out of Africa by your progenitors was an ancestor of mine—for I am of a mixed breed, an infinitely shaded and exquisite mongrel. I'm not one of your sham meerschaums that you can color in a week. No, my complexion is the patient art of eight generations. Well, in my own time, I had acquired a lot of my kin—by purchase, and swapping around, and one way and another—and was getting along very well. Then, with the inborn perversity of your lineage, you got up a war and took them all away from me. And so, again am I bereft, again I am forlorn; no drop of my blood flows in the veins of any living being who is marketable.

At the end of his speech, he acknowledges that the Pilgrims were not so bad after all but suggests that they could be improved by "having them born in Missouri." This early "joking about ancestry, starting with his own," Louis Budd suggests, may be not only characteristic of Mark Twain's irreverent humor but also an indication of his social anxieties,

---

there was but one course for you to pursue—leave that room the moment you found yourself the only representative of your sex in it?" In Salsbury, *Susy and Mark Twain*, 319. For an interesting discussion of Sam's relationship with his daughters, see Peter Stoneley, *Mark Twain and the Feminine Aesthetic* (Cambridge, Eng., 1992); and J. D. Stahl, *Mark Twain: Culture and Gender; Envisioning America Through Europe* (Athens, 1994).

his sense of being an outsider, his fear of (and, at times, his compen-
satory insistence upon) being taken as a mere buffoon when he longed
to be recognized as a gentleman and a moralist.[15] Yet even though the
optimistic nationalism of the post–Civil War (and pre-Bourbon) years,
the refurbished hope in the nation's future, and the attempt to imagine
U.S. identity in terms of assimilation—so predominant in his sketch of
the Bay—continue to inform Mark Twain's humor in the above excerpt,
there is a sharper bite here, a more complacent racism, a clear sense of
himself as a defeated (hence racially marked) southerner, and a caustic
jibe at Gilded Age marketability in the final sentence. No one was more
aware than Mark Twain of the persistence of certain kinds of marketability in the post–Civil War United States.

The corruptions (real or imagined) of Reconstruction constituted in
the minds of many Anglo-Americans a crisis of character that was
linked, very tightly, to Reconstruction ideals of assimilation. The principle of universal male suffrage—which established no distinction
among voters based on property or education—was seen by many
(including Mark Twain) as the source of Reconstruction governmental
corruption and a harbinger of mob rule. "We know there is Unrestricted
Suffrage," he wrote, "we *think* there is a Hell: but the question is, which
do we *prefer?*" As might be expected, a number of political philosophers
and historians arose to reassure the worried or to fan the flames of
hysteria among the people John Fiske called "the English race in America." In 1880, Fiske delivered in England a series of lectures, among
them one entitled "Manifest Destiny." In this lecture on U.S. cultural
prospects, he characterized the "English race" as assimilationists but
with an interesting qualification: "It is a race which has shown a rare
capacity for absorbing slightly foreign elements and moulding them
into conformity with a political type which was first wrought out
through centuries of effort on British soil. . . . The American has absorbed considerable quantities of closely kindred European blood, but
he is rapidly assimilating it all, and in his political habits and aptitudes

15. Mark Twain, "Plymouth Rock and the Pilgrims," in *Mark Twain: Collected Tales,
Sketches, Speeches & Essays, 1852–1890,* ed. Louis Budd (New York, 1992), 782, 783–84,
785; Louis Budd, *Our Mark Twain: The Making of His Public Personality* (Philadelphia,
1983), 59.

he remains as thoroughly English as his forefathers in the days of De Montfort, or Hampden, or Washington."[16]

This logic suggested to many of that era that those qualities held to be most representative of the U.S. character—self-governance, self-reliance, strong family bonds based on affection, individual ownership of property, a strong work ethic, preference for arbitration over force as a solution for disagreements, gregariousness, practicality, and so on—were "bred in the blood" of the descendants of the English. In short, the reassuring phrase "thoroughly English" connotes for Fiske a tradition of self-government of such long and uninterrupted duration that it constituted a "blood" (or biological) inheritance and was virtually inalienable—except, perhaps, through "dilution" by the "blood" of "slave" or "servile" races (*i.e.*, those without a comparable tradition of self-rule). The conclusion was unavoidable: the assimilation of elements more than "slightly foreign"—southern Europeans, Asians, Africans—could seriously jeopardize the future of the United States. The cosmopolitanism of the post–Civil War decade was giving way to nativism and xenophobia among some white Americans of British ancestry.

Samuel Langhorne Clemens, himself an Anglo-American, was in the center of these events, sometimes marching sedately, sometimes acting up. He had set off for England in 1872 with the intention of having "Mark" satirize the British, but both of them returned with serious cases of Anglomania (prompted, it seems, by British appreciation of Mark Twain) to coauthor *The Gilded Age*, whose object was the governmental and moral corruption in the United States under Radical Reconstruction.[17] In the late 1870s and early 1880s, he read voraciously in British and European history.[18] *The Prince and the Pauper*, published in

16. Budd, *Our Mark Twain*, 59; John Fiske, "Manifest Destiny," in *American Political Ideas Viewed from the Standpoint of Universal History* (New York, 1885), 105.

17. Justin Kaplan, *Mr. Clemens and Mark Twain* (New York, 1966), 154–55. According to W. D. Howells, "It was after his first English sojourn that I used to visit him, and he was then full of praise of everything English: the English personal independence and public spirit, and hospitality, and truth. . . . He . . . was not blind to the defects of their virtues: their submissive acceptance of caste, their callousness with strangers, their bluntness with one another," in W. D. Howells, *My Mark Twain: Reminiscences and Criticisms* (New York, 1910), 12.

18. For information about Mark Twain's reading, see Everett Emerson, *The Authentic Mark Twain: A Literary Biography of Samuel L. Clemens* (Philadelphia, 1985), 90, 106–107,

1881, was begun in 1877. Although critical of British class distinctions, it exhibits a typical Anglo-American identification with the cultural and political heritage of Great Britain, as would *A Connecticut Yankee in King Arthur's Court* (1889) and *The American Claimant* (1892). Even *The Adventures of Tom Sawyer* and *The Adventures of Huckleberry Finn*, for all their concern with the unfortunate hold on the South of the "sham grandeurs, sham gauds, and sham chivalries of a brainless and worthless long-vanished society," illustrate the shared history of Great Britain and the United States, and the belief that the United States ought to constitute a further and finer development of British republicanism.[19] This Anglophilia waned as the 1880s advanced, but the optimistic assimilationism of the 1860s and early 1870s had also vanished.

Joel Williamson observes that "it is one of the great ironies of American history" that "when the nation freed the slaves, it also freed racism." After the mid-1870s, the political and economic racism associated with the Reconstruction years—fears that whites would be disfranchised in the South and would lose economic control of the region—began to be transformed or reconfigured by an increasingly insidious rhetoric of race as a "metonym for culture," culture biologized.[20]

One of the most prolific of the new "scientific racists" was Nathaniel Shaler, who published in the *Atlantic Monthly* in 1884 (the same year *The Adventures of Huckleberry Finn* appeared) an essay entitled "The Negro Problem." In it he protests that the ideals of Reconstruction were attributable to the "rash confidence" that followed a military victory, but that a wiser generation will understand that men "are what their fathers have made them, and that resolutions cannot help this rooted nature of man." So Shaler argues and Mark Twain agrees, but despairingly. One hardly needs to imagine what Mark Twain would make of the dictum that men are the product of their inheritance, or that trans-

---

160, 219; Alan S. Gribben, *Mark Twain's Library* (Boston, 1980); Philip S. Foner, *Mark Twain: Social Critic* (New York, 1958), 13; *Mark Twain's Letters*, II, 489–90; Albert Bigelow Paine, *Mark Twain: A Biography* (New York, 1912), II, 790–91.

19. Mark Twain, *Life on the Mississippi: The Writings of Mark Twain* (25 vols.; Hartford, 1899), IX, 304.

20. Williamson, *Crucible*, 109; Anthony Appiah, "The Uncompleted Argument: DuBois and the Illusion of Race," in *"Race," Writing, and Difference*, ed. Henry Louis Gates, Jr. (Chicago, 1985), 36.

formation would take generations. He wrote very particularly about the effects of inheritance and delusions of the "new man" throughout the 1880s and early 1890s. Where the two diverge is in Shaler's focus on blacks as the victims of history—it isn't so much the troublesome inheritance of the black man that concerned Mark Twain as that of the white one. Whereas Shaler predicted that it would take generations to transform blacks into reputable citizens of the United States, Mark Twain seems more interested in the time it would take to transform whites into reputable Americans. Of most danger, Shaler felt, was the conservative policy of removal of blacks into their own segregated communities. Such a policy could produce nothing more than the degeneration of the black population into the savagery that was supposedly their birthright. Nor could blacks be "uplifted" by miscegenation. Look at Jamaica, he said, where "the mingling of the races has brought with it a fatal degradation of the whole population that puts those peoples almost out of the sphere of hope." [21] On the other hand, the association of black with white in Mark Twain's work seems more often to uplift the white character.

As might be expected, Mark Twain's uses of race change during this period. By the mid-1880s, he is less likely to depict the robust American as racially or ethnically mixed and seems less inclined to base his humor on overt claims of kinship between himself and blacks. As a matter

21. Nathaniel Shaler, "The Negro Question," *Atlantic Monthly*, LIV (November, 1884), 697, 698. For other accounts of scientific racism, see John S. Haller, Jr., *Outcasts of Evolution: Scientific Attitudes of Racial Inferiority, 1859–1900* (Chicago, 1971); Philip Appleman, ed., *Darwin* (New York, 1970); Paul F. Boller, Jr., *American Thought in Transition: The Impact of Evolutionary Naturalism, 1865–1900* (Chicago, 1969); John W. Burrow, *Evolution and Society: A Study of Victorian Social Theory* (London, 1966); David G. Croly and George Wakeman, *Miscegenation: The Theory of the Blending of the Races, Applied to the American White Man and Negro* (New York, 1864); Joseph A. Gobineau, *The Moral and Intellectual Diversity of Races, with Particular Reference to Their Respective Influence in the Civil and Political History of Mankind* (Philadelphia, 1856); Thomas F. Gossett, *Race: The History of an Idea in America* (Dallas, 1963); Richard Hofstadter, *Social Darwinism in American Thought* (Rev. ed.; Boston, 1955); Jordan, *White over Black;* August Meier, *Negro Thought in America, 1880–1915: Racial Ideologies in the Age of Booker T. Washington* (Ann Arbor, 1963); Vernon Louis Parrington, *The Beginnings of Critical Realism in America, 1860–1920* (New York, 1930), Vol. III of *Main Currents in American Thought;* Stow Persons, *Evolutionary Thought in America* (New Haven, 1950); William Stanton, *The Leopard's Spots: Scientific Attitudes Toward Race in America, 1815–59* (Chicago, 1960); Forrest G. Wood, *Black Scare: The Racist Response to Emancipation and Reconstruction* (Berkeley, 1968).

of fact, he has picked up the ugly habit of depicting the *corrupt* American as "colored" or "slavish," a habit apparent in two political and moral essays written during the Cleveland-Blaine presidential campaign of 1884: "Turncoats" and "Mock Oration on the Dead Partisan." But the habit (along with his preoccupation with Magnetic Blaine) remained for a few years and is visible in "The Character of Man," "The New Dynasty," and "Consistency."[22]

Part of the change may have to do with the satisfactions of having been taken up by the eastern literary establishment as more than a humorist, as a moralist.[23] The role of "funny man" had been tempered with a greater seriousness of purpose incompatible in that time with a black persona. Mark Twain had been a contributor to the *Atlantic Monthly* for several years. The respectable readers liked his irreverence, but Mark Twain also liked his respectability. However, a good deal of the change in Mark Twain's persona must have been a reflection of and reaction to political and cultural changes—a sense of Reconstruction having failed, of immigration getting out of hand, of assimilation no longer a boon but a possible threat to the development of a national character.[24] "Isn't human nature the most consummate sham and lie that was ever invented?" Mark Twain asked Howells in 1884.[25]

Scientific racism transformed the debate about political and economic rights for black Americans from a discussion of the education and training for citizenship of people who had been slaves into a discussion of the impact of a supposed genetic inheritance which unfit them for that citizenship and had a profound impact on black Americans. It provided the basis for reconstituting a kind of slavery, for one thing, leading to restrictive legislation that required blacks to work

22. All three of these sketches are in *Mark Twain: Collected Tales, Sketches, Speeches, and Essays, 1852–1890*, ed. Louis Budd. It is also visible throughout the rest of Mark Twain's career, most notably in the fine essay "In Defense of Harriet Shelley," Pts. 1–3, *North American Review*, CLVIX (1894), 108–19, 240–51, 353–68.

23. This transformation is recounted by a number of biographers, including Louis Budd, *Mark Twain: Social Philosopher* (Bloomington, Ind., 1964) and his *Our Mark Twain;* Emerson, *The Authentic Mark Twain;* and Kaplan, *Mr. Clemens and Mark Twain,* 148–49, 193–96, *passim;* See also *Mark Twain's Letters*, I, 263 (letter of October 19, 1875).

24. Many scholars have discussed these events of the 1870s and early 1880s. See John Higham, "The Age of Confidence," in *Strangers in the Land: Patterns of American Nativism, 1860–1925* (New Brunswick, 1988), 24–34.

25. *Mark Twain's Letters*, II, 443.

where they were told, to carry passes, and that curtailed their rights to vote and to testify in courts, thus circumscribing their freedom of movement and choice considerably. It also had a profound effect on all Americans, because what it did was to make the "body" the chief trope for discussions of race and political or economic rights. During the 1880s and 1890s, the Reconstruction drama of racially mixed congressional houses is transformed into the Redemption-era nightmare of racially mixed private homes where the human body, represented by the mulatto, is seen as the battleground of the two races.[26]

Mark Twain, like many other southern writers of the post–Civil War South, becomes more interested in the 1880s and thereafter in the trope of the racially marked body. It is important to remember, however, that the tendency to take for granted the familiar Freudian model of personality that decontextualizes or essentializes the personality as the product of a "natural" familial order is a feature of our own age, not of Mark Twain's. According to many twentieth-century readers, the "black body" in the literature and art of the white racist of Mark Twain's generation is the repressed sexual shadow, a psychological representation. Any political or economic context for that body is of somewhat secondary interest, and the unfortunate implication is that if whites could only rid themselves of their sexual repressions, racism would vanish from the face of the earth.[27]

Without underestimating the impact of personal psychology or sexuality on the manifestations of racism, one must acknowledge that such dedicated psychoanalytical models can distort a more complex intersection between individual psychology and social order. And this was not the model of personality Mark Twain would have internalized. Not only was Freud just beginning his work in Vienna in the 1880s, but Mark Twain was also much more "sociological" than "psychological" in his understanding of personality, more inclined to understand "mental phenomena from mores, social relationships, and cultural discourses rather than from postulates about the internal dynamics of individual minds."[28] In Mark Twain's work, action seems more often a matter of

26. See Berzon, *Neither White nor Black*; Nancy Tischler, *Black Masks: Negro Characters in Modern Southern Fiction* (University Park, Pa., 1969).

27. Kovel, *White Racism*.

28. George E. Marcus, "'What did he reckon would become of the other half if he killed his half?': Doubled, Divided, and Crossed Selves in *Pudd'nhead Wilson*; or, Mark

social role than psychological dynamic. Nevertheless, the result of this appeal to a biological and genetic metaphor for the body politic is an internalization (not necessarily rendered "psychologically") of the debate over race and inheritance, an internalization that will account for many of the most perplexing features of *Pudd'nhead Wilson and Those Extraordinary Twins*.

The readability of *Pudd'nhead Wilson and Those Extraordinary Twins* has been under hot dispute since Hershel Parker threw down the gauntlet in 1981: "While the published *Pudd'nhead Wilson* is thus patently unreadable, anyone who knows literary critics will know that a simple fact like that has not deterred them from trying to read the book and bragging about having done so." The usual response is like that of Susan Gillman and Forrest Robinson, who argue in the introduction to their collection of essays on *Pudd'nhead Wilson and Those Extraordinary Twins* that rather than seek merit or interest in "a hidden unifying structure," like the New Critics—or textual critics like Parker—readers might see incoherence as "political symptom" rather than "aesthetic failure," searching, with Myra Jehlen, for "the novel's most basic and unacknowledged issues."[29]

Of course, some read the text's apparent incoherence as aesthetic strategy, arguing that there does exist a very well hidden "unifying structure." This is not impossible to do, provided the "text" is defined not by the prescriptions of genre but more broadly in terms of a fluid relationship between text and context (the kinds of contextual readings Eric Sundquist, Susan Gillman, Myra Jehlen, and others offer), or even among different stages of the text, these being precisely the kinds of relationships that had always interested Mark Twain and would eventuate in the radically experimental *Autobiography*, where the author insisted upon taking a number of risks with "conventional form and method." Among those risks was an insistence upon having the *Autobiography* published in the order in which it was composed rather than in the chronological ordering of event.

Twain as Cultural Critic," in *Mark Twain's "Pudd'nhead Wilson": Race, Conflict, and Culture,* ed. Susan Gillman and Forrest Robinson (Durham, 1990), 195.

29. Hershel Parker, *Flawed Texts and Verbal Icons: Literary Authority in American Fiction* (Evanston, Ill., 1984), 136; Susan Gillman and Forrest Robinson, Introduction to *Mark Twain's "Pudd'nhead Wilson": Race, Conflict, and Culture* (Durham, 1990), vii.

Mark Twain's determination on this point frustrated a number of his editors, most particularly Charles Neider, whose edition of the *Autobiography* attempts to reorganize the work in "autobiographical time," or chronologically according to date of event rather than date of recollection. But for Robert Atwan, altering the intent of Mark Twain in his *Autobiography* is comparable to correcting Huck Finn's grammar; the literary value of the work itself is to be found in the way "Twain's preoccupation with mental processes and his deliberate rejection of conventional narrative sequence make [the autobiography] not so much a failed autobiographical effort but an important precursor of modern self-consciousness." Arlin Turner points out that it is one of the characteristics of Mark Twain's aesthetic that "his books were less planned than allowed to *grow*." [30]

Whatever his attitude toward "growth," the trope of narrative "drift" had certainly been important to Mark Twain's fictional work as well as to his lectures, essays, and to the final autobiographical writings. In the *Autobiography*, speaking ostensibly of autobiography but with some relevance to fictional narrative as well, Mark Twain writes:

> Narrative should flow as flows the brook down through the hills and leafy woodlands, its course changed by every bowlder it comes across and by every grass-clad gravelly spur that projects into its path; its surface broken, but its course not stayed by rocks and gravel on the bottom in the shoal places; a brook that never goes straight for a minute, but goes, and goes briskly, sometimes ungrammatically, and sometimes fetching a horseshoe three-quarters of a mile around, and at the end of the circuit flowing within a yard of the path it traversed an hour before; but always going, and always following at least one law, always loyal to that law, the law of narrative, which has no law. [31]

30. Robert Atwan, "The Territory Behind: Mark Twain and His Autobiographies," in *Located Lives: Place and Idea in Southern Autobiography*, ed. Bill Berry (Athens, Ga., 1990), 42, 43; Arlin Turner, "Mark Twain and the South: An Affair of Love and Anger," *Southern Review*, IV (1968), 500. Italics mine.

31. *Mark Twain's Autobiography*, ed. Albert Bigelow Paine (New York, 1925), I, 237. On June 21, 1879, James Garfield, a Ohioan and leader of the House of Representatives, answered a fellow legislator: "It was said . . . by a great and eminent politician of Mississippi . . . that there were some things which were subject to the laws of science; that there were some things which could be controlled by man's ingenuity and man's devices; but that the Mississippi was not one of those things. He said that God Almighty, when he made [it] and bade its great floods flow from the mountains to the sea, said, 'Let her

Mark Twain's method, then, if we are to take him at his word here, is one of narrative movement (but not necessarily evolution) through improvisation upon necessity. And if we do take him seriously, we might find in the inconsistencies an example of a structure "ungrammatical" but nevertheless viable. We might find, in narrative's junctures and irruptions, signs of those "bowlders" that alter direction, or create "shoals" where the passage is dangerous, aesthetically as well as politically dangerous, but as much a part of the story as those smoother, more "developmental" passages.

Many have, in fact, already made similar claims for *Pudd'nhead Wilson*, admittedly intriguing to readers for its willful thwarting of narrative conventions, for an authorial hinge that calls the reader's attention to the process of composition and represents the author as "jackleg," and to the "evolution" of a supposedly failed novel from "a very little tale, a six-page tale . . . which [the author] is not acquainted with, and can only find out what it is by listening as it goes along telling itself." [32] There is, as George Marcus has observed, something unmistakably modern about this self-consciousness (as there is in the late-Romantic idea of the author as paraclete, or medium through whom "order" is revealed). However, since F. R. Leavis first observed that Samuel Clemens was not a "systematic thinker," we may have been altogether too quick to read Mark Twain's literary experiments, where they are most successful, as serendipitous (as if literary experimentation must be systematic), and where they are least successful, as evidence of his dwindling energy and control; and perhaps to overlook some of the most interesting features of Mark Twain's post-1890 work. [33] The late work might indeed repay some renewed attention, provided we are willing to take it on its own terms rather than as a falling away from the high-water mark of *The Adventures of Huckleberry Finn*.

The text of *Pudd'nhead Wilson* has a complicated history, too com-

---

rip; there is no law to govern it.' " Mark Twain, speaking in *Life on the Mississippi* of his conception of narrative, borrows the Mississippi's freedom from "natural law" to authorize his own narratives. See Howard Horwitz, *By The Law of Nature* (New York, 1991), 97.

32. Mark Twain, *Pudd'nhead Wilson and Those Extraordinary Twins*, ed. Sidney E. Berger (New York, 1980), 119. All subsequent citations are to this edition.

33. F. R. Leavis, "Mark Twain's Neglected Classic: The Moral Astringency of *Pudd'nhead Wilson,*" *Commentary*, XXI (February, 1956), 128.

plicated for complete review at this point.[34] One might reiterate, however, that the writing of what became *Pudd'nhead Wilson* began with the
writing of the story of *Those Extraordinary Twins*. What we read in portions of Chapters 5 through 8, and in Chapter 11 through part of Chapter 14 of the text we now have (*i.e.*, those portions concerning the arrival
of the Extraordinary Twins and their introduction to the town of Dawson's Landing), was written first, before the story of child-switching,
before Roxy became a major character. At this stage of composition,
Tom Driscoll is the *white* child of Percy Driscoll, a sorry excuse for a
child, with all of the vices most associated with the decadent Cavalier—
gambling, drinking, moral irresolution, and so on—but without the
"fatal drop" that will eventually mark him racially. The next, second
stage of composition produced Chapters 15 through the end of the
book—the sections concerning the election, Tom's racial classification,
his indebtedness, the murder of Judge Driscoll, the ensuing trial, and
the final revelation of Tom Driscoll's racial identity to the townspeople.
The third stage of composition is recorded in the first five chapters,
which concern the genealogies of the town's leading citizens, the arrival
of David Wilson and his acquisition of the epithet "Pudd'nhead," and
the story of Roxy's switching of the babies (which is the background
for Tom's racial classification).

Since the writing of *Pudd'nhead Wilson* began with the writing of
Those Extraordinary Twins, and one of my intentions is to reread the text
as Mark Twain would have us read the *Autobiography*—in the order in
which it was composed, as a kind of metanarrative—I should like to
begin my analysis there. *Those Extraordinary Twins* was designed as a
short farce about the arrival of a pair of Italian Siamese twins, a dark
one named Luigi and a fair one named Angelo, in a small slaveholding
town in Missouri, their reception by various townspeople, including
the morally compromised—and white—heir to the fortune of the
town's chief citizen, and their subsequent political fortunes in that
town.

Initially, the Twins write from St. Louis, which they describe as "way

34. See Anne P. Wigger, "The Composition of Mark Twain's *Pudd'nhead Wilson and
Those Extraordinary Twins:* Chronology and Development," *Modern Philology,* LV (1957),
93–102; and Daniel Morley McKeithan, "The Morgan Manuscript of Mark Twain's
Pudd'nhead Wilson," *Essays and Studies on American Language and Literature,* No. 12 (Cambridge, Mass., 1961), 1–64.

off yonder in the dim great world to the North." They claim to be "of the old Florentine nobility," to have been "seized" as children for the debts stemming from their parents' illness and "placed among the attractions of a cheap museum in Berlin," where "it took [them] two years to get out of that slavery"—details that configure their personal history within the context of nationalist efforts to unify Italy in the 1850s.[35] But in its broad outlines—within the context of national unification and self-government—the history recounted by the European Twins articulates the history that the residents of Dawson's Landing consider in some senses to be a version of their own national history. This recounting makes them especially appealing to a U.S. populace enamored, for very patriotic reasons, of the sentimental tale of the displaced heir, a tale so well and satirically mined by Mark Twain in *The American Claimant*.

Reading the personal history of the Twins in terms of the romance of the American Revolution, they are freed and come to a new, "free" world where they attempt to start over again. Of course, their attempts at re-making are thwarted in Mark Twain's more pessimistic farce, where both die so that one can be adequately punished, but the earlier sale of the Twins into slavery also recapitulates the story of the events that led up to the American Revolution. Many of us have internalized the story: our ancestors, the finest and sturdiest of England's "aristocracy of talent," crossed the ocean to the New World and are taxed to pay the debts of a culturally "ill" motherland, forced to work for the greater glory of the British Empire, which has indeed transformed its colonies into a museum displaying the artifacts and records of its most glorious history. It takes us a while to "get out of that slavery," but when we do we are "masters" indeed and our "prodigious slam-banging" is still heard far and wide in the land.

The personal history of the Twins recapitulates the nationalistic romance of the United States. However, in their own constitution, the Twins are perfectly constructed to function as tools for the anatomizing of U.S. pretensions toward a redemptive national unity. They are doubled—in the image of the United States—Angelo a de facto Puritan devoted to keeping his corporate body on the road to salvation, and Luigi a Cavalier devoted to the Cavalier virtues of honor and bravery

---

35. Twain, *Pudd'nhead Wilson and Those Extraordinary Twins*, 25–28.

and to the Cavalier pleasures of drink and carousing. In light of the postbellum ideology of national reunification, such a constitution is indeed monstrous and erases any possibility of social or moral progress. What moral reforms Angelo might make during those times he controls the body, Luigi will undermine the following week. The unity, or the coherence, of national, racial, and even municipal "selves" is shown to be a delusion; and the nationalist narrative of reunion and progress is strategically unwritten by the effect on the progressive Angelo of the hanging of his recalcitrant brother Luigi.

In this first stage of composition, the text is largely devoted to the hunger of the most prominent townsfolk of Dawson's Landing to legitimate their own claims to place and hereditary status by hitching up with the European nobles. Judge Driscoll, one of the four most visible of the F.F.V. (First Families of Virginia), is particularly susceptible to this desire, acting as quasi-official booster for Dawson's Landing's municipal glories. Initially, then, although the story—the farce—may have been intended as a satire of the reconciliation of North and South into a once-more unified (but not progressive) entity, its narrative scope is municipal.

For all of its concern with national reunification—and it is concerned with national reunification—the story is set in a small town and focuses on national issues through the lens of the municipality. This does make sense in light of the parochialism that defined U.S. life in the late nineteenth century. The pace of immigration had certainly picked up after the Civil War, but U.S. towns and cities were hard pressed to assimilate the newcomers. Writing in 1889 for James Bryce, Brooklyn mayor Seth Low observed that his contemporary U.S. city "is confronted not only with the necessity of instructing large and rapidly-growing bodies of people in the art of government, but it is compelled at the same time to assimilate strangely different component parts into an American community." Such is the task that faces Dawson's Landing, only more singularly:

> The political campaign in Dawson's Landing opened in a pretty warm
> fashion, and waxed hotter and hotter every week. . . . But as the canvass
> went on, troubles began to spring up all around—troubles for the Twins,
> and through them for all the parties and segments and factions of parties.
> Whenever Luigi had possession of the legs, he carried Angelo to balls,
> rum shops, Sons of Liberty parades, horse races, campaign riots, and

everywhere else that could damage him with his party and his church; and when it was Angelo's week he carried Luigi diligently to all manner of moral and religious gatherings, and did his best to get back the ground which he had lost before. As a result of these double performances, there was a storm blowing all the time, and it was an ever rising storm, too— a storm of frantic criticism of the Twins, and rage over their extravagant and incomprehensible conduct." [36]

The judge's xenophobia during the trial of Luigi and Angelo in *Those Extraordinary Twins* mirrors the antiforeign sentiment in many U.S. towns and cities during the postbellum years: "This court is not run on the European plan, Mr. Wilson; it is not run on any plan but its own." [37] For all of its relevance to the supposedly successful reconciliation of North and South in "Redemption" and for the changing discourse of race and slavery in the United States—and both are profoundly relevant—the story that became *Pudd'nhead Wilson* seems more immediately concerned with Dawson's Landing; and it retains a focus on the transformation of a small unincorporated town into a municipality. It is not irrelevant that Dawson's Landing receives a city charter during the course of the tale and mounts a mayoral election.

Had Mark Twain stopped with *Those Extraordinary Twins*, it would no doubt be ranked among his minor efforts, but he didn't. Consistent with his philosophy of narrative, he digressed, he drifted. He drifted into *Pudd'nhead Wilson and Those Extraordinary Twins*, which James Cox has called Mark Twain's last "American novel" and his last major work in the trilogy begun with *The Adventures of Tom Sawyer*. [38] Mark Twain's disclaimer at the end of the resurrected farce—that the two stories are not connected, possess "no interdependence, no kinship"—is more provocation than explanation, in light of the fact that they were originally twinned in the same mother-text and that Mark Twain the literary midwife did choose to retrieve the somewhat-mutilated orphan for publication with its more fortunate sibling. [39] Who can resist trying to discover a secret of repressed kinship between two texts published to-

36. Seth Low, "An American View of Municipal Government in the United States," in *The American Commonwealth*, ed. James Bryce (New York, 1889), I, 621; Twain, *Pudd'nhead Wilson and Those Extraordinary Twins*, 167.

37. Twain, *Pudd'nhead Wilson and Those Extraordinary Twins*, 149.

38. Cox, *The Fate of Humor*, 225.

39. Twain, *Pudd'nhead Wilson and Those Extraordinary Twins*, 170.

gether, joined in the middle by an authorial ligature, each one dealing with the subject of kinship?

As *Pudd'nhead Wilson* evolved (or descended) from *Those Extra-ordinary Twins*, perhaps the most significant transitions were the "south-ernization," or growing complicity with the slaveholding system, of the Yankee tinker David Wilson; the "reclassification" of the southern aristocrat Tom Driscoll from master to slave; and the transformation of the slave Roxy into the prime mover, the authorial mother in this female-identified text, a transformation that has serious implications for the way Mark Twain insists that we understand authorship (and identity) in the United States.

The most pronounced feature of these transfigurations is that each inverts the principle of evolutionary progress as it was used to buttress the ideology of a redemptive U.S. nationalism during the Civil War and early Reconstruction periods: according to that ideology, abolition was to have freed masters as well as slaves from slavery, former slaves would become free of their servility in the free air of the United States, and the self-reliant American who had been in grave danger through his intimacy with slaves was to have been saved. In *Pudd'nhead Wilson*, however, the master as well as the slave is reduced to slavery, the eman-cipated slave (Roxy) is reduced to servility, and the self-reliant Ameri-can is corrupted by slavery.

David Wilson was *the* central character for white readers of the 1890s, particularly so because he is, when he arrives in Dawson's Land-ing, somewhat naïve, apparently "untouched" by the legacy of slave-holding, about as decent a white man as the late nineteenth-century American Mark Twain could imagine.[40] At least one critic characterizes him as an example of the kind of hero who "epitomizes all of the hope for popular government which Mark Twain's long years of observation at home and abroad had allowed him to retain, a hope modified but not vitiated by experience."[41] Most readers of the 1890s, and many readers of our own time, agree. Wilson is long suffering, and his cal-endar is a compendium of endearing folksy satire. However likeable

---

40. Of course, that he was incapable of imagining a very innocent white man is indicated by Livy's admonition to her husband to "consider every man colored until he is proven white." See Bernard De Voto, *Mark Twain's America* (Boston, 1935), 66.

41. Robert Regan, *Unpromising Heroes: Mark Twain and His Characters* (Berkeley, 1966), 219.

he might be, this is too optimistic a take on David Wilson's character. For James Cox, his impact on the text is "repressive."[42] He is "brought in," Clemens himself has said, "to help work the machinery;" and one of the most serious tragedies in *Pudd'nhead Wilson* is that Wilson's technical cleverness with his fingerprinting scheme does not bring a murderer to justice. Instead, it serves only to implicate the Yankee in the moral morass of slavery, in what Mark Twain knew was a fundamentally immoral social order, to enable Wilson to make a name for himself in Dawson's Landing.[43]

In the final pages, when David Wilson becomes a hero after having "unmasked" Tom Driscoll, he is fêted by the citizens of Dawson's Landing. They "require a speech, and shout themselves hoarse over every sentence that fell from his lips—for all his sentences were golden, now, all were marvelous. His long fight against hard luck and prejudice was ended, he was a made man for good."[44] Wilson has revealed the murderer to have been born a slave; the creditors conclude that a slave is incapable of murder and that the real guilty party is "an erroneous inventory." Wilson's tinker-thought (meaning his fixation on the capacity of his fingerprinting scheme to uncover a fixed identity) in no way solves any of the conundrums surrounding questions of identity in this text.[45] The tragic irony is that David Wilson might be, in fact, a "made man" in Dawson's Landing, but the transfer of linguistic power to Wilson does not transform him into a satisfactory authorial agent. David Wilson is never invested with creative authority. His intentions are not underwritten by the text.

Part of the difficulty that some critics experience in trying to come to terms with *Pudd'nhead Wilson* stems from a reluctance to read it as the work of a postbellum southerner, "desouthernized" as Howells noted, but a southerner nonetheless, a man who had grown up the child of Virginia slaveholders and most of whose best work used the setting of the antebellum frontier South as the site from which to comment on the tensions of his own newly reunified United States. Although the

42. Cox, *The Fate of Humor*, 246.
43. Mark Twain, *Pudd'nhead Wilson and Those Extraordinary Twins*, 169.
44. *Ibid.*, 114.
45. Cox, *The Fate of Humor*, 233–46. Cox argues this point from a psychoanalytic perspective.

text of *Pudd'nhead Wilson* seems on the surface to be so different from texts like *The Grandissimes* or *Absalom, Absalom!*, it is in many respects like them—in its treatment of the theme of racial classification, in the kinds of characters who surround the racially troubled (and troubling) protagonist(s), and in the nature of the conflicts among those characters. One finds in each of these texts the same clustering of character types: the northern immigrant; the black man who appears white; his white "twin" or "brother"; the aristocratic or entitled slaveholder who is loyal to the old regime; and, most interestingly, the European. All are engaged in a drama that is best characterized the way H. H. Boyesen characterized *The Grandissimes*, as a "külturroman," a novel about the clash of cultures in the United States. The consequence—in all of these works—is the exile or death of the Europeans and the black man or, to be more exact, the "imitation white." [46] In the popular fiction of the time, this outcome was most often represented as a politically and culturally happy consequence that leaves the United States free to pursue its "manifest destiny," to redeem history, to regenerate the savage and the senile cultures of the Old and New Worlds. But in the hands of writers like Cable, Mark Twain, and Faulkner, this removal of the European and the African more often constitutes a tragedy that ties the United States all the more tightly to the sins of history.

To reiterate, during the years that Mark Twain was writing, a great deal was being said in the national press about the dangerous legacies of southernness in the progressive New World nation. It was in the South, supposedly, that the political and moral ideals of U.S. republicanism had been most deeply (or at least visibly) compromised by the corruptions of slavery, corruptions seen by most Americans as having originated in Europe and Africa rather than in Great Britain, regardless of Great Britain's role in the slave trade. That moral bequests from "the blood of a dozen generations of slaveholders" might manifest themselves in the newly reunified nation was of some concern—and connected with anxieties about the demands for citizenship from freedmen and from the increasing numbers of immigrants from eastern and southern Europe. The former slaveholder, like the former slave and the

---

46. H. H. Boyesen to George W. Cable, February 18, 1877, quoted in Arlin Turner, "A Novelist Discovers a Novelist: The Correspondence of H. H. Boyesen and George W. Cable," *Western Humanities Review*, V (August, 1951), 345.

foreign immigrant, might be characterized as willful and violent, possessing "prejudices against work" formed during slavery, "habits of extravagance," and "false loyalty to the worn out ideas of a forgotten system,"[47] all qualities that Tom Driscoll possesses in one way or another (and two of which Samuel Clemens possesses).

In some senses, then, the former slaveholder, in the rhetoric of post-Reconstruction nationalism, shared with the freedman and the immigrant dangerous inheritances, destructive potential, and the burden of history. One has only to remember Rebecca Harding Davis' *Waiting for the Verdict,* or Henry James's *The Bostonians,* or John W. DeForest's *Miss Ravenel's Conversion,* in which the white southerner is a somewhat unthinking and morally compromised figure shadowed by slavery and by a degenerate Europe, a kind of wandering second son (or spoiled daughter) whose plantation ethic has been displaced by the town ethic of the northern and mid-Atlantic areas, a type desperately in need of regeneration by what Cable called "Anglo-American spirit and inspiration."

The development of the white Tom Driscoll of the first stage of the composition is consistent with this stereotype. He is the dissipated and mean-spirited heir of a slaveholder; he is, appropriately, challenged in his courtship of the silly southern belle by the European visitors who so appeal to her sense of caste and entitlement. He is also a man who, uninvited (Mark Twain repeats the "uninvited"), follows the Twins and Pudd'nhead to a gathering of forces for the pro-rum party, the Sons of Liberty, and who ends by being kicked by Luigi Capello "clear over the footlights and landed . . . on the heads of the front row of the Sons of Liberty," from which position he is passed right out the door.[48] The implications are clear: for all of the traditional prestige of the F.F.V., Tom Driscoll, even in his white manifestation, has no political or romantic future in the growing and changing Dawson's Landing.

The text remains perplexing, particularly for critics of this generation who long to find some definitive answer to the question of whether *Pudd'nhead Wilson and Those Extraordinary Twins* is or is not a "racist"

---

47. C. Vann Woodward, *Origins of the New South, 1877–1913* (Rev. ed.; Baton Rouge, 1971), 153.

48. Mark Twain, *Pudd'nhead Wilson and Those Extraordinary Twins,* 56.

text and possess a number of new analytical strategies with which to search for an answer. Does *Pudd'nhead Wilson and Those Extraordinary Twins* suggest that Tom's criminality is due to the one drop of black blood that he possesses (and that supposedly possesses him), or that the criminality is traceable solely to his upbringing as slaveholder? Finally, does *Pudd'nhead Wilson and Those Extraordinary Twins* suggest that the *blood* of his slaveholder fathers, his "white" blood, is behind Tom's criminal behavior? Although Roxy attributes Tom's cowardice to his slave ancestry, much of the textual evidence points to Tom's inheritance and training as a spoiled and self-indulgent slaveholder, combined with his feelings of betrayal when he discovers that he is, legally, a "bastard" as well as a slave, as the factors that motivate him to murder the man who has raised him and who could, at any moment, disinherit him:

> In his broodings in the solitudes, he searched himself for the reasons of certain things, & in toil & pain he worked out the answers:
>
> Why was he a coward? It was the "nigger" in him. The nigger *blood*? Yes, the nigger blood degraded from original courage to cowardice by decades and generations of insult & outrage inflicted in circumstances which forbade reprisals, & made mute & meek endurance the only refuge & defense.
>
> Whence came that in him which was high, & whence that which was base? That which was high came from either blood, & was the monopoly of neither color; but that which was base was the white blood in him debased by the brutalizing effects of a long-drawn heredity of slave-owning, with the habit of abuse which the possession of irresponsible power always creates & perpetuates, by a law of human nature. So he argued.
>
> But what a totally new & amazing aspect one or two things, in particular, bore to Tom, now that he found himself looking at them from around on the other side! For instance—nigger illegitimacy, yesterday & today. Yesterday, of what consequence could it be to a nigger whether he was a bastard or not? Today the reflection "I am a bastard" made the hot blood leap to Tom's very eyelids. Yesterday, if any had asked him, "Which is more honorable, more desireable, & more a matter for a nigger to be proud of—to be a nigger born in wedlock, or a white man's bastard?" he would have thought the questioner was jesting. It was of course an honor to be a white man's bastard & the highest honor a nigger could have. Who could doubt it? The question would astonish the nigger

himself—go ask him & you will see. But today—today! to be a nigger was shame, but compared with this millionfold obscener infamy it was nothing. "And I am a nigger *and* that other thing!" It was only thought, he could not have uttered it, for his throat was dry & his tongue impotent with rage." [49]

Mark Twain excised the above from *Pudd'nhead Wilson* when he performed the famous "caesarian" that extracted *Those Extraordinary Twins*, but it is nevertheless telling. On the one hand, it confirms the argument that in Mark Twain's mind, "heredity and training" were not considered as alternatives. Instead, consistent with the tenets of neo-Lamarckianism, one "inherited" from the experience of one's ancestors and passed on one's own experiences, through heredity, to one's children. [50] Consequently, American republicanism was bred in the bone of those Americans whose ancestors came from England and Scotland; and it was also generally thought that the degradations of enslavement would take generations to transcend. Radical racists took neo-Lamarckianism a step further by arguing that blacks had already reached the limit of their evolutionary capacity. [51] On the other hand, the above excerpt also suggests that Tom is more upset by his illegitimacy than by his racial inheritance—a response that attests to the complexity of racist discourse in Victorian America by showing how the rhetorics of "science" and law were connected in the idea of the nation-state. It also points to the text's real issue, which is whether and how former slaves, former slaveholders, and their descendants were to be defined within the United States—as legitimate citizens or as illegitimate and alienated within the national family.

For all the relevance of its antebellum setting, then, the novel is constructed upon the divisions in American political and cultural life

49. Wigger, "Chronology and Development," 36–37.

50. See Brooks Thomas, "Tragedies of Race, Training, Birth, and Communities of Competent Pudd'nheads," *American Literary History*, I (Winter, 1989), 754–83. Thomas argues that whereas we tend to read "Training is everything" optimistically—as evidence that the present environment can thoroughly shape each individual regardless of the environment in which that individual's ancestors lived, "within Twain's world the phrase 'Training is everything' has repressive, not liberating, connotations . . . [and] evokes the fear that a natural self does not exist," suggesting that one is always completely at the mercy of "communal opinion" (762).

51. John S. Haller, Jr., *Outcasts from Evolution: Scientific Attitudes of Racial Inferiority, 1859–1900* (Chicago, 1971), 100–101.

in the post–Civil War period. Eric Sundquist and others have discussed the import of growing racism and black disfranchisement to the text, underscoring Mark Twain's continuing concern with racial divisions in the United States.[52] And race is, without doubt, at the very center of the text. *Pudd'nhead Wilson and Those Extraordinary Twins* comments critically and very directly upon U.S. racism; but it also uses race as a figure of speech, a trope for the fundamental divisions within or divisiveness of the United States during the 1880s. In situating this drama of miscegenation and child switching within the contexts of immigration, the coexistence in the U.S. mind of the fact of municipal growth with the habit of parochialism, and the growing hegemony of the party system following the Civil War, and tying it to a story of a pair of foreign and strangely constituted twins who differ fundamentally in temperament but are just as fundamentally linked, Mark Twain exhibits not only how powerfully the U.S. ideology of race in the era shaped the understanding of political, economic, and cultural identity but also the relationship of the past to the future and the nature of change in the United States.

Pudd'nhead Wilson and Those Extraordinary Twins is considerably more readable if one starts from the premise that it is not so much a study of racial essences as an anatomy of the fiction of white racial purity and its attendant moral virtues, as that fiction was developed in the nineteenth-century United States. In other words, one might examine the centrality of those "fictions" that make one "white" rather than focusing so much attention on those that make one "black." The fact of a shifting color line preoccupies a number of post–Civil War white southerners, from George W. Cable to Rebecca Harding Davis to Kate Chopin, Lafcadio Hearn, and Alice Morris Buckner. One can certainly look for the reasons for that preoccupation in the way the assimilationist legacies (attenuated as they were) of the Deep South and Mississippi Valley frontier intersected with the segregationist ideology of post-

---

52. Among the many treatments of race in Mark Twain's fiction are the following: Susan Gillman, *Dark Twins: Imposture and Identity in Mark Twain's America* (Chicago, 1989); Arthur Pettit, *Mark Twain and the South* (Lexington, 1974); Forrest Robinson, *In Bad Faith: The Dynamics of Deception in Mark Twain's America* (Cambridge, Mass., 1986); and Sundquist, "Mark Twain and Homer Plessy," 102–28.

bellum nationalism during a time when the future of the white southerner in the newly reunified nation was unsure. What were the "fictions
of law and custom" that defined "whiteness" in the time and the place
in which *Pudd'nhead Wilson* was conceived and published? How did
those "fictions of law and custom" differ from those that defined
"whiteness" in the time and the place in which *Pudd'nhead Wilson* is
set? What was one saying about a person when one described that
person as "white"?

As a matter of historical fact, it would have been almost impossible to
identify Tom Driscoll (or his mother) as racially black on the grounds
of "nature" or "assignment" in Missouri in the 1850s, however counterintuitive this assertion might at first seem. Our tendency to accept this
anachronism stems from a modern misreading of the "one-drop" rules
as they existed in the antebellum period. We tend to assume that "a
drop" meant "any admixture however minuscule" and to comprehend
these laws through the mediation of the pseudoscientific racism that
biologized race in the years following the Civil War.

In other words, we tend to read antebellum law and racist ideology
in terms of postbellum law and racist ideology. This is a mistake. In
1889, concurrent with the outbreak of radical racism and only a year
or so before Mark Twain began writing *Pudd'nhead Wilson*, Charles
Chesnutt published in the New York *Independent* an essay entitled
"What Is a White Man?": "The fiat having gone forth from the wise
men of the South that the 'all-pervading, all-conquering Anglo-Saxon
race' must continue forever to exercise exclusive control and direction
of the government of this so-called Republic, it becomes important to
every citizen who values his birthright to know who are included in
this grandiloquent term." Chesnutt points out that the color line (like
Mark Twain's Mississippi River, I might add) had changed location, or
"drifted" (to continue a metaphor), a great deal since the end of the
Civil War. In many states prior to the Civil War, a person of less than
one-fourth African ancestry was deemed incapable of being enslaved
and capable of inheriting property, was legally "white." Of course, law
and practice were not always consistent; but the Missouri law of 1855
(the state where and about the time when Tom Driscoll of *Pudd'nhead
Wilson* is supposedly identified as a slave and sold down the river)

stipulates that in order to be called a "mulatto," one must have a "Negro" grandparent.[53]

What this means is that one who does not have a Negro grandparent—one who, say, has a "mulatto" grandparent—is "white" and free. A similar standard governed in Mississippi and Louisiana, as in Michigan and Ohio (all states with some significant French colonialist influences). It is hard to believe that Mark Twain, of Missouri origins and experience in the antebellum South as a pilot, who took steamboats for several years up and down the lower Mississippi between New Orleans and St. Louis, did not know this. On the other hand, a Louisiana law of 1892 (passed during the time Mark Twain was working on *Pudd'nhead Wilson and Those Extraordinary Twins*) defined racial classification on the basis of the state's ability to identify an ancestor with any admixture of African "blood," a much stricter definition and one which not only made it impossible for certain descendants of certain families to inherit property but also underlay the U.S. Supreme Court's 1896 segregation decision, one that formalized long-standing assumptions about nationalist genealogy in the United States. What happened in the post-Reconstruction South was a reconfiguration of a racist discourse grounded in a slave culture with strong French colonialist (*i.e.*, assimilationist) influences into a racist discourse suitable to a nationalistic, nonslaveholding but profoundly racist culture; it enabled a reconfiguration of "slavery" and "mastery" (previously understood as irreconcilable *legal* conditions) into the discourse of "black" and "white" as irreconcilable *racial* conditions.[54] The result was that during the post-Reconstruction period, many people who had been stipulated as "free" prior to the Civil War found themselves "redefined." In the late nineteenth century, an individual of one thirty-second (or one sixty-fourth) African ancestry might well be a "master" (like Tom Driscoll)

53. Charles Chesnutt, "What Is a White Man?" New York *Independent*, May 30, 1889, pp. 5–6.

54. I do not in any way intend to ignore the profound racism that accompanied slavery in the New World. Jordan's *White over Black*, and especially the first chapter, "First Impressions," discusses the racism of British and Anglo-American cultures from the beginning of the era of colonialism. It should not be ignored, however, that Jordan's work is based on the British and Anglo-American experience in the New World. French and Spanish racisms were different, and did influence the growth of slaveholding cultures along the French Arch.

one day—that is, the beneficiary of a legitimating cultural genealogy and capable of claiming property—and "nonwhite" the next, "sold down the river."

It is exactly this transfiguration of racist discourse from a preoccupation with the impact of *slavery* upon the United States to a preoccupation with the impact of *racial difference* that underwrites the riddle as to Tom Driscoll's moral culpability and makes it clear that the problem is not to solve the riddle of whether his criminality and cowardice are the inheritances of his black or white ancestry, but to avoid asking it, because to do so makes one complicitous with the narrative of exclusion. A master does not exist without a slave, nor a slave without a master.

Chesnutt's remarks—together with New Historicism's interest in the intersections between constructions of subjectivity, race, and nation—can provide a long-overdue new perspective on southern racial histories and the function of southern racisms. The plural is useful to underscore one of the most immediately illuminating possibilities— the breaking up of both "South" and "race" as monolithic and essentializing concepts in southern studies, particularly in southern literary studies, where the perception (among some scholars) of the "South" as a fundamentally unified region and of "race" as a homogeneous genetic or social determinant of identity within that region (*i.e.,* of subjects as "either" black or white at all places and at all times in the history of the South) have perhaps done more to oversimplify complex social and *textual* realities than any other concept, with the possible exception of "natural" or "universal" gender roles.

In fact, both the idea and the ideal of a homogeneous South and of racial purity or racial definitiveness were more rhetorical constructs than realities of life in southern communities either before or after the Civil War. It has often been noted that the proportion of "mulatto" to "black" slaves increased dramatically between about 1830 and the beginning of the Civil War. Less often noted but equally true is that white fathers in some southern communities managed to free their slave children and to bequeath property to those children. And very seldom acknowledged, but true as well, children of mixed Anglo- or Euro-African ancestry were not infrequently absorbed into white families, especially in the creole Deep South and in those border states along the French Arch (*i.e.,* up the Mississippi and into the Great Lakes regions) where frontier conditions made social control more difficult (or at least different), and French colonialist legal policies and the remnants of a legal code based on Roman Civil Law rather than English Common Law permitted some petitioners to be stipulated as white under certain conditions.[55]

When Cable read Chesnutt's essay, he wrote to Chesnutt that his entire career had been devoted to exploring just this issue: "What is a white man?" One might make a similar claim of Mark Twain because, for all of his interest in black voices, his work is much more concerned with those discrepancies between the ideology of racial whiteness and the heterogeneous reality of the free population of the United States than with the ideology of race itself. There is actually no comment on the essential "race" character or nature of anyone in *Pudd'nhead Wilson*, although there are many occasions on which the impact of "slavery" on character is assessed (in Tom's rumination excerpted above, for example). It is intriguing to speculate that Mark Twain might have read Chesnutt's essay, or that he might have otherwise recalled that a Missouri law of 1855 would have preserved Tom's freedom.

Although I find it difficult to believe that Mark Twain could have been unaware of those laws that would have made of Tom Driscoll a white man in Missouri in the 1850s, I find it even more difficult to believe that Mark Twain presents Tom Driscoll as anything *but* a representation of the American morally compromised by his associations with a fundamentally immoral system of slaveholding. Perhaps the most convincing evidence that Tom Driscoll, imposter, is white is the fact that Driscoll was initially conceived as racially "unmarked" (which was, and still is, to be considered white). In the first version of the manuscript, Driscoll was racially unmarked, a minor character, and as thoroughly wicked as he could be. The incorporation of "blackness" as biological taint may be an effect of radical racism's tendency to represent cultural degeneration in terms of genetic amalgamation. Chambers suggests as much when he acknowledges that he and Roxy are of no use whatsoever as "imitation niggers." In this text, neither is Tom Driscoll of any such use. Where he is useful is as an imitation white, as a defamiliarized mirror through which whites might see themselves—in

55. See n. 32, Chap. 1. For an interesting discussion of the concept of race, see also Appiah, "The Uncompleted Argument," 21–37.

much the same way that Luigi and Angelo function as defamiliarized mirrors in which the residents of Dawson's Landing can see a flattering image of their own history and identity. The indeterminacy of Tom Driscoll's motivations, insofar as they might be traced to an essential racial self or to training is, I believe, integral to the nature of a text committed to this problematizing of racial—and most other forms of— identification. As Susan Gillman points out, everyone in *Pudd'nhead Wilson* is, in one way or another, an "imitation white man." [56]

Under these circumstances, it is certainly not necessary—nor even warranted in light of the "open" nature of the manuscript—to read the racially unmarked Tom of the first stage of composition and the racially marked Tom of the second stage as being distinct or unrelated to each other.[57] One might even speculate as to the influence of the transfor- mation of Tom Driscoll, from the legitimate "white" son of Percy North- umberland Driscoll to the illegitimate child of the slave Roxy and the cipher Cecil Burleigh Essex, upon Mark Twain's decision to divide the Siamese twins into two distinct bodies. During the second stage of com- position, after Tom acquires the "taint" that makes him black and trans- forms him from spoiled, amoral white heir into a tragically motivated black criminal, the twins have not yet been pulled apart. The conse- quent description of them as "side-show riff-raff, dime museum freaks" (which remains as one of the vestiges of the earlier inscription, even in the published version) would seem to announce that Mark Twain in- tended to configure them as confidence men of the likes of the King and the Dauphin of *Huckleberry Finn*. But after the Twins arrive and sit down to play the piano, the townspeople in this slaveholding com- munity (unlike those in Bricksville) realize "that for once in their lives they were hearing masters." [58]

There is no travesty of art here, as there is in the King's and Dau- phin's rendition of Shakespeare in the earlier book. Nevertheless, even

---

56. Twain, *Pudd'nhead Wilson and Those Extraordinary Twins*, 35; Gillman, *Dark Twins*, 78.

57. Gillman and Robinson note this fact in the Introduction to *Mark Twain's "Pudd'n- head Wilson,"* ix. James Cox, in "Puddn'head Revisited," which appears in the Gillman and Robinson collection, admits to wanting the "published text to take precedence over whatever deletions or changes can be detected in the manuscript" (8), a convention of traditional scholarship which I realize I am violating in this chapter.

58. Twain, *Pudd'nhead Wilson and Those Extraordinary Twins*, 30.

though they are not finally developed as con artists, the details of their personal history do at least attest to their appropriation by a capitalistic system that "sold" such aristocratic "oddities" to an American public hungry for entitlements. It may be that the physical outlandishness of the Italian Siamese Twins, in comparison with the moral outlandishness of the citizens of Dawson's Landing, is minor; that in this narrative the confidence games connected with the remnants of aristocratic order and privilege are so intricately a part of the community order that by contrast the Twins, despite their monstrous physical constitution, appear remarkably authentic. At any rate, the confidencing that is always so much a part of Mark Twain's work is attributable chiefly to Tom Driscoll, who at this stage of the composition is unmarked racially, not to the Siamese twins nor to the subsequently developed black manifestation of Tom Driscoll. What I mean to suggest is that Tom Driscoll's criminality and cowardice are developed during the first inscription of the novel; it is only the hint of a motivation (not pursued in the final published version) that is developed during the second inscription, after Tom is transformed into a changeling. One might suggest here that to the extent that Mark Twain is exploring the idea of the "white nigger," it is not in its meaning of mulatto but in its meaning of morally compromised white man.

Mark Twain has some subtle fun with the U.S. desire for "title" in *Pudd'nhead Wilson and Those Extraordinary Twins*. The claims of Dawson's Landing's chief citizens to an "aristocratic" status based on their descent from the F.F.V. can be debunked merely through a "genealogical" reading of their proud, but somewhat chaotically conferred, names. The name of Tom's shadowy father, Cecil Burleigh Essex, is, for instance, an amalgamation of the names of loyal members of the court of Queen Elizabeth I and those of various would-be usurpers of her authority. William Cecil Burleigh (1520–1598) was an English statesman who advised Queen Elizabeth I for forty years and persuaded her to execute Mary Queen of Scots. But Robert Devereux Essex, second earl of Essex, was an English courtier who hoped to usurp the place of Burleigh. He must have been somewhat upset when Elizabeth conferred authority on Burleigh's son Robert Cecil, because Robert Devereux Essex was then executed after trying to effect a coup to seize power from the queen. Odd lineage for Tom's father, who (if the metaphor of the individual as a biologized manifestation of cultural inheritance is accepted) seems to have been constructed as an entity divided against itself, a "dividual." Then, of course, Sir Henry Percy (1366–1403), alias Hotspur and the son of the first earl of Northumberland, for whom Percy Northumberland Driscoll might have been named, was also a would-be usurper—of Henry IV, and was killed at Shrewsbury. Pembroke Howard may have been conceived as a conglomerate descendant of Thomas Howard, fourth duke of Norfolk (b. 1538), who was executed for intrigues against Queen Elizabeth in troubles between England and Scotland; and William Herbert, first earl of Pembroke, who was also implicated by advocating marriage between Mary, Queen of Scots and Thomas Howard. And York Leicester Driscoll, the Judge, is a nominal descendant of the royal house of York, which produced Kings Edward IV and V and Richard III, and the earl of Leicester, a courtier to Queen Elizabeth (who had at one point betrayed her by plotting to install another on the throne). Naming is subversive in this text, for each man's name attests to a somewhat chaotic or misinformed appropriation of the genealogies of various loyalists and would-be usurpers of the British throne in the Elizabethan era. Thus we seem to have suggested the possibility that the F.F.V., who have been so nominatively amalgamated from former enemies and competitors, carry with them the insignia of division, and that Mark Twain, who was so interested in the history of England and Scotland, might have used the context of the Scottish struggle for independence (or supremacy) against England as a kind of submerged trope for the struggles between various parties (personal and political) in *Pudd'nhead Wilson*. He certainly would not have been the first southerner to do so. Acknowledging that Mark Twain is, as Leavis notes, "not a systematic thinker," I think we can still see that Thomas à Becket Driscoll, "from the moment of his usurpation," may be no more or less than the willful child who challenges the father's design (much as the real Thomas à Becket challenged King Henry II) and is martyred.[59]

In a letter of February 3, 1893, Mark Twain admitted to Fred Hall that he didn't know exactly what to do with the manuscript of *Pudd'nhead Wilson*. His own publishing house, Charles Webster and Company, no longer had any subscription machinery—which was the only real

59. See n. 18 above for sources for Mark Twain's reading.

moneymaking option—but he sent the story anyway. One month later, he followed it to the United States, where he presumably discussed its possibilities with Hall. At any rate, after that consultation, he went back to the manuscript once again and performed the caesarian that would extract the greater portion of the narrative of *Those Extraordinary Twins* and leave the story focused on the story of David Wilson's unraveling of the mystery surrounding the murder of Judge Driscoll and the revelation of Tom Driscoll as Chambers, the "black" son of Roxy and Cecil Burleigh Essex.

"This time 'Pudd'nhead Wilson' is a success!" Clemens wrote on July 30, 1893, to Hall:

> Even Mrs. Clemens, the most difficult of critics, confesses it, and without reserves or qualifications. Formerly she would not consent that it be published either before or after my death. I have pulled the twins apart and made two individuals of them; I have sunk them out of sight, they are mere flitting shadows, now, and of no importance; their story has disappeared from the book. Aunt Betsy Hale has vanished wholly, leaving not a trace behind; aunt Patsy Cooper and her daughter Rowena have almost disappeared—they scarcely walk across the stage. The whole story is centered on the murder and the trial; from the first chapter the movement is straight ahead without divergence or side-play to the murder and the trial; everything that is done or said or that happens is a preparation for those events. Therefore, 3 people stand up high, from beginning to end, and only 3—Pudd'nhead, 'Tom' Driscoll and his nigger mother Roxana; none of the others are important, or get in the way of the story or require the reader's attention. Consequently, the scenes and episodes which were the strength of the book formerly are stronger than ever, now.
>
> When I began this final reconstruction the story contained 81,500 words; now it contains only 58,000. I have knocked out everything that delayed the march of the story—even the description of a Mississippi steamboat. There ain't any weather in, and there ain't any scenery—the story is stripped for flight![60]

This letter, with its emphasis on marching and flying and "movement straight ahead without divergence or side-play," is odd indeed for a writer whose entire sense of narrative had been built on the image of the winding and changing Mississippi River and whose meaning re-

60. *Mark Twain's Letters*, II, 354–55.

sides so often in digression (as in "His Grandfather's Old Ram"). There may be any number of reasons why, at this time, Mark Twain seemed much more willing than before to appropriate or at least to profess an aesthetic of "flight," one so different from the aesthetic of "drift" that had governed his best work. The financial problems Clemens was suffering during the 1890s may account, in part, for that willingness. But I suspect that there was more to the reconstruction of *Pudd'nhead Wilson* than simple economics, and that Clemens' aesthetic instincts had not been completely destroyed by financial desperation. He *did* try to get the Morgan manuscript published and resorted to the final caesarian only in desperation.[61] Furthermore, as the subsequent publishing history suggests, Mark Twain was not entirely satisfied with the work as it appeared in *Century*. Within a year he had resurrected the mutilated body of the story of *Those Extraordinary Twins*, attached it with an introductory and self-reflective authorial "hinge" to *Pudd'nhead Wilson*, and published, through the American Publishing Company, the book that we know as *The Tragedy of Pudd'nhead Wilson and the Comedy of Those Extraordinary Twins*.

"Mark Twain," posing as "jack-leg," tells us that he initially planned to pen one story, not to "build" a novel but "to tell a little tale, a very little tale." [62] Unfortunately, "it is a tale which he is not acquainted with, and can only find out what it is by listening as it goes along telling itself" (119). This puts the "jack-leg" in a potentially embarrassing position, a position in which he is likely to be taken advantage of by the unscrupulous and the ambitious.

> [In the story of *Those Extraordinary Twins*,] other people got to intruding themselves and taking up more and more room with their talk and their affairs. Among them came a stranger named Pudd'nhead Wilson, and a woman named Roxana; and presently the doings of these two pushed up into prominence a young fellow named Tom Driscoll, whose proper place was away in the obscure background. Before the book was half finished those three were taking things almost entirely into their own hands and working the whole tale as a private venture of their own—a tale which they had nothing at all to do with, by rights. (120)

The author pleads his case before a panel of readers. "Do not judge me

---

61. Wigger, "Chronology and Development," 98–99.
62. Twain, *Pudd'nhead Wilson and Those Extraordinary Twins*, 119.

too harshly," he seems to say; "I am, after all, a 'jack-leg,' an amateur, small-potatoes." Now a real novelist, a born novelist (like a real American, a born American), not only has a story, but *knows* his story, and this protects him. The jack-leg was not stupid. He did see the problem in advance and he tried to resolve it. Mark Twain begins *Pudd'nhead Wilson* with the mock legal and genealogical authentication of "A Whisper to the Reader," a kind of deposition:

> Given under my hand this second day of January, 1893, at the Villa Viviani, village of Settignano, three miles back of Florence, on the hills . . . and given, too, in the swell room of the house, with the busts of Cerretani senators and other grandees of this line looking approvingly down upon me as they used to look down upon Dante, and mutely asking me to adopt them into my family, which I do with pleasure, for my remotest ancestors are but spring chickens compared with these robed and stately antiques, and it will be a great and satisfying lift for me, that six hundred years will. (2)

"A Whisper to the Reader" operates on the level of the discourse between writer and reader (albeit ironically) as an attempt to legitimate the jack-leg and his product, to provide a tradition that will give him the "lift" he needs in order for *Pudd'nhead Wilson: A Tale* to be authenticated as his own work and accepted by the reader as authoritative in its minutest particulars.

Paternity is a vexed issue on many levels in *Pudd'nhead Wilson and Those Extraordinary Twins*. On the level of plot, Tom Driscoll's original position as the legitimate son of Percy Northumberland Driscoll and his shadowy wife is abolished as the story "spreads itself along." Tom acquires a trace of African ancestry, and his slave mother displaces his master father as the acknowledged parent. At that point, paternity is unofficially transferred to the deceased Cecil Burleigh Essex (as much a cipher in the story as Driscoll's deceased wife). In effect, the father disappears as *Those Extraordinary Twins* engenders *Pudd'nhead Wilson*, to be replaced by a guardian and eventually, after Tom is found out, by a "proprietor." "Proprietorship" turns Tom Driscoll from son into saleable property. In short, "A Whisper to the Reader" purports to ensure that title to the "saleable property" of *Pudd'nhead Wilson: A Tale* is given over to Mark Twain as legitimated (if not authentic) "author."

Of course, "A Whisper to the Reader" and the preface to *Those Extra-*

ordinary Twins really constitute master-strokes (or freedom-strokes) that enable Mark Twain to take advantage of the new status quo of writing and publishing in order to authorize his art by de-authorizing it.[63] This is part of what makes Mark Twain so representative, so authentic, an "American author" in this work.

Victor Doyno has argued that *The Adventures of Huckleberry Finn* is shaped by the author's concerns with "literacy and copyright," and that the novel interweaves those issues with "the topics of slavery and freedom, heredity and environmental determinism."[64] It is possible to make a similar argument for *Pudd'nhead Wilson and Those Extraordinary Twins,* although one would want to make it clear that "authorship" itself is contested in *Pudd'nhead Wilson and Those Extraordinary Twins* to a much greater degree than in *Huckleberry Finn.*[65] From the perspective of the U.S. author, the situation that preceded the passage in 1891 of the International Copyright Law was one in which foreign (chiefly British) publishers pirated U.S. books, seldom paying the author for the privilege of reprinting the work, and sometimes issuing only fragments of those books under the guise of publishing the text in its entirety, sometimes interspersing fragments of one text in another and altering prefatory matter (title page, contents page, etc.) in order to disguise the book's origin. On a trip to Britain, an outraged Mark Twain once noticed a British publisher selling under the name "Mark Twain" titles that he had never written. This was the situation the International Copyright Law was designed to remedy by providing for an initial period of copyright (twenty-eight years, with the privilege of renewing for another fourteen), stipulating that all manufacturing of books sold in the United States had to be done in the United States, and prohibiting the importation of more than two copies of foreign copyrighted books for use in the United States.[66]

63. Gillman, *Dark Twins,* 31. Her analysis has been invaluable for my own study.

64. Victor Doyno, *Writing "Huck Finn": Mark Twain's Creative Process* (Philadelphia, 1992), 70.

65. There are two unpublished dissertations that take up this issue as it figures in other texts: David Barrow, "Mark Twain and the Oral Economy," Duke University, 1991; and Nancy S. Cook, "Marketing Mark Twain, or, Samuel Clemens and the Selling of 'The Innocents Abroad,' " SUNY Buffalo, August 17, 1991.

66. John Tebbel, ed., *The Expansion of an Industry, 1865–1919* (New York, 1975), 640–41; Vol. II of Tebbel, *A History of Book Publishing in the United States,* 4 vols.

Nevertheless, even though the desired effect of international copyright law was to protect authorial rights, to make bowdlerization of an author's works more difficult and to ensure the integrity of both "author" and "work," there were limits to its effectiveness in an age of cheap production and mass distribution. In the last years of the nineteenth century, changes in printing technology—the introduction of better and faster presses, cheaper ways of making paper, and new "ways of duplicating and multiplying materials"—as well as changes in the organization of the publishing business itself, particularly the growth of large publishing corporations, provided male authors in the United States with a new site from which to explore old anxieties about gender, the nature and status of authorship, and the genealogical control of texts.[67] Edward Said has articulated the basis of this anxiety in his observation that "underneath" the "genealogical connections" between "author" and "text" and "meaning" that maintain "the unity or integrity of the text" lies "the imagery of succession, of paternity, or hierarchy."[68]

As Michel Foucault has observed, "the coming into being of the notion of the 'author' constitutes the privileged moment of *individualization* in the history of ideas."[69] What Foucault does not state directly—at least in this essay—and what ought to be stated, is that the individualization of the author was one aspect of the ideology of the progressive state, with its agenda of investing agency in the male head of a household. In short, the individualization of the author was one consequence of the "emergence of private property and class inequality," which also subordinated women to male control.[70] Under the circumstances it

---

67. Russell Nye, *The Unembarrassed Muse: The Popular Arts in America* (New York, 1970), 2. In my thesis, I say "male authors," of course, to underscore the very heavily gender-marked discourse of authorship in the nineteenth century and to acknowledge that the woman writer's relationship to changes in publishing and printing was very different. In short, women writers as a group seem not to have been threatened by and in fact to have benefitted from new technologies and ways of organizing the production and reproduction of books. See Sandra M. Gilbert and Susan Gubar, *The Madwoman in the Attic: The Woman Writer and the Nineteenth-Century Literary Imagination* (New Haven, 1979), 45–92; Baym, *Women's Fiction.*

68. Edward Said, *Beginnings: Intention and Method* (New York, 1985), 162.

69. Michel Foucault, "What Is an Author?," in *The Foucault Reader,* ed. Paul Rabinow (New York, 1984), 101.

70. See Joan Kelly's discussion of Engels' thesis in "The Social Relations of the Sexes," in *Women, History, Theory: The Essays of Joan Kelly* (Chicago, 1984), 10.

should be no surprise that those changes in publishing and printing that appeared to threaten the individualization of the author would be represented as "feminization" of the author, of his appropriation by a larger, more empowered, "corpus."

During this period, authors associated certain changes in publishing and printing technology with loss of property rights (*i.e.*, control over the text). They feared (with some justification) that the "work" had been commodified to such a degree that its "exploitation and availability" were becoming more highly valued than "its presumed moral services and capacities for ideological instruction and integration," that the social construction of the "author" and his or her relationship to text and reader were becoming more a matter of authorial "mediation" than of authorial "mastery."[71] Essentially, they feared that their relationship to their work was becoming more and more like the relationship of women or slaves to theirs.

Yet some seem to have been as much intrigued as frightened by new possibilities. Mark Twain, for instance, in his post-1890 texts launches a series of attempts to redefine his relationship to text and reader in ways that enable him to take advantage of the possibilities of authorial mediation rather than mastery, to disrupt "genealogical connections" and to undermine narrative hierarchies and lines of succession. Although Mark Twain had always been interested in role-playing and confidence games, in bastardy, inheritance, and challenges to the status quo, late texts like *Pudd'nhead Wilson and Those Extraordinary Twins*, "The Mysterious Stranger" manuscripts, and the fragments "Which Was It?" and "Which Was the Dream?," as well as the *Autobiography*, are not only interested in these issues but are also "constituted" or structured according to genealogical disruptions of the text, false claims to title to and property in the text, and authorial "bastardy." Rather than pursue conventional kinds of textual "integrity" (with its inevitable suggestions of beginnings, middles, and endings; closure, determinacy, authority), they attempt to take advantage of those challenges to textual and authorial integrity made possible by new technologies of printing and distribution.

Most readers would agree that Mark Twain's best and most impor-

71. Robert Weimann, "Realism, Ideology, and the Novel," *Boundary 2*, XVII (Spring, 1990), 194.

tant work is set along the Mississippi River. Many readers have also observed both the displacements of geographical and temporal settings in Mark Twain's late works as well as the apparent loss of authorial control, the fragmentation of narrative, the fragmentation of character, and the disturbing recapitulations of character or plot or motif in different geographical and temporal contexts. I am thinking in particular of stories that begin, break off, begin again, to remain either unfinished or seemingly forced to premature or otherwise unsatisfactory conclusion (as the end of *Pudd'nhead Wilson,* for example); of characters or figures duplicated and reduplicated in ways that seem to defy reason (as No. 44, the Mysterious Stranger is duplicated through several related but distinct narratives).

Although traditional literary criticism has taken these features of the late texts as little more than signs of the originating author's loss of creative power and discipline, there is more to it. What is so apparent when one looks at these texts from a New Historicist perspective is that the fragmentation of narrative seems to accompany the displacement of "white" and "American" or "nationalist" voices by black and extranational or prenational ones, as in "Which Was It?," where the mulatto Jasper's voice displaces the white George Harrison's, or in *No. 44: The Mysterious Stranger,* where in medieval Austria No. 44 takes on the voice of a black singer from South Carolina. Of all Mark Twain's late works, *Pudd'nhead Wilson and Those Extraordinary Twins* might be the most complex—and most successful—example of this use of "black" and "foreign" voices (or voicings) to explore and to explode the myth of the racially "pure" or determinate and culturally innocent American, a myth that had a great deal of currency in the 1890s. It is a complex example of the use of black and white, foreign and domestic, northern and southern social bodies to examine the myths of racial purity, national unity, and individual autonomy, upon which the ideal of authorship was constructed in Victorian America. It is, after all, the story of several strategic "arrivals" in a complacent southern town—David Wilson, the Scottish tinker/thinker, and a pair of Italian twins, who are initially inscribed as Siamese twins and who proceed to catalyze a satire of U.S. boosterism. All this, of course, is hitched to a story of child switching and race mixing among the locals. The difficulties that the "old" historicism has been unable to surmount in attempts to read *Pudd'nhead Wilson* stem from the text's radical "openness" around these questions of race, nation, and subjectivity, its thwarting of any attempt at closure. Perhaps the only way to read this text is as a subversive *un*writing (rather than *re*writing) of the allegory of the American pilgrim's progress toward a redemptive nationalism that will "transcend" difference.

In *Pudd'nhead Wilson and Those Extraordinary Twins*, the slave Roxy, her changeling son, and the Italian twins catalyze a drama that displaces the Anglo-American from his traditional role of mastery and problematizes mastery itself as inconsistent with freedom. To be a "master" in this text means to be or to have been a "slave." The false Tom Driscoll is born into slavery, becomes a master, and is returned to slavery. The false Chambers is born a master, becomes a slave, and is then returned to mastery (which is not freedom). Despite these strategic substitutions, the cultural ideal of "mastery" is deconstructed in *Pudd'nhead Wilson and Those Extraordinary Twins* by a vision of radical incoherence around entities that were thought to be fundamentally coherent (the person, the community, the nation, the state). In other words, the issue is not simply the substitution of a chattel slave for a master but the identity of the "chattel" as "chattel" and the identity of the "master" as "master." Chambers, although "white," is certainly no master; Roxy, though a slave, is perhaps the most "masterful" of anyone throughout most of the story. It may, in fact, be that "mastery" which precipitates her into the lowest moral point of "slavery" in the text, a development understandable within Hegel's analysis of the dialectic of master and slave.[72] In other words, this is a narrative that challenges conventional post-Reconstruction, Anglo-American nostalgia for "mastery."

But "mastery" operates more resonantly on an abstract or symbolic level to signify the expected relationship of an artist to the medium. The narrator uses the word "masters" to refer to the Twins when they sit down to play the piano. "Mastery" also signifies the expected relationship of the author to the text, and by far the most telling subversions of "mastery" in *Pudd'nhead Wilson and Those Extraordinary Twins* take place around the operations of "authorship" itself.

In the United States (and in Britain), realism is based on the fun-

---

72. Georg Wilhelm Friedrich Hegel, *Phenomenology of Mind* [*ca.* 1807], trans. J. B. Baillie (2nd ed.; New York, 1955).

damental principle that the author, like the ideal reader, is blessed with a fixed identity (a known or knowable quantity), holds property in himself and his products, is empowered as an agent of the national culture in which he moves (*i.e.*, is neither a bastard nor a slave), and is capable of improvement.[73] In this text the aesthetic logic of the realist ethos, with its faith in the integrity or mastery of the author, as in the integrity or mastery of the national culture within which that subject was held to move freely and autonomously, is undermined by the "author's" protests that he is not to be taken for the master of narrative in *Pudd'nhead Wilson and Those Extraordinary Twins*. In other words, the author rejects any legitimating genealogy in the claim that he not only doesn't "know" his story but that he doesn't even *have* one. In this text not having a story turns out to be a dangerous and racially weighted state of affairs, as it was in the discourse of U.S. nationalism wherein the text was produced. Apparently, *Pudd'nhead Wilson and Those Extraordinary Twins* leaves us without an author willing to take responsibility for his work, a frustrating situation for readers raised to expect narrative regulation according to the principles of literary realism, with its faith in fixed identities and stable stories.

So when Mark Twain questions his own control over his intentions, abandons the ruse of authorial intentionality, suggesting that "a little tale" might "[go] along telling itself . . . till it spreads itself into a book," and that he, the author, has no power to do more than to listen and to submit to the abolition of his original intention, he is not only positing a very different social contract between author and text—a contract

---

73. Daniel Singal, *The War Within: From Victorian to Modernist Thought in the South, 1919–1945* (Chapel Hill, 1982). Edward Said, in *Beginnings* and more recently in *Culture and Imperialism*, (New York, 1993), does a brilliant job of linking the agenda of literary realism, with its faith in the unified [or unifiable] subject to the imperialist agenda. See also Amy Kaplan, "Romancing the Empire: The Embodiment of American Masculinity in the Popular Historical Novel of the 1890s," *American Literary History*, II (Winter, 1990), 663.

Pudd'nhead Wilson has been repeatedly assessed and evaluated in terms of its adherence to or divergence from the principles of literary realism. Recently, critics have argued that it is not an instance of realism, but throughout most of the scholarship one still finds the assumption that it is an example of a failed realist novel taken for granted. See John C. Gerber, "*Pudd'nhead Wilson* as Fabulation," *Studies in American Humor*, II (April, 1975), 21–31; Introduction to Gillman and Robinson, eds. *Mark Twain's "Pudd'nhead Wilson"*; Parker, *Flawed Texts and Verbal Icons*.

unlike that imagined by the Romantics, for whom the author is a paraclete who conducts the spirit of a nation or a people upward or outward into visibility and power, to the extent that it suggests that the author, like the nation, might not in fact be coherent, autonomous, unified. The nation/human subject might well be "doubled, divided, and crossed," even populated with broken or partial identities, complicitous and contingent. The author becomes at best more mediator among quarreling selves than sovereign or master, more conduit than originator, more impersonator (and occasionally imposter) than rightful heir. The consequence, of course, is that "work" becomes "text." The hierarchy that gives the author what one might call "paternal" rights over a "work" is overturned; and "proprietorship," being provisional, remains unsatisfactory. The clever author might, however, demand "proprietorship"—as Mark Twain does in his "Whisper to the Reader," where with stately (and ironic) legalese, the "jack-leg" attests to his adoption of "Cerretani senators and other grandees of this line" and to his own elevation by virtue of that adoption. But Mark Twain understands (as he asks the reader to understand) that proprietorship is not paternity. In a letter of 1890, "Reply to the Editor of 'The Art of Authorship,'" he argues that "deliberate and consciously methodological training" was never his way; so if he has methods, "they begot themselves, in which case I am only their proprietor, not their father."[74]

In so many of Mark Twain's post-1890 works, the aesthetic logic of the Victorian ethos in America, with its faith in the integrity of the person as in the integrity of the culture, is undercut by a vision of radical incoherence around entities that were thought to be fundamentally coherent (the person, the community, the state). By extension, the narrative of "psychological development," according to which a fully realized protagonist is changed—and usually for the better—by his experience, is displaced by what might best be called the narrative of dramatic recapitulation, according to which one figure on the narrative terrain is displaced by another who "duplicates" him, with a difference. In *Pudd'nhead Wilson*, for example, the narrator (who is Mark Twain)

---

74. Twain, *Pudd'nhead Wilson and Those Extraordinary Twins*, 119; Twain, "Reply to the Editor of 'The Art of Authorship,'" in *Collected Tales, Sketches, Speeches, and Essays, 1852–1890*, ed. Louis Budd (New York, 1992), 946.

goes to some trouble to make his chief actors capable of remarkable metamorphoses. Tom and Chambers are so much alike that a change of clothes enables master to pass as slave and slave as master; the Italian Twins Luigi and Angelo are "exact duplicates," except that "one was a little fairer than the other." Mark Twain referred to them as his "conglomerate twins."[75] Tom can disguise himself as a young girl or a young woman. Even the device of David Wilson's fingerprinting scheme as a means for revealing an authentic identity signifies on the trope of repetition with a difference—the revelation, however clever its discriminations, does nothing to restore any old order. Instead, the southern heir becomes a slave and the slave becomes the southern heir, and authenticity is nowhere to be seen.

As might be expected, the closest we come in this story to an authentic creative agent is in the voice of a racially marked woman, the commanding Roxy. It is intriguing to speculate about a possible model for the figure of Roxy in Maria McLaughlin, Clara Clemens' final wet nurse, "the unique, the sublime, the unapproachable." But whether or not McLaughlin was to any extent a model for Roxy, Mark Twain's later creation, the most complexly rendered female character in his corpus is comparable to the wet nurse in her unruly but glorified genealogy, her resourcefulness, and her profound impact on the children in her charge, particularly on the false Tom Driscoll, who receives the bulk of her attention.

In Roxy's case, one of the "children" in her care is the text itself. She is, in fact, the authorial mother of this female-identified text. On a few occasions prior to *Pudd'nhead Wilson and Those Extraordinary Twins*, Mark Twain had tried out (or tried on) a female authorial persona, in "A True Story," for example. One instance is especially intriguing. He responded to William Dean Howells' review of *Roughing It* with the following: "I am as uplifted and reassured by [your review] as a mother who has given birth to a white baby when she was awfully afraid it was going to be a mulatto." Evan Carton suggests that Howells must have found Mark Twain's reaction to the review "deeply unsettling" to the extent that it compares authorship to "a lustful and secretly de-

---

75. Twain, *Pudd'nhead Wilson and Those Extraordinary Twins*, 27; Emerson, *The Authentic Mark Twain*, 181.

graded maternity" that "entangle[s] and confuse[s] the identity of the offspring."[76] It is, however unsettled Howells might have been by it, a comparison that is characteristically Twainian in its ostensible degradation of authorship. At the same time it must be acknowledged that the word "degraded" might be replaced with less damning terms like "promiscuous," or merely "unrepressed," even "exuberant." (And having said all this, I should concede that Samuel Clemens would not necessarily have been as comfortable with these possibilities as we are, but neither would "Mark Twain" have been as uncomfortable with them as Samuel Clemens.)

In any case, the writerly Roxy turns out to be a figure who can play the role of master, of slave, of man, or of woman. On the other hand, she cannot remake herself or her son. Unlike Maria McLaughlin, she cannot "march in a procession by herself." She cannot, any more than Huckleberry Finn or the young Samuel Clemens, maintain the freedom she found on the Mississippi River during her years of chambermaiding on a steamboat. Like Mark Twain's art, hers resides more in mimicry than in originality and damns her (as it damned him) to return to the site of her origins.

Ralph Ellison once observed that "when the white man steps behind the mask of the [black] trickster his freedom is circumscribed by the fear that he is not simply miming a personification of his disorder and chaos but that he will become in fact that which he intends only to symbolize; that he will be trapped somewhere in the mystery of hell ... and thus lose that freedom which, in the fluid, "traditionless," "classless" and rapidly changing society, he would recognize as the white man's alone."[77]

In this essay, Ellison might have been speaking directly of Mark Twain, whose *Pudd'nhead Wilson* does indeed threaten his authorial freedom, threaten to trap him "somewhere in the mystery of hell." For when Mark Twain steps behind the mask of Roxy as "trickster"—when he invests Roxy with the creative agency necessary to transform her son into "master" rather than with the creative agency necessary to free

76. *Mark Twain–Howells Letters*, ed. Henry Nash Smith and William M. Gibson (Cambridge, Mass., 1960), I, 10–11; Evan Carton, *"Pudd'nhead Wilson* and the Fiction of Law and Custom," in *American Realism: New Essays*, ed. Eric Sundquist (Baltimore, 1982), 62.

77. Ralph Ellison, "Change the Joke and Slip the Yoke," in *Shadow and Act* (New York, 1972), 53.

him (or herself)—Mark Twain's own "authorial freedom" must pur-
port to be circumscribed through an imaginative identification of the
authorial self with the trickster. The revelation of Tom Driscoll as Roxy's
son in the courtroom scene has an intense effect on his and Roxy's use
of language in the final pages. Tom is not only silenced, but his silence
is also taken as confession; Roxy's words "struggle," but they struggle
not to exert any apparent mastery—to display or to demand understanding from Wilson or the readers—but to ask for mercy. "Roxy flung
herself upon her knees, covered her face with her hands, and out
through her sobs the words struggled—'De Lord have mercy on me,
po' misable sinner dat I is!'" [78]

Roxy's final words constitute an admission of guilt in a text in which
guilt has more often been disputed, denied, or repressed; but those final
words are also a "minstrel cry" and not to be taken at face value.[79] This
is not to say that Roxy is dissimilating; it is to say that they are part of
the performance, and the guilt they acknowledge does not, by rights,
belong to Roxy alone. What these final words reveal, of course, is the
dynamic through which guilt is not only displaced onto blacks in the
postbellum United States but contained by minstrelsy (which under-
went many changes in its form and its significance after the Civil War).
In a sense, there is an ironic—a disguised—mastery Roxy exerts over
the story in her final minstrel cry. One thinks of Ellison's *Invisible Man*,
of the protagonist there learning to direct pain into laughter and to
contain the electricity in that way. Although imaginative identification
with the black trickster was dangerous—perhaps especially so for a
man like Samuel Clemens, whose ambivalence about his dual (often
contradictory) roles of humorist and moralist was so powerful—it was
also cathartic.[80]

What, the scholarship leads us to ask, is Mark Twain's relationship
with the black characters and black voices in his work? Is he a white
minstrel exploiting the stereotypes for fun and profit? Is his relationship

78. Twain, *Pudd'nhead Wilson and Those Extraordinary Twins*, 113.

79. Cox, *The Fate of Humor*, 246, 230.

80. Beginning in the 1890s, the expression "white nigger," as Williamson has reminded us, could be used not only to designate the mulatto, but also to refer to the white
man morally compromised by associations with blacks. The role of trickster was somewhat empowering (at least emotionally) for slaves, but not for "masters"; it might have
been symbolically liberating, but not empowering.

to blacks proprietary or paternalistic, or is it "predial" and "akin"? Is it a relationship of likeness or difference, or both? Is there an element of the "uncanny" about it? Much of the discussion of the significance of race in his fiction posits either a humane and sympathetic Mark Twain gently arguing (from a secure position of racial and cultural respectability, *i.e.*, from a paternal distance) for black rights or an exploitative Mark Twain appropriating black voices for his own profit. At best, critics have drawn a portrait of a disillusioned and self-doubting Mark Twain implicated—generally and vaguely—in abstract questions of character and identification that are catalyzed by racial theorizing in the period. I would suggest, as an alternative, the existence of a Mark Twain constructed by race mixing, a kind of symbolic "mulatto" who at once performs and anatomizes the drama of black and white confluence and conflict in the United States. This alternative enables us to recognize the "blackness" in the persona along with the "whiteness," and to deconstruct any hierarchy that might be supposed to stabilize their relationship with each other. Most importantly for my purposes, it enables us to engage the color line less as static boundary than as symbolic and rhetorical force in the late nineteenth-century United States.

Despite the rhetoric of autonomy that characterizes official political and moral discourse in Dawson's Landing (and Victorian America), the kinship between *Those Extraordinary Twins* and *Pudd'nhead Wilson* seems to rest on the principle of interdependence itself. Insofar as *Those Extraordinary Twins* is concerned, the issue seems to be whether and how to determine separate identities for brothers who share a pair of legs and the control over those legs, whether or how to assign responsibility for a crime to one twin or another and to punish the appropriate twin without violating the rights of the other (an imperative which proves impossible). Insofar as *Pudd'nhead Wilson* is concerned, the issue is much the same—whether it is possible to discover Tom Driscoll's cowardice and criminality as the effect of one identity or another, his slave inheritance or his inheritance as a slaveholder. In short, both *Those Extraordinary Twins* and *Pudd'nhead Wilson* are constructed around questions of the extent and nature of one's complicity with one's history and on the difficulties of assigning moral responsibility in one quarter where interdependence is the rule.

Pudd'nhead Wilson differs from *Those Extraordinary Twins* in that it deploys these questions about complicity within the context of U.S. chattel slavery rather than within the context of immigration. But together, both texts bring the legacy of assimilation in the New World to bear on the nationalist ideology of segregation for the purpose of critiquing the reassertion of ideals of racial and national "purity," "definitiveness," "integrity," or "mastery" in the post-Reconstruction years. Consequently, Leslie Fiedler's suggestion that Mark Twain stopped, through reticence, just on the verge of *creating* "a monstrous poem on duplicity" is not exactly true.[81] There is little doubt that Mark Twain created one—he simply had some trouble publishing it, settling (for a while) for the publication of *Pudd'nhead Wilson* in *Century*. He did, however, return to the story and reconstruct it for publication in book form, and in a form that is indeed a "monstrous poem" on duplicity, a profound challenge to the ethos of authorship and, by extension, to the ethos of self-making in the late nineteenth-century United States.

81. Leslie Fiedler, "As Free as Any Cretur . . . ," *New Republic*, August 15, 22, 1955, pp. 7–8.

4

WILLIAM FAULKNER AND THE DISCOURSE
OF RACE AND NATION

" . . . as if it were the voice which he haunted . . . "
      —*Absalom, Absalom!*

                         William Faulkner (actually "Falk-
ner"at this time) was born three years after the publication of *Pudd'n-
head Wilson and Those Extraordinary Twins*, into a South alienated from
the rest of the nation, impoverished, defensive, and provincial. He did
not come of age amid the upheavals of Reconstruction or the optimistic
white rhetoric of the Reconciliation and Redemption eras. He was born
two years after Booker T. Washington delivered the famous "Atlanta
Compromise" speech, which shook hands with Jim Crow and sealed
the segregationist compact. But as is true for the other authors included
in this study, the major problem in Faulkner's work is genealogy in a
new age and the challenges it presents to conventional notions of the
relationship between author and narrative. The context, in this instance,
is the context of white racist paranoia in a South that had begun to
move into the twentieth century in a United States where a future imagined in terms of political, economic, and hence cultural isolation was
no longer convincing.

The years between 1890 and 1930 had been, in the South, years of
hysterical white reaction to any possibility of integration, which was
seen as a dangerous infection of the white cultural body and a threat
to the very foundations of Anglo-American civilization. In fact, 1920
was the final year in which the U.S. Census provided a separate category for "mulattoes"; after that date, one was "either" black or white.

Since about 1890, it had been the figure of the mulatto, and the possibilities (or impossibilities) of "passing," that had preoccupied writers dealing with the issue of race in the United States. The reason is that this figure, more than any other, embodied the threats and promises of integration in a racist culture that had defined itself chiefly through tropes of mastery (transcendence, redemption, sublimation) rather than through tropes of equality and difference (reconciliation, compromise, multiplicity).

It is around this figure that writers of the era construct powerful and resonating dramas of national and racial identity—white writers through dramas of retaliatory segregation and (many) black writers through dramas of failed integration. Like the earlier ones, these texts challenge traditional ideals of heredity and entitlement, seeking more to critique the ideology of whiteness than that of blackness, the ideology of mastery rather than slavery. William Faulkner began to write late in this era. *Light in August* was published in 1932, *Absalom, Absalom!* in 1936; both are retrospectives on racism, with special relevance to the era of radical racism.

In *Absalom, Absalom!*, the hubris of an American innocent, Thomas Sutpen, creates, in the 1820s, a retributive agent in the figure of Charles Bon, a mystery whom we never see (any more than we see his father), who never speaks except through the mouths of those who tell his story, who has no identity independent of their projections.[1] That "durn French feller" appears suddenly in the middle of frontier Mississippi.[2] He comes (at least initially we are told he comes) from New Orleans, the site of the colonialist culture represented by so many of the octoroons in U.S. literature. And like so many of them he possesses a fatal (and fatalistic) creole sophistication and later, much later, for some

1. In calling Thomas Sutpen an "American innocent," I follow critics like Cleanth Brooks and Carolyn Porter, for whom Sutpen is, in Porter's words, "no less American for being Southern, and no less Southern for being American." Carolyn Porter, *Seeing and Being: The Plight of the Participant-Observer in Emerson, James, Adams, and Faulkner* (Middletown, Conn., 1981), 209. See also Cleanth Brooks's important discussion of the character of Thomas Sutpen in *William Faulkner: The Yoknapatawpha County* (New Haven, 1963), 11–20, 296.

2. William Faulkner, *Absalom, Absalom!* (New York, 1936), 133. All subsequent citations are to this edition.

speakers (and only for some speakers), the "taint" of African ancestry—a detail that is considered fact by most Faulkner scholars and
probably comes as close to fact as any other detail concerning Bon,
which is to say not very close at all. The real fact, of course, is that the
conversation that supposedly reveals Bon as black is not included in
the text. This leaves open the possibility that Quentin might have mis-
construed or invented such a conversation for his own purposes. The
reason for the murder of Charles Bon by Henry Sutpen in 1865 becomes
one of the novel's central mysteries, as central as the mystery of Thomas
Sutpen's character to which that murder is intricately tied; and the need
to create a satisfactory explanation for that murder becomes an obsession for each speaker.

As a reader, one does not know exactly why Henry Sutpen killed
Charles Bon. All one can be sure of is that, for all of the speakers except
Miss Rosa, Henry was driven by some necessity for preserving his
family's (i.e., the nation's) purity. In fact, what one is more than likely
meant to know is that the story of the murder constructed by each
speaker is remarkably representative of that speaker's sense of his own
defeat within a specific historical context. In other words, whether the
"purity" that Henry is seen as protecting is constructed in terms that
are nationalistic, familial, or racial depends upon who the speaker is
or, rather, *when* he is. Repeatedly, Faulkner warns us that the story is
"invented" by the tellers of the tale, and "true enough" to boot, but
that the telling of the story is a matter of "hearing and sifting and
discarding the false and conserving what seemed true, or fit the preconceived."[3] Under the circumstances, Faulkner's decision to embed
the truth in the drama of performance, to bind information so tightly
to interpretation, leads the reader to ask not only who or what Charles
Bon was—black or white, possible son or would-be husband—but to
ask who and what the speakers are with respect to the Charles Bon
they construct. And it is clear that who and what they are has everything to do with history as it unfolded in the Deep South between the
years of the cession of the Louisiana Territory and the early twentieth
century. It is the relationship of two postwar generations, represented
by Jason Compson and his son Quentin, to that history, which in this
text takes the form of the "preconceived," that makes the tale. The final

---

3. *Ibid.*, 316.

irony is that whatever the rationale, the murder itself did happen; and instead of releasing the Sutpens and those whom they represent from the tragedies of their own history, it serves to accelerate their decline into that history.

There is little doubt that Faulkner wrote *Absalom, Absalom!* out of a deep familiarity with the political and cultural situation in New Orleans and in Haiti, especially as it was perceived by and important to nineteenth- and early twentieth-century southerners like the ones Jason and Quentin Compson were modeled on. It should not be surprising that he did so. His Deep South origins; the arrival of his own most famous ancestor, William Clark Falkner, in the southwestern frontier during the first half of the nineteenth century, when Mississippi was still very much frontier and creole New Orleans was a newly acquired southern terminus (hardly sixty miles south); as well as Faulkner's own years in the French Quarter of New Orleans and in France may account in part for this context.

Thomas Sutpen is in French Haiti from the early 1820s to 1833. He serves for a while as overseer on a sugar plantation owned by a French planter; he "subdues" an uprising of Haitian slaves who threaten the planter with their voodoo in what is probably one of the many skirmishes that made up the long and bloody Haitian revolution of the late eighteenth and nineteenth centuries; he marries Eulalia, the planter's daughter by a Spanish Creole; and his son, Charles Bon, is born in 1829. Sutpen makes the discovery that causes him to repudiate Eulalia in 1831, two years before he arrives in Yoknapatawpha County and not long before his spurned wife arrives, with their son, in New Orleans—still a logical destination for a West Indian Creole (especially a white one) at this time.

That a man like the young Sutpen, obsessed with his redemptive design, should end up in the West Indies is probable. Despite the United States' refusal to recognize Jean Paul Boyer's mulatto government, Haiti, of all the West Indian islands, was of the most economic importance to the United States during this time. The Caribbean was the logical theater for dreams of U.S. expansion in the pre–Civil War era (as it would be once again in Quentin's era), since the desire for expansion had certainly not been exhausted by the acquisition of the Louisiana Territory. What did happen between that time and the years preceding the Civil War was the development of a more articulate ideology of expansion in which the idea of the design as redemptive was more pronounced and more entangled with the ideology of race and slavery. Throughout the pre–Civil War era, dreams of worldly wealth for white Americans and dreams of a millennial civilization or terrestrial paradise, where even the enslavement of darker peoples could be seen as a step toward lifting them out of such darkness and into the light of God's righteous millennium, were united in that rhetoric. By extension, it was of great importance to preserve the United States from contamination by decadent Europe and its leveling influence, already visible in the formation of Haiti as the first mulatto government in the New World. The question, of course—the same question that Americans put to themselves in their debate over national assimilation of white Creoles—was whether such preservation was possible. It was a question that would be readily appropriated by the postbellum white American as a way to explain the South's defeat as somehow preordained. But just as important, it was a question that would be readily appropriated by William Faulkner as the key to the construction and reconstruction of Charles Bon and the means through which Faulkner might explore the implications of his own generation's imperialist designs.

In the light of Faulkner's critique of millennialist ideology, it is certainly of some ironic import that the architect for Sutpen's mansion should be a colonialist Frenchman from Martinique, because in so many ways the slave culture that the Anglo planter in the Deep South inherited (if not the slave culture he envisioned) was established upon a West Indian—predominantly French and Spanish—foundation. During the time that Sutpen's mansion is going up, the architect "in his formal coat and his Paris hat and his expression of grim and embittered amazement lurked about the environs of the scene with his air something between a casual and bitterly disinterested spectator and a condemned and conscientious ghost—amazement . . . not at the others and what they were doing so much as at himself, at the inexplicable and incredible fact of his own presence." Later, Charles Bon will share not only a French cultural identification but also the Frenchman's spectral relationship to the U.S. slaveholder:

> From the moment when he [Bon] realized that Sutpen was going to prevent the marriage if he could, he [Bon] seems to have withdrawn into a mere spectator, passive, a little sardonic, and completely enigmatic. He

seems to hover, shadowy, almost substanceless, a little behind and above
all the other straightforward and logical, even though (to him) incomprehensible, ultimatums and affirmations and defiances and challenges
and repudiations, with an air of sardonic and indolent detachment like
that of a youthful Roman consul making the Grand Tour of his day
among the barbarian hordes which his grandfather conquered.[4]

Like the French architect (who may be, at least rhetorically and symbolically, the "grandfather" referred to), Bon is a ghostly spectator who
seems condemned to haunt the site of a former life. Despite the intricate
historical relationships among New World slave cultures, the expansion of the United States during the early nineteenth century placed
the colonialist cultures of Europe in just this position with respect to
the developing nation in the New World, a nation that defined itself
as the working out in a New World wilderness of a providential design
impossible in the corrupt atmosphere of Europe. That this French architect should so clearly prefigure Charles Bon suggests that Faulkner
was well aware of the inevitable persistence of the displaced in any
design seeking to transcend a historical relationship among various
cultures and peoples.

It is the persistence of history in the New World—in the discourse
of New World speakers—and its capacity to undermine official U.S.
innocence that Faulkner seems most interested in. Faulkner's rich historicism is strikingly apparent in his handling of the voices that construct and reconstruct the story of Charles Bon, constructing and reconstructing themselves in the process. According to Rosa Coldfield,
who came of age in the antebellum South (and for whom the Civil War
is a consequence rather than a cause), Bon's murder is inexplicable
except as the inevitable consequence of Sutpen's—the American Innocent's—own demonic nature. For Rosa, Bon is "Charles Good,
Charles Husband-Soon-To-Be," an unseen prince who is nothing less
than a miracle, a civilized man on the Mississippi frontier; for her, the
marriage between Judith and Bon is "forbidden without rhyme or reason or shadow of excuse."[5] But according to those speakers who came
of age after the Civil War (Jason Compson and his son Quentin), the
murder is made necessary by Bon's nature, not by Sutpen's—at least

4. *Ibid.*, 38, 93.
5. *Ibid.*, 15, 18.

that is the kind of motivating cause they pursue with greatest energy. Not surprisingly, for them the Civil War has become a kind of originating moment wherein the Sutpens, like the Compsons their textual descendants, find their motive and rationale.

Jason Compson and Quentin are nevertheless very different as speakers. Their stories of Bon—*i.e.*, of the South's (and of the U.S.'s) repressed history—diverge, especially insofar as race figures into the stories, chiefly because for Faulkner they represent two distinct generations whose understanding of the United States and of their own relationship to it, and to the history of slavery and race in the Deep South, is very different. Although both imagine Bon as a Creole possessed of the expected creole decadence and capable of corrupting the innocence of the Sutpens, it is only in Quentin's narrative that Bon is constructed as black. Jason's understanding of Bon and of the South's defeat seems to have developed free of the impact of U.S. imperialism and radical racist ideas of race and culture, which became popular only in the late 1880s, long after Jason would have first heard of Bon and begun to formulate his own understanding. Bon is simply "the curious one" in this U.S. frontier, "apparently complete, without background or past or childhood," a man who invades an "isolated puritan country household" and seduces both brother and sister in a way more inevitable than deliberate.

For Jason, preoccupied with the scene of a colonizing and corrupting European empire and its impact on the U.S. Deep South, the Creole Bon is representative of a retributive power perceived as culminating in his inheritance of the French architect's ability to "curb the dream of grim and castlelike magnificence" toward which Sutpen aims. The difference between Jason and his antebellum forebears, of course, is that the postbellum Jason Compson identifies *himself* more closely with the Creole Bon than with the Sutpens. Charles Bon is, in Donald Kartiganer's words, Jason Compson "writ large," a man "equipped with a cynicism that rivals Mr. Compson's own;" fundamentally, he is a man who shares with Jason Compson the kind of cultural superfluity that results from having inherited, like the French aristocrats in Faulkner's early manuscript *Elmer,* "an old and splendid thing worn out with time." Kartiganer's reading is convincing, for the South's defeat in the Civil War has left Compson in the very position he constructs for Bon— "complete [yet] without background . . . a mere spectator," and so on.

Jason's heroic ancestors are separated from him not only by time or death but by a kind of political legitimacy that he, like the white Creole, can no longer aspire to. Unlike him, they are "not dwarfed and involved but distinct, uncomplex who had the gift of loving once or dying once instead of being diffused and scattered creatures drawn blindly limb from limb from a grab bag and assembled, author and victim too of a thousand homicides and a thousand copulations and divorcements."[6] In this passage Jason reveals his own sense of confused and violent origins, as well as the alienation of the southerners whom he represents from the ordering power of a nationalistic discourse, an alienation traceable to 1865 and, in this text, to the murder of Bon.

When Jason attempts to explain that murder, he resorts predictably to the terms of his own compelling narrative of the encounter of the nationalistic American and the colonizing European. Henry Sutpen, the "legitimate" ("puritan") son of Thomas Sutpen, might have found that Bon had to be killed for the fatal French assimilationism that allowed him to maintain, in a semblance of legitimacy, an octoroon woman and their son—a story that recapitulates the response of the segregationist United States to the existence of the intermediate caste of Creoles of color in the Caribbean and reflects, in terms of domestic/sexual history, U.S. distrust of the French as authors of the black revolutions in the Caribbean. In murdering Bon, then, Henry (according to the logic of Jason Compson's version of events) might have been attempting to preserve Sutpen's vision of order and hierarchy from the example of Europe. That Bon maintained a black family, and perhaps even carried their daguerreotypes with him, must have seemed to Henry a violation of the very terms upon which civilization must be established. One must note, however, that for Jason the threat (and the seductive promise) of "race mixing" is situated in the female octoroon, whom he imagines as a creature utterly powerless to challenge or threaten the white estate except as tool of the colonist. The relish with which Jason describes her home in New Orleans, closed and hidden, its crumbling walls and old doorkeeper like a figure from a French woodcut, confines her threat within the displaced colonialist culture—far removed by the

6. *Ibid.*, 93, 38; Donald M. Kartiganer, *The Fragile Thread: The Meaning of Form in Faulkner's Novels* (Amherst, 1979), 81–82; William Faulkner, "Elmer," *Mississippi Quarterly,* XXXVI (Summer, 1983), 410; Faulkner, *Absalom, Absalom!*, 89.

ideology of race, gender, and nation from any possibility of a serious claim to the white estate, except through the agency of the European colonist.[7]

It is Quentin's appropriation and deployment of this horror of confused and violent origins in his reconstruction of Charles Bon as "white nigger" that is of greater significance, however. It is, after all, Quentin Compson as "commonwealth," as heir of southern history, its final dying original, who completes—and is himself completed by—the story begun by Rosa Coldfield and continued by Jason.[8] It should not be surprising that a white southerner of Quentin's generation, caught between a history that associates him with Africa and with Europe and a political rhetoric that would assimilate him to a nationalistic, increasingly imperialistic, and racist ideal, would dramatize his situation with respect to the very best representative of that situation, the creole man of mixed blood.

Central to Quentin's reconstruction of Bon are the preoccupations of his own turn-of-the-century South with questions of white racial purity and the U.S. mission. In his revision, black Haiti replaces white creole New Orleans as the locus for Bon, who eventually becomes a representative of that troubled "mulatto nation" as well as a harbinger of the United States' own assimilation to a like future through the inevitable "amalgamation" that racists of Quentin's generation felt would result from any recognition of blacks as equal citizens of the United States.

The extent and the nature of this cultural hysteria are most visible in the work of radical racists like Thomas Dixon, Jr., and Robert Lee Durham. There is little question that in the work of these writers the mixed blood has been characterized very differently than by Cable and other Deep South writers of his generation, even by Mark Twain. The figure is marked in this fiction by an inclination to sexual excess and violence associated with images of "African" savagery, the white skin nothing more than a mask to hide the destructive fires associated with a heavily sexualized "dark continent," a place that ostensibly exists prior to history and political order, the site of a radical chaos that is presented as a danger to the U.S. redemptive mission. Of course, Quen-

---

7. Faulkner, *Absalom, Absalom!*, 100, 112–13.
8. *Ibid.*, 12.

tin's narrative eventually does work its way around to this sexualized vision of an African Bon, but the development of this Bon as part of a longer historical process of "inventing" Bon serves as a means of textual containment and commentary on that vision.

Actually, it is really not very far, in terms of metaphorical development, from Jason's creation of Bon (and by extension of *himself*) as cynical or fatalistic European charged with the seduction of the South through the unveiling of the white Negro, the beautiful octoroon woman or "apotheosis of chattelry," to Quentin's creation of Bon (and by extension of *himself*) as the white Negro, a man who has inherited the violence and the illegitimacy, and whose blood demands vengeance.[9] Both are dramatizations of the white southerner's sense of his own construction by postbellum history. By extension, one might also note that Bon's capacity to contain all of history in this new role of "nigger" (corrupt European and dispossessed elder brother as well as slave), as if the "white nigger" is indeed the "supreme apotheosis" not only of chattelry but also of all of history, offers one some sense of the extremity of Quentin's position as both American and as southern heir to a past he cannot transcend.

Equally important to the reconstruction of Bon is the context of U.S. imperialism. What Theodore Roosevelt called "new nationalism" may have been the logical outcome of the reunion of North and South after Reconstruction. By the end of the century, however, nationalism had become imperialism—at least what Benedict Anderson calls "official nationalism" had become useful rhetorically for the agenda of empire. And at the turn of the century, the imperialistic designs of the United States tapped the same racist ambitions and anxieties in white Americans that the expansionist designs of slaveholders had tapped half a century before. The concurrent rise of U.S. imperialism abroad and radical racism inside the United States, which held that blacks, freed from the civilizing influences of slavery, were retrogressing into savagery and would eventually die out in the competition with whites, was no coincidence. One might read the hysteria of radical racism as an appropriation on the domestic front of the imperialistic agenda of redemption, the burnings and dismemberments of black bodies a dramatization on the physical body of the effects of colonization on the

9. *Ibid.,* 112.

black cultural bodies of Cuba, Puerto Rico, and the Philippines, acquired by the United States in the Spanish-American War. The U.S. agenda was quite clear. Albert Beveridge may have said it best:

> God has not been preparing the English-speaking and Teutonic peoples for a thousand years for nothing but vain and idle self-contemplation and self-admiration. No. He made us master organizers of the world to establish system where chaos reigned. He has given us the spirit of progress to overwhelm the forces of reaction throughout the earth. He has made us adept in government that we may administer government among savage and senile peoples. Were it not for such a force as this the world would relapse into barbarism and night. And of all our race He has marked the American people as His chosen nation to finally lead in the redemption of the world.[10]

Beveridge made this speech to the U.S. Senate at the turn of the century, marshaling in only a few lines the kind of rhetoric that William Faulkner would conjure with in his development of Quentin as both victim and agent of such imperialist ideology.

Quentin's narrative begins in the winter following his discovery of Henry Sutpen in the old mansion. What this means is that it begins after he has supposedly learned that Bon was black. Nevertheless, Quentin does not reveal this putative solution to the text's various mysteries until very late in the story, allowing the detail of miscegenation to *seem* to be arrived at by a process of deduction from the premise of Bon's origins in a colonialist slave culture—a process that recapitulates the psychopolitical drama of the white southerner in the novel, whose own origins in a colonialist slave culture eventually lead to his defeat and alienation. At first, we know only that Charles Bon is a mysterious French Creole, but as Quentin's story unfolds, Bon is transformed from colonialist Creole into Sutpen's elder son into "the nigger that's going to sleep with your sister." [11] In other words, Quentin's narrative transforms Bon from a man who had, at a prior stage of history (*i.e.*, Jason Compson's), some (albeit negligible) claim upon the white estate—a claim to assimilation—into someone who cannot possibly, according to the conventional logic of U.S. radical racism, sustain any such claims.

10. Anderson, *Imagined Communities,* 83–111; Albert Beveridge, quoted in Ernest Lee Tuveson, *Redeemer Nation: The Idea of America's Millennial Role* (Chicago, 1968), vii.

11. Faulkner, *Absalom, Absalom!,* 358.

It is here that the extent of Quentin Compson's own alienation from the ordering power of the nationalist discourse becomes most evident. Quentin's Charles Bon (Quentin Compson "writ large") wants the father's recognition more than he wants his father's daughter. His lawyer (never mentioned in Jason's story and certainly more believable as a product of the imaginations of two turn-of-the-century college students than as a realistic representation of antebellum legal counsel) is more intent on pressing the claims of the (at this point) white and creole Bon on the American father's estate than in pressing his suit of love. In fact, the *"daughter? daughter? daughter?"* is hardly more than a means for acquiring some portion of entitlement to that estate.[12] Bon's ultimatum, implicit but nevertheless clear enough, is recognition by the American father and all it entails or incestuous marriage to the daughter. It is also implicit, but clear enough, that the ultimatum is designed to lead to the father's recognition of Charles Bon and not to Bon's marriage to Judith. What it does lead to, as Quentin imagines it, is Sutpen's revelation to Henry that Charles Bon is not white. That revelation changes everything. Bon's claims to the white estate are rendered absolutely monstrous, and Bon is transformed from alienated son into "the nigger who's going to sleep with your sister," an agent for the destruction of the white estate.

The post-1890 context out of which Quentin constructs his story becomes clearest here. The phrase that Bon uses during his final confrontation with Henry—"the nigger that's going to sleep with your sister"—would not likely have been used in the South of 1865, when Charles Bon is supposed by Quentin Compson to have uttered it. It had, however, become a racist rallying cry by the turn of the century, when Quentin Compson constructs this imaginary scene. (It is indeed fascinating that Quentin attributes that line to Charles Bon himself, as if giving the character an opportunity to comment, somewhat prematurely, upon his own development as a construct.) In Quentin's South, growing more and more isolated from the rest of the country, the terms *black* and *brother* became, in the rhetoric of radical racism, which claimed that the black man wanted nothing so much as the white woman, just reconcilable enough, just possible enough to function as the white southerner's ultimate nightmare of alienation. As African, as

12. *Ibid.*, 309.

"black beast," as "the nigger that's going to sleep with your sister," and yet as brother nonetheless, Charles Bon represents all that the post-1890 white southerner most feared: the gradual usurpation of political, familial, and economic purity—that is, legitimacy, recognition by the national body, or father—by a mulatto brother or brother-in-law, a usurpation almost always associated with the degeneration of a proud civilization into a "mongrel" future.

What this substitution of "nigger" for "brother" suggests is the existence in Quentin's narrative of a perceived necessity, played out in a rhetorical maneuver, of denying the Fifteenth Amendment, of denying, in effect, that one can be *both* black and brother. In 1913, Senator James K. Vardaman of Mississippi spoke directly to this point: "I unhesitatingly assert that political equality for the colored race leads to social equality. Social equality leads to race amalgamation, and race amalgamation leads to deterioration and disintegration."[13] What Vardaman and those whom he spoke for reveal in such statements is the fear of the degeneration of their own political lines. Under the circumstances, it is relatively easy to see that what the white racist is attempting to protect by refusing to acknowledge a black man as brother or "social equal"—the purity of the family line being a kind of metaphor for citizenship and rights to govern—is, in *Absalom, Absalom!*, exactly what such a policy does not protect, and precisely because of the possibility that an unrecognized (and unrecognizable) black son might, through passing unknown into the white family, violate laws against miscegenation as well as incest. Ironically, Sutpen's refusal to acknowledge his mulatto son, to give him the father's name, which would "place" him with respect to his lineage (a placing that had been possible in the Caribbean cultures that preceded the coming of Americans like Sutpen into the Deep South), is exactly what precipitates the dual threats of incest and miscegenation.

If one recalls, for a moment, Quentin's often-discussed obsession with his sister Caddy, the incestuous desires that lead him in *The Sound and The Fury* to transform his own virginity into the sign of incest consummated and reified, the nexus of issues of racial (familial) purity and national legitimacy in the novel becomes clearer as the site of the white southerner's own struggle for cultural redemption, that is, for an escape

---

13. James K. Vardaman, quoted in Williamson, *The Crucible of Race*, 379.

from history into the millennial New World nation of the United States. Bon is Quentin "writ large," in the language of his own defeat, as a construct who almost but not quite gets away with the incest Quentin imagines that he has committed, longs to have committed, and fears desperately that he has committed. It is an incest that, as John Irwin has suggested, operates as a metaphor for origination and authority in Quentin Compson but also carries with it the threat, as well as the promise, of death. "Amalgamation is incest," wrote one Mississippian as early as 1854. "Impurity of race is against the law of nature. Mulattoes are monsters. The law of nature is the law of God. The same law which forbids consanguinous amalgamation forbids ethnical amalgamation. Both are incestuous." It is a powerful equation when read in terms of Quentin's narrative of race and sex, where the monster who must be destroyed, the figure who "owns the terror," *is* both black and brother, despite the rhetoric that would deny that relationship; in other words, it is a dramatization of the white racist's most nightmarish vision of his future under the new dispensation. If the "supreme apotheosis" of slavery is the octoroon woman, the supreme apotheosis of emancipation, in the mind of a radical racist, may be the "white nigger." It is particularly important for one's reading of Quentin Compson's paradoxical desire for and rejection of the "black" brother that this is a phrase used at this time not only to refer to the octoroon but also to describe certain kinds of traitorous whites who exhibited what was perceived as "morally black" behavior—incest, for example.[14]

Quentin's incestuous desires are thus configured as the logical outcome of his own loss of cultural legitimacy, which could effectively "name" and thereby "place" him (in a parallel of the black Creole's loss of such legitimacy during the cession years), and they do indeed redefine him as a "white nigger," as "morally black." They make him, in a sense, "the nigger that's going to sleep with your sister" (in a kind of inversion of the Reconciliation romance). In fact, Shreve McCannon, Quentin's audience and co-creator for the story, suggests this very thing. "You've got . . . one nigger Sutpen left," he tells Quentin at the end of *Absalom, Absalom!:* "I think that in time the Jim Bonds are going

14. John Irwin, *Doubling and Incest/Repetition and Revenge: A Speculative Reading of Faulkner* (Baltimore, 1975), 64, 82–94; Henry Hughes, *A Treatise on Sociology: Theoretical and Practical* (Philadelphia, 1854), 31; Williamson, *The Crucible of Race*, 466.

to conquer the western hemisphere. Of course it won't quite be in our time and of course as they spread toward the poles they will bleach out again like the rabbits and the birds do, so they won't show up so sharp against the snow. But it will still be Jim Bond; and so in a few thousand years, I who regard you will also have sprung from the loins of African kings." The subtext, of course, is that Quentin himself has already, in some sense, "sprung from the loins of African kings." Shreve's prophecy makes it apparent that already, through a process of constructing the story in terms of the most deadly fear—assimilation/amalgamation—it is the white southerner himself who finally and ironically "owns the terror" because he has been transformed (or has transformed himself), through the rhetoric of defeat as it is used in a racist and nationalistic culture, into the victim, into the European and African ghosts the United States, obsessed with its own ahistorical uniqueness, fears so intensely.[15]

In other words, when a nation envisions itself in ahistorical and millennialist terms, as new and as redemptive, it denies its relationships to the past, even to the history of its making. For a white southerner who had been, prior to his defeat by the United States, at the very center of a southern nationalism that envisioned itself in terms remarkably similar to those of the United States (*i.e.*, as redemptive), the consequence is that, by the logic of his own rhetoric, he has become through his defeat the inheritor of history and the bearer of prior displacements in his own.

In the climactic scene between Henry Sutpen and Charles Bon at the gate to Sutpen's mansion, the segregationist ideal is enforced. No marriage takes place between Charles Bon and Judith Sutpen. By all the lights of radical racist ideology, this is preservation, the laying of foundations for a sunny future. But in Faulkner's text, the segregationist dream is subverted into its own nightmare. Instead of progress, redemption from the sins of the fathers, and transcendence of history, one is left with degeneration, damnation, and submergence into history. The fact is that Quentin fails. It is not so much that he fails to penetrate the mysteries of the past—that failure is inevitable—the more significant failure is that he reconstructs Charles Bon in the same terms, ac-

15. Faulkner, *Absalom, Absalom!*, 378, 369–70.

cording to the same economy of exclusion that his fathers had used in their construction of the United States on the preposterous ideal of transcendence of history. Like his fathers, he is incapable of reading his own kinship with those populations alienated by nationalistic ideology as anything other than a sign of his own degeneracy. Quentin's is a failure of imagination, an inability to rewrite the old stories. Quentin solves no mystery of Charles Bon; he solves no murder. Bon remains invisible; the murder remains unexplained; and Quentin remains as much a victim of the past as his many fathers.

One of the most profound achievements of *Absalom, Absalom!* is its power of commentary on the construction and deployment of "creole" identity in the postbellum South. In *The Grandissimes,* for example, lying beneath the scapegoating of unacceptable legacies in the exile of the quadroon woman and the suicide of the octoroon man, one discerns a faint suggestion that the white heroes might someday once again have to face their own troublesome history. It is a suggestion that becomes reality in *Absalom, Absalom!,* where the economy of U.S. national innocence is itself thematized and the economy of the text is one of historical reclamation. That Charles Bon should, in following his U.S. father (and Martinican grandfather) into the frontier wilderness of Mississippi, be transformed from "Charles Good, Charles Husband-Soon-to-Be" into decadent white Creole, into brother, into "the nigger that's going to sleep with your sister"; and that he should then eventuate in the figure of Jim Bond, the "one nigger Sutpen left," whose howling in that wilderness has no direction, cannot be traced toward New Orleans, toward the West Indies, nor finally eastward toward Europe—in no direction, in fact, except inward— is the final reclamation of a damning history by Quentin Compson, as he himself lies displaced and shivering in a "cold known land."

But if Quentin's status as a victim of history makes him a compelling representation of the southerner of Faulkner's generation, it also makes him equally as compelling as a representation of Faulkner's future American. Certainly, Shreve's metaphor of migration suggests that the implications of amalgamation are not exclusive to that region of the United States known as the "South," although the alienated status of the U.S. South at this period is essential to the story. The reality of implication suggests, instead, that in *Absalom, Absalom!,* the South is not only a discrete region within the geographical borders of the United

States, but also a phase within the narrative of nationalism, a "tropic" site. The power of *Absalom, Absalom!* is to be found in its capacity to critique, on southern terrain, those rhetorical strategies the United States has used to constitute itself as a coherent and culminating entity, distinct from its colonialist past and from slavery. Carolyn Porter observes that in *Absalom, Absalom!*, "by the time we find out what is going on, we are already implicated in it."[16] For all of its engagement with the alienating discourses of racial, national, and regional difference, *Absalom, Absalom!* is a study in implication.

One generation after Quentin Compson lay shivering in a Harvard dormitory room, reconstructing history with his roommate Shreve, Joe Christmas—a white racist deep in the middle of a nightmare—begins the last leg of his tormented journey along the color line. While the pregnant Lena Grove pauses in her search for the dark-complected drifter who has abandoned her, Joe Christmas cuts Joanna Burden's throat, leaving her with "her head turned clean around like she was looking behind her." This detail leads Byron Bunch to conclude, mistakenly, that if she had been able to do that "when she was alive, she might not have been doing it now."[17]

A few days later, Christmas is hunted down, shot, and mutilated by "a captain in the state national guard." Percy Grimm is a young man born too late to have fought in the "European War" and will "never forgive his parents for that fact":

> It was the new civilian-military act which saved him. . . . Then suddenly his life opened definite and clear . . . uncomplex and inescapable as a barren corridor, completely freed now of ever again having to think or decide, the burden which he now assumed and carried as bright and weightless and martial as his insignatory brass: a sublime and implicit faith in physical courage and blind obedience, and a belief that the white race is superior to any and all other races and that the American is superior to all other white races and that the American uniform is superior to all men.
>
> "We got to preserve order," he said. "We must let the law take its

16. Porter, *Seeing and Being*, 49.

17. William Faulkner, *Light in August* (New York, 1932), 85. All subsequent citations are to this edition.

course. The law, the nation. It is the right of no civilian to sentence a man to death. And we, the soldiers in Jefferson, are the ones to see to that."

"Freed now of ever again having to think or decide," Grimm can act alone, confident that he is acting on behalf of "the law, the nation":

> When the others reached the kitchen they saw the table flung aside now and Grimm stooping over the body. When they approached to see what he was about, they saw that the man was not dead yet, and when they saw what Grimm was doing one of the men gave a choked cry and stumbled back into the wall and began to vomit. Then Grimm too sprang back, flinging behind him the bloody butcher knife. "Now you'll let white women alone, even in hell," he said. But the man on the floor had not moved. He just lay there, with his eyes open and empty of everything save consciousness, and with something, a shadow, about his mouth. For a long moment he looked up at them with peaceful and unfathomable and unbearable eyes. Then his face, body, all, seemed to collapse, to fall in upon itself, and from out the slashed garments about his hips and loins the pent black blood seemed to rush like a released breath. It seemed to rush out of his pale body like the rush of sparks from a rising rocket; upon that black blast the man seemed to rise soaring into their memories forever and ever. They are not to lose it, in whatever peaceful valleys, beside whatever placid and reassuring streams of old age, in the mirroring faces of whatever children they will contemplate old disasters and newer hopes. It will be there, musing, quiet, steadfast, not fading and not particularly threatful, but of itself alone serene, of itself alone triumphant. Again from the town, deadened a little by the walls, the scream of the siren mounted toward its unbelievable crescendo, passing out of the realm of hearing.[18]

Again, as in *Absalom, Absalom!*, a young man acts on behalf of the white family to protect what he imagines as the purity of the bloodline, and the result is tragic. We are left with a sound we can no longer hear well enough to locate but which is there nevertheless: it is a scream, a howling, of "blood." This "blood" is not, of course, a "taint" that belongs in any way to any African ancestor; it has nothing to do with any innate incompatibility between persons of African ancestry and persons of British or European ancestry; it is not manifested in the color of one's skin. It is neither black nor white but red like all blood, and it

18. *Ibid.*, 425–27, 439–40.

is based on the memory of the violence upon which U.S. nationalism is based.

During these years, the dependence of the "nation" upon exclusion, a kind of political excision of the offending "I," is visible in the prevalence of lynching. Through this ritualized violence white mobs divested black and sometimes white men and women of eyes, ears, noses, lips, hands, feet, and/or genitalia—of any organ which might see, hear, smell, speak, or touch—in a hysterical attempt to contain the threat to the "purity" of the national body. When in 1935 Faulkner declined a request from *Vanity Fair* to write an article on lynching, saying "I never saw a lynching and so couldn't describe one," he was probably telling the truth.[19] There is absolutely no evidence that Faulkner ever witnessed a lynching. But even though he may never have seen or described one in his work, he had grown up during those years when lynchings were almost weekly occurrences throughout the South, and he had heard the tales and read the stories.[20] In September, 1908, when Faulkner was eleven, Nelse Patton had been lynched in Oxford, Mississippi, by a mob led by a former U.S. senator, W. V. Sullivan, a politician Faulkner's family had supported years before. Patton had cut the throat of a white woman, almost decapitating her, and threatened her daughter. A mob killed him, mutilated his body, and then hanged him from a tree in the Oxford Square. On May 22, 1917, when Faulkner was nineteen years old—and not long after the United States entered World War I—a lynching took place not far from Memphis. Eell Parsons had been charged with the decapitation of a white girl named Antoinette Rappel, and the crowds gathered to observe the burning and mutilation of Parsons.[21]

Threats of intended lynchings (*Intruder in the Dust*) as well as retrospective responses to lynchings ("Pantaloon in Black") are not infrequent in his work, but Faulkner's treatment of white mob violence against black characters is never particularly "descriptive." Percy Grimm's pursuit and murder of Joe Christmas in *Light in August* is not,

19. Joseph Blotner, *William Faulkner: A Biography* (2 vols.; New York, 1974), 880.

20. In 1905 his first-grade teacher, Annie Chandler, had given him a copy of Thomas Dixon's *The Clansman*—a book that he owned when he died and, significantly, one in which no lynching is described. In Blotner, *William Faulkner*, 94.

21. *Ibid.*, 113–14, 189–90.

strictly speaking, a lynching, since it is the act of a single individual and does not take place in public for an appreciative white audience. The murder and mutilation of Joe Christmas does, however, gain significance when read against the background of lynching, which was a kind of quasi-official "civilian-military act." [22] Grimm's is an effort, not by a mob, but by one white man similarly motivated, one who longs to be a soldier in the war to redeem the United States, to declare a personal and highly symbolic war, appoint himself commander-in-chief, and dramatically save the nation by mutilating and murdering a "white nigger." The irony is the same irony that attended the mutilation of Bras-Coupé and will attend Henry Sutpen's murder of Charles Bon at the entrance to Sutpen's Hundred; instead of saving the United States, it dooms the United States to remember and to reproduce the violence. Joe Christmas becomes, like Charles Bon three generations before him and Bras-Coupé three generations before that (and even like the false Tom Driscoll and the Italian Siamese Twins), an interpretant, a ghostly presence who will continue to haunt the site of his violent death, who will be remembered if not known: "It will be there, musing, quiet, steadfast." As in *Absalom, Absalom!*, the site of that former life is less geographical than temporal, a phase within the narrative of nationalism as it has been written and rewritten in the United States since the end of Reconstruction.

Joe Christmas, a white man in the middle of his own nightmare, has killed Joanna for reasons not unlike those for which he is killed a few days later. Joe's murder of Joanna is an attempt to preserve his autonomy, to maintain the fiction that he has lived thirty years "to make me what I chose to be." Like so many of the individualistic heroes in U.S. literature, he wants no marriage, no child, no ancestors and no descendants, no history and no future, "since tomorrow to-be and had-been would be the same." He doesn't know who his parents are, not even "that one of them was part nigger," although he believes that one

22. See Brooks's discussion of this point in *William Faulkner*, 51–52. Lynching is commonly understood to be the taking of an alleged criminal by a mob which conducts, for an audience, an elaborate ritual of torture and mutilation prior to killing the victim. For further discussions of this practice, see Trudier Harris, *Exorcising Blackness: Historical and Literary Lynching and Burning Rituals* (Bloomington, 1984), and Williamson, *Crucible of Race*, especially pp. 183–89.

of them was. But "memory believes before knowing remembers" in *Light in August*, suggesting that what is "known," or thought to be known, is built upon the human tendency to believe what is remembered, to inherit first the beliefs rather than the knowledge of the past.[23]

In an effort to implicate Joe in her own past (as well as to implicate herself in his future) and in the history of the South, to give him a place and an identity (and to find both for herself), Joanna Burden recounts to Joe Christmas her own genealogy. It is not unlike that of the Grandissime family or that of Dawson's Landing in its preoccupation with dreams of racial purity superimposed upon the reality of mingling of black and white, Anglo-American and European, on the southwestern frontier:

> Calvin Burden was the son of a minister named Nathaniel Burrington, the youngest of ten children, he ran away from home at the age of twelve, before he could write his name (or would write it, his father believed) on a ship. He made the voyage around the Horn to California and turned Catholic; he lived for a year in a monastery. Then years later he reached Missouri from the west. Three weeks after he arrived he was married, to the daughter of a family of Huguenot stock which had emigrated from Carolina by way of Kentucky. On the day after the wedding he said, "I guess I had better settle down." He began that day to settle down. The wedding celebration was still in progress, and his first step was to formally deny allegiance to the Catholic Church. He did this in a saloon, insisting that every one present listen to him and state their objections; he was a little insistent on there being objections, though there were none; not, that is, up to the time when he was led away by friends. The next day he said that he meant it, anyhow; that he would not belong to a church full of frogeating slaveholders. That was in Saint Louis. He bought a home there, and a year later he was a father. He said then that he had denied the Catholic church a year ago for the sake of his son's soul; almost as soon as the boy was born, he set about to imbue the child with the religion of his New England forbears. There was no Unitarian meetinghouse available, and Burden could not read the English Bible. But he had learned to read in Spanish from the priests in California, and as soon as the child could walk Burden (he pronounced it Burden now, since he could not spell it at all and the priests had taught him to write it laboriously so with a hand more apt for a rope or a gunbutt or a knife than a pen) began to read to the child in Spanish from the book which

23. Faulkner, *Light in August*, 250–51, 266, 240.

he had brought with him from California, interspersing the fine, sono-
rous flowing of mysticism in a foreign tongue with harsh, extemporised
dissertations composed half of the bleak and bloodless logic which he
remembered from his father on interminable New England Sundays, and
half of immediate hellfire and tangible brimstone of which any country
Methodist circuit rider would have been proud. The two of them would
be alone in the room: the tall, gaunt Nordic man, and the small, dark,
vivid child who had inherited his mother's build and coloring, like
people of two different races. When the boy was about five, Burden
killed a man in an argument over slavery and had to take his family and
move, leave Saint Louis. He moved westward, "to get away from Dem-
ocrats," he said.[24]

The story that Joanna recounts for Joe Christmas recapitulates the story
of Anglo-American expansion in the first half of the nineteenth century
into what had been French and Spanish territories. During the 1820s
and 1830s, the Anglo-American moved southward and westward, en-
countering French and Spanish Creoles, living with them, learning
from them, even becoming somewhat "colonized" by a European slaveholding economy and by Catholicism.

When he marries, the Anglo-American chooses a woman of French
Huguenot ancestry — dark, European, but at least a Protestant. It is the
fact of marriage that prompts him to try to reclaim his Anglo-American
tradition, to become, as it were, a Puritan and a nationalist with a vengeance. (One of the differences between the colonial history of France
and Spain in the New World and that of England was that the English
brought their families with them with every intention of "settling
down," whereas the French and Spanish colonists to the south and west
were largely male and peripatetic, at least more so than the English.)
He renounces the Catholic Church and slavery, renunciations in keeping with nationalist ideology in the mid-nineteenth century, and begins
"to imbue [his] child with the religion of his New England forbears."
Of course, the irony, and the source of the tragedies that follow, is that
the father's desire is the nationalist's desire to transcend the debris of
history (the debris of his own history in the West and the Southwest in
particular), to redeem himself and his children from complicity with
that history, which he (like Daniel Nelson in Beaumont's *Marie*) projects
shamelessly onto the dark mother, Evangeline. Nonetheless, the Anglo-

24. *Ibid.*, 228–29.

American father knows (perhaps as a consequence of his own habituation to English Common Law, which could determine inheritance through the mother) and fears that the child is as much the French creole mother's as the English father's, having inherited the mother's body type and her coloring. For the father, this suggests that the child has also inherited dangerous predispositions, what Thomas Jefferson, (who was less religious), identified as the habits of "unremitting despotism" that would undermine the national ideal of a republican paradise, the "polity of the free mind." [25]

And when the son Nathaniel flees his father, he flees once again toward the southwest, where he marries a Spanish Creole, Juana. She looks (to Nathaniel's father at least) just like his French wife, Evangeline: "The boy who could hardly remember his mother at all, had taken for a wife a woman who looked almost exactly like her." But the father's sight has begun to fail; he could be mistaken.

> After supper that night, with the woman and the child in bed, Nathaniel told them. . . . There were no ministers out there where he had been, he explained; just priests and Catholics. "So when we found that the chico was on the way, she begun to talk about a priest. But I wasn't going to have any Burden born a heathen. So I begun to look around, to humor her. But first one thing and then another come up and I couldn't get away to meet a minister; and then the boy came and so it wasn't any rush anymore. But she kept on worrying, about priests and such, and so in a couple of years I heard how there was to be a white minister in Sante Fe on a certain day. So we packed up and started out and got to Sante Fe just in time to see the dust of the stage that was carrying the minister on away. So we waited there and in a couple more years we had another chance, in Texas. Only this time I got kind of mixed up with helping some Rangers that were cleaning up some kind of a mess where some folks had a deputy treed in a dance hall. So when that was over we just decided to come on home and get married right. And here we are."
>
> The father sat, gaunt, grizzled, and austere, beneath the lamp. He had been listening, but his expression was brooding, with a kind of violently slumbering contemplativeness and bewildered outrage. "Another damn black Burden," he said. "Folks will think I bred to a damn slaver. And now he's got to breed to one, too." The son listened quietly, not even attempting to tell his father that the woman was Spanish and not Rebel.[26]

25. Simpson, *Mind and The American Civil War*, 14.
26. Faulkner, *Light in August*, 233–34.

Here are the traces of the kind of "memory" that "believes before knowing remembers," a genealogy of overdetermined associations where
might be discovered the source and the direction of the internal divisions, the self-doubts and self-hatred that will continue to plague the
Burdens and, by analogy, the nation itself, and will eventually lead to
the murders of Joanna and Joe.[27] For the grandfather Calvin, as for
many other Anglo-Americans, the French, the Spanish, the Rebel, and
the Negro "belong to the same party." He points out, "But we done
freed them now, both black and white alike. They'll bleach out now. In
a hundred years they will be white folks again. Then maybe we'll let
them come back into America."[28]

Apparently, this conversation takes place at the very end of the Civil
War; Calvin doesn't know that it will take less than ten years for the
South to return to the Union. A few years later, the grandfather Calvin

---

27. André Bleikasten has observed, that Joe and Joanna are linked by the terms of
the "curse," and it is this that brings them together in the mutually destructive (and self-
destructive) dramatic enactment of that curse:

> Whereas Joe has known neither of his parents, Joanna bows under the "burden"
> of a family tradition; but they share an abiding obsession with race, transmitted to
> them at a very early age and closely associated with the indelible memory of a father,
> a grandfather, or both. These figures are in turn surprisingly similar. Though alleged
> to be from New England, Joanna's grandfather Calvin is in his theological fanaticism
> a worthy match for Doc Hines: both regard the black man as the accursed of God and
> the emblem of white man's guilt; the abolitionist's militant negrophilia and the white
> supremacist's demented negrophobia are antithetical rationalizations of the same racist
> delirium. Furthermore, if Joe's father, according to rumor, might have been a Mexican,
> Joanna has been named after Juana, her father's first Mexican wife, who looked exactly
> like Evangeline, her father's French Huguenot mother. In the chronicle of the Burdens,
> as recounted by Joanna to Joe in the middle of Chapter XI, these women and their
> progeny are evoked as if they belonged to another race, and the physical contrast
> between Calvin and his son Nathaniel is heavily emphasized: "the tall, gaunt, Nordic
> man, and the small, dark, vivid child who had inherited his mother's build and col-
> oring, like people of two different races."
>
> Even more revealing are Calvin's outraged remarks when he sees Juana's son for
> the first time: " 'Another damn black Burden,' he said. 'Folks will think I bred to a
> damn slave [sic] and now she's got to breed to one too.' "

(*The Ink of Melancholy* [Bloomington, 1980], 318). But Calvin does not, as Bleikasten's
misprint suggests, say "slave"; it is "slaver," and that detail reiterates the fact that the
slave and slaveholder were, in Puritan rhetoric, linked as two sides of the same spiritual
coin.

28. Faulkner, *Light in August*, 234.

and his namesake, hardly twenty, are killed "over a question of negro voting," their graves hidden by Nathaniel, who fears that they might be desecrated by white Redemptioners. Why didn't Joanna's father Nathaniel kill the man who murdered his own father and his son, Joe asks. "He was French," she answers. "Half of him. Enough French to respect anybody's love for the land where he and his people were born and to understand that a man would have to act as the land where he was born had trained him to act. I think that was it." [29]

A contemporary reader might expect Joanna to have said that her father was "enough" *southern* "to understand that a man would have to act as the land where he was born had trained him to act," since that fatality is, today, associated with the southerner's much-discussed "sense of place" and sociability. That Joanna associates such fatality with the French blood underscores the conceptual genealogy that ties the South to the slaveholding creole cultures of the Deep South and French Arch, that binds white slaveholder to the slave and to the French and Spanish colonists who first brought slaves into the Louisiana Territory, and, finally, that sets them all against Anglo-American nationalism.

Eric Sundquist has identified the fundamental question of *Light in August* as "how can a white man be a black man?" In his discussion of southern paranoia during the years in which *Light in August* is set, Joel Williamson provides the beginnings of an answer when he points out that such paranoia "had its genesis in the Radical mind during the red-hot fights of that age when Radicals drew a clear, firm line between those who were on the right side of the race line and those, white or black, who were on the wrong side. This extreme intolerance of deviation among their white brothers was so strong as to breed a new definition of blackness in the South. Whites who sided too closely with blacks, were, as the phrase went 'white niggers.' One could be perfectly white genetically and yet be black morally." Williamson further notes that "southerners came to fear hidden blackness, the blackness within seeming whiteness" and "began to look with great suspicion upon mulattoes who looked white, white people who behaved as black, and a whole congeries of aliens insidious in their midst." A white man (or woman) might be relocated with respect to the color line by being as-

29. *Ibid.*, 235, 241.

sociated with blacks economically, politically, or socially; or by violating moral conventions. It is within this context of white paranoia that
the fact that Joe Christmas and Joe Brown/Lucas Burch end up doing
a "negro job" at the sawmill turns out to be such an issue for their
white coworkers when Brown begins to work himself up to quit:

> "Lay into it, you slaving bastards!" Brown said, in a merry, loud voice
> cropped with teeth.
> Mooney looked at Brown. Then Brown's teeth didn't show. "You ain't
> calling me that," Mooney said, "are you?" [30]

Obviously, one way a white man could be a black man, or rather a
slave, in the Deep South in the 1920s and 1930s was through illegitimacy. If the father of an illegitimate child is unknown—a stranger—
the child might be the carrier of what the white racist would have
understood as social and cultural contagion.

In this sense, *Light in August* problematizes Jim Crow. But the central
issue is not so much the difficulties of a light-skinned person of African
ancestry "passing" into "white" America as (considering that the writer
was a white man and a southerner who grew up during the era of
radical racism, when whites were obsessed with preserving their own
"whiteness" from contamination with "blackness") it is the threat that
the impossible principle of racial purity represented *for men who had
known themselves and been known as "white."*

In short, the Spanish-American War and World War I changed the
relationship of race and class in the South. Allen Tate observed that the
South reentered the world during the years of World War I; what he
did not remark upon, at least directly, was the effect of that reentry
on the traditional relationship of black and white southerners and on
the ways white southerners defined themselves as "white" and as
"American."

Blacks had begun moving northward during the war years in order
to take advantage of the employment opportunities in northern factory
towns. In 1910, 89 percent of African Americans lived in the South, but
by 1930 that proportion had dropped by more than 10 percent. The
economic consequences for the white South were immediate and serious; it is within this economic context that one may place the fact that

30. Eric Sundquist, *Faulkner: The House Divided* (Baltimore, 1983), 71; Williamson,
Crucible of Race, 464–65; Faulkner, *Light in August*, 31, 41.

both "Joes" of *Light in August* end up doing a "nigger" job at the Jefferson sawmill. There seems to be no shortage of work, provided one is willing to take the work that is available. The era actually *did* witness a breakdown in economic segregation. Restless African Americans began to form organizations (like the Progressive Farmers and Household Union of America) devoted to gaining political and economic rights. Later, in the 1920s, Senator Vardaman worried about the sexual consequences of the return of black soldiers who had been "ruined" by the degenerate ways of French women.[31] In light of this postwar "deracination" that made traditional methods of identification increasingly problematic, it is no coincidence that the early years of the twentieth century saw growing efforts on the part of federal and state governments to record an individual's racial classification. Not since Reconstruction days, when tales of enforced "social equality" began to terrify white southerners, had the threat of "Africanization" seemed so present.

Within this complex of racial tensions, the old fear of the rape or seduction of white women by black men—mined so well by the radical racists of the turn-of-the-century South—persisted into the 1920s. The icon of the innocent white woman was of much use to radical racists during the era of lynchings. There is no more powerful, no more historical representation of that cultural icon than that trusting, pregnant, and unmarried young woman in *Light in August*. And there is no more powerful an icon with which Faulkner can explore U.S. obsessions with race, nation, and genealogy. Even her origins in the working class are significant in situating her within this context, for during these years of *Volksgeist*, the icon was not so much the "lady" as the wife and daughter of the beleaguered white working man and farmer.

Leonidas F. Scott wrote during the era of radical racism of the danger the "black beast" posed to the daughters of the working (white) man:

> It will alarm any thoughtful mind to notice the awful extent of these most awful of all crimes, and notice that they excite only a "news special" from the community where the crime is committed. If the brute is caught, if the Victim has many friends, he is lynched, if a poor white woman or girl, the law is allowed in some instances "to take its course," and the

---

31. James K. Vardaman, quoted in George B. Tindall, *The Emergence of the New South, 1913–1945* (Baton Rouge, 1967), 151.

Sheriff complimented by the reigning governor for maintaining "law and order" when the land is full of murder, outrage, and arson and all sorts of crime.[32]

And this is by no means rare. Rebecca Latimer Felton spoke to an annual convention of farmers in 1897, warning them against leaving their wives and daughters alone and unprotected on isolated farms: "If it takes lynching to protect woman's dearest possession from drunken, ravening human beasts, then I say lynch a thousand a week if it becomes necessary."[33] In the same speech she linked rape to the corruption stemming from the buying of black votes by powerful interests, a clear rhetorical appeal to the increasingly important—and restless—white working man. Clearly, there exists in these calls to arms as much a plea for the empowerment of the white working class as for the safety of white womanhood. The two are so closely bound that it would be a misrepresentation not to read the icon of white womanhood in the form of the innocent and healthy working-class girl as an apotheosis of working-class ambitions for political influence and economic stability.

The opening of *Light in August* depicts Lena Grove sitting alongside a Mississippi road and thinking that she has in fact come "a fur piece. All the way from Alabama a-walking." Her mother and father are dead; her brother is struggling to take care of his own growing family; and her seducer is a dark-complected drifter named Lucas Burch. She is supposedly in search of him, but it might be that she's "just travelling."[34] In *Light in August,* it is the image of Lena—rather than Joanna Burden (in whose name, if not in whose honor, the lynching is committed)—that provides the ironic contrast upon which the story of "death and destruction" attains significance.

Lena Grove is usually read as a kind of fertility goddess. For Cleanth Brooks, "Lena is one of Faulkner's several embodiments of the female principle. . . . Her rapport with nature is so close. She is never baffled as to what course of action to take. She is never torn by doubts and indecisions. There is no painful introspection." In fact, she leads "a charmed life." Myra Jehlen writes that "Lena Grove in no way speaks to the issues embodied in Christmas. She represents only an abstract

32. Williamson, *Crucible,* 127.
33. *Ibid.,* 128.
34. Faulkner, *Light in August,* 1, 480.

affirmation, an allegory in which a spirit of the life-giving earth passes through a scene of death and destruction and causes the flowers to bloom once more." Even Eric Sundquist, somewhat less inclined to permit anyone or anything to remain unhistoricized, writes that Lena's "story provides the frame and the filtered domestic warmth that makes Christmas's story all the more terribly ironic."[35]

This tendency to read Lena Grove as an ahistorical, apolitical representative of an essential "female principle" associated with flowers and "domestic warmth" obscures a great deal of the drama of origination and inheritance in the text. Lena Grove is white, but she is also unmarried, pregnant by an unknown drifter, and incredibly footloose. All this makes her one of the most terrifying possibilities imaginable by a culture as preoccupied with racial purity as was the white South in the 1920s. There is no image as powerful in its capacity to evoke the dangers of a new world for white southerners than that of an unmarried and pregnant working-class white woman searching for the drifter who has abandoned her or, even more frightening, is "just traveling." That image, more than any other, taps the xenophobia associated with social and political change in the South during the 1920s, when plain folk had begun to move out of the backwater as Lena is on the move, in search of a legitimating identity as Americans and as participants in the national mission. Her innocence is beyond dispute (and recapitulates Thomas Sutpen's singleminded quest for a legitimating order), but so is the isolation and vulnerability that result from having come so far from her people. In this sense, she is a particularly apt representation of the white southerner of the early twentieth century, when old forms of social identification were, like Lena's mother and father, dead or dying. Memory and knowledge were increasingly problematic: the rich, albeit crippling, presence of a remembered past that so characterizes Joanna Burden is absent for Lena, as it is for so many of the other working-class characters of *Light in August*. Byron Bunch, for example, is at once provincial and alienated, given no family, no home. We know that he is mountain-bred, like so many of the sawmill workers, and that he is involved with the choir in a country church, but this hardly constitutes a fully realized genealogy. The same is true of Lucas Burch/Joe

35. Brooks, *William Faulkner*, 67–68; Myra Jehlen, *Class and Character in Faulkner's South* (New York, 1976), 93; Sundquist, *Faulkner*, 75.

Brown, who is described as "another stranger . . . travelling light . . . [with] a way of jerking his head quickly and glancing over his shoulder like a mule does in front of an automobile on the road . . . as though the man were reiterating and insisting all the while that he was afraid of nothing that might or could approach him from behind." And certainly the novel's avatar of alienation, the orphan Joe Christmas, is "rootless, as though no town nor city was his, no street, no walls, no square of earth his home."[36] Predictably enough, such movement away from traditional communities would bring them, like Lena Grove, closer and closer to the color line, which still represented for the white American (and especially for the white southerner) the indisputable boundary between civilization and chaos.

Lena is a troublesome figure throughout the text. Her own personal history mimics that of Joe Christmas. Brooks notes that both are orphans who flee their homes through a window, but both are also sexually involved with partners who are less than respectable, and both are on the road.[37] In a work so concerned with the redemptive power of memory (when united with "knowing"), Lena is—like Joe and like Lucas Burch and Byron Bunch—somewhat remarkable for her historical and personal deracination. Her mother hardly exists, her father's death removes her to the home of a shadowy brother, and her pregnancy links her both to Milly Hines and to Joanna Burden, one the mother of and the other the lover of Joe Christmas. Furthermore, the murder of Joanna Burden is interestingly juxtaposed, temporally and spatially, with Lena's delivery, in a Negro cabin, of her illegitimate child. Many have argued that the substitution of Lena Grove and Byron Bunch for Joanna Burden and Joe Christmas—of birth for death, white characters for black—attests to the comic nature of *Light in August*. But the "natural vitality and fecundity" that Lena Grove supposedly represents is surrounded and qualified by such overwhelming violence that any attempt to classify *Light in August* as "comic," or even as cautiously optimistic, is problematic.

In *Light in August,* the narrative moves from the presentation of this pregnant young woman, unmarried and without family to speak of,

---

36. Faulkner, *Light in August,* 32, 27.
37. Brooks, *William Faulkner,* 55.

into the story of Joe Christmas. We get to the story of Joe Christmas (*i.e.*, to the story of the unknown character who does not know what he is, black or white) in an interesting and oblique way: we move from a community of respectable white farmers and mill workers (whose racial identification is not at issue) into a world of alienated and rootless figures whose racial identification becomes more and more trouble-some.[38]

Initially, Lena Grove crawls through the window of a brother's house and takes to the road. That her own racial identification is not at issue—indeed, that race is no issue at all for quite a while—might obscure the fact that through her mediation we are moving closer and closer to the place where race does become an issue. She is assisted at first by a married white farmer, Armstid, and his wife; then by Byron Bunch, another "good" man and white, if a bachelor and somewhat on the fringes of the community himself. It is Byron who feels the most responsibility for Lena, who stands between her and the Joe Brown/Joe Christmas scandal into which she could so easily have been drawn—with some dire consequences for her future. What is subtly rendered is a gradual movement toward the site within the social struc-ture where segregation becomes most difficult, where black and white were actually most likely to come into contact. The young, fatherless, working-class white woman's impregnation by an unknown drifter of obscure origin initiates that journey. Her complaint that people are con-fusing her child with Christmas has then some rhetorical force.

Rather than read the story of Lena Grove as an essentializing frame for the tragedy of Joe Christmas, we should read her story as intricately bound to his, being as relevant to the story of his victimization by a racist ethos as Aurora de Grapion's perennial innocence is relevant to the victimization of Bras-Coupé. Without the figure of innocent white

38. Historians and sociologists have noted that much of the race mixing that brought "black blood," to use that strange phrase, into the white community occured within the working class and the poor white group. The scenario of the beautiful octoroon marrying into the white aristocracy is a literary revision of the reality, a revision that underscores the fluidity of class sensibility in the South in the sense that within a culture which classifies people chiefly by race, those of the master race are, by fiat, "aristocrats." (Look at Charles Chesnutt's genealogy, for example.) The literary representation of the white planter as "aristocratic" is fascinating when one looks at the lives and genealogies of real planters in the South, who were more often of the middle classes.

womanhood in Lena Grove, the "lynching" of Joe Christmas would possess much less resonance.

One might object at this point that Lucas Burch is white, that there is never any suspicion on the part of any character in the text that he is anything but a white man. On the level of plot, this is true. It is important, however, to remember that the way the text engages "blackness" is through suspicion and fantasy, through a kind of dream logic comparable to a "memory" that "believes before knowing remembers," in other words, through a kind of logic based on faith rather than evidence. Even though no one in this text points a finger of suspicion at Lucas Burch or suggests in any direct way that he might not be a white man, there is a narrator who describes or delineates a context within which Lucas Burch's "whiteness" is problematic: he is a drifter like Christmas; he is "dark-complected" like Christmas; he is employed in a "nigger job" like Joe Christmas; his alias "Joe Brown" not only echoes "Joe Christmas" but marks the color term, "brown," that will eventually distinguish Christmas from the white community; and, like Christmas, he is implicated in the brutal murder of a (falsely) pregnant/menopausal white woman. Finally, the telling "scar" by his mouth is shadowed at the moment of Christmas' castration and death by the fleeting shadow that can only suggest a symbolic kinship with Lucas Burch. In short, Joe Brown, being preceded by and so closely associated with Christmas, is exactly the kind of white man whose association with a black man marks him as "white nigger."[39] Furthermore, it is suspicion, self-doubts played upon by an apocalyptic fundamentalism, that prompts Joe Christmas to suggest to Joe Brown that he has "nigger blood in him." And Joe Brown, in an attempt to protect himself from the suspicion of murdering a white woman, relays the suspicion of Christmas' "black" ancestry to the sheriff. What all of this suggests is

---

39. One is reminded of George Schuyler's novel *Black No More* . . . (1931; rpr. College Park, Md., 1969) about the discovery of a drug that can make blacks white, a discovery that results in a kind of racist hysteria in which the newly minted "whites" are the most vociferous in lynchings of those fellows who are discovered to have taken the drug. It is a crying of wolf that identifies the "criminal" all right, but the criminal turns out to be the cryer himself. One might look at Lucas' charge that Joe has "nigger blood in him" in much the same way. No one knows whether or not Joe has any African ancestry (any more than we know whether Lucas Burch does), but the suspicion—once aroused—can become the reality and that is the issue.

that we might look not for evidence of African ancestry in this text, since such a search is repeatedly and intentionally frustrated, but for "faith" in one's social identification comparable to faith in one's spiritual status.

This dramatic context of suspicion constitutes a background, a tissue of dramatic possibility that, like the documentary realism underlying the story of Bras-Coupé in *The Grandissimes*, is never realized in the text itself. At the same time, the impact of that background in making sense of the text cannot be overstated. In a text like *Light in August*, centered on a drama that arises from suspicion, one ought not too quickly to dismiss the fictional possibilities of suspicions that are aroused, even if quickly denied or apparently denied. On the level of plot, one *knows* that Joe Christmas is not the father of Lena's child, but when one reads into the structure of the text, one also discovers that paternity has been at issue from the very beginning of the story: that Lucas Burch, the biological father of Lena's child, is Joe Brown, a partner in Joe Christmas' moonshining business, leads Sheriff Kennedy to suggest that Christmas may be the father of Lena's child; that Gail Hightower assists in the delivery of a black child is sufficient cause for some townspeople to suspect him of fathering that child; that Milly Hines's lover may be Mexican or black means that he is black. And Joanna Burden's genealogy, for all of its preoccupation with racial and cultural purity, integrates black and white in a subversion of the paternal repressions that would protect that genealogical purity.

"Red Leaves" is set where so many of Faulkner's genealogies begin, in the Deep South in the early to mid-nineteenth century. On the one hand, it delineates another failure of imagination, this time of the Chickasaws, who in this story are more burghers than braves. On the other hand, it may have represented for Faulkner a turning point in his understanding of the impact of the history of race and nationalism on authorship in the modern South (and in the modern world). "Red Leaves" is set little more than one generation following the cession of the Louisiana Territory from France to the United States. Like *The Grandissimes*, it takes up the history of the Deep South—slavery, the color line, dreams of nationalism within a postcolonialist context, and the forms and functions of resistance within this context. The Chickasaws, as representations of the white South, are grotesques, living among the debris left by their French allies when they were abandoned at the cession. Their new chief, Moketubbe, is degenerate both physically and mentally, preoccupied with the impossible task of trying to get his large feet into a pair of red slippers left by the French. Presumably the slippers are fetishized for him, containing the authority of the displaced colonizers. The Chickasaws talk a lot, but their talk, like the rhythm of their days, is aimless and trivial. Three Berry and Louis Basket, agents for "the Man" (*i.e.*, the chief), conduct throughout the story an idle dialogue that touches on the possibility that Issetibbeha, the former chief, might have been murdered; on his son Moketubbe's laziness and obesity; on whether the tribe ought to eat their slaves in order to get some use out of them; on speculations that the skin of Africans was turned black through sweat, and so on. Most damning, however, is that they have no real knowledge of their past, hence no desire for life in the present and no future.

By contrast, their slaves have little use for talk, although their knowledge is palpable:

> "If he lives past sundown, he will live until daybreak," one said.
> "Who says?"
> "Talk says."
> "Yao. Talk says. We know but one thing." They looked at the body servant as he stood among them, his eyeballs a little luminous. He was breathing slow and deep. His chest was bare; he was sweating a little. "He knows. He knows it."
> "Let us let the drums talk."
> "Yao. Let the drums tell it."
> The drums began after dark. They kept them hidden in the creek bottom. They were made of hollowed cypress knees, and the Negroes kept them hidden; why, none knew. They were buried in the mud on the bank of a slough; a lad of fourteen guarded them. He was undersized, and a mute; he squatted in the mud there all day, clouded over with mosquitoes, naked save for the mud with which he coated himself against the mosquitoes, and about his neck a fiber bag containing a pig's rib to which black shreds of flesh still adhered, and two scaly barks on a wire. He slobbered onto his clutched knees, drooling; now and then Indians came noiselessly out of the bushes behind him and stood there and contemplated him for a while and went away, and he never knew it.[40]

40. William Faulkner, "Red Leaves," in *The Collected Stories of William Faulkner* (New York, 1977), 315, 328–29. All subsequent citations are to this edition.

Although at least one reader has protested that the silence of the slaves—"the thoughts sealed inscrutable behind faces like the death masks of apes"—renders "the complexity of Negro characterization . . . inaccessible," "Red Leaves" is less a story of character than one of culture. Even though the silence of the slaves also leaves a great deal of the complexity of the culture inaccessible, that may indeed be the point.[41] The slaves remain unassimilated, their lives "transplanted whole out of African jungles," exiles dreaming of Africa: "They were like a single octopus. They were like the roots of a huge tree uncovered." Faulkner relies heavily on images of "muteness" to characterize them, but in taking the story as an allegory dealing with the transmission of and dispersal of cultural legacies, silence here is more a sign of authenticity than repression.

"Red Leaves" focuses on one of these slaves, a man from Guinea, abducted from Kamerun at the age of fourteen and brought to America, where he has served as Issetibbeha's personal servant for twenty-three years. When Issetibbeha is on his deathbed, the slave learns that the Chickasaws plan to sacrifice him so that he can accompany Issetibbeha in death. The story told is that of the slave's failed flight and heroic transfiguration in the face of death, and it is underwritten both by legends of Bras-Coupé and by the context of lynching in Faulkner's South. Faulkner had arrived in New Orleans in early January, 1925. He hoped to make arrangements to get to Europe inexpensively but spent six months in New Orleans before setting sail. During that time he lived in the French Quarter, where he became acquainted with various members of New Orleans' literary community. Among them was Lyle Saxon, who had been raised on a plantation outside of Baton Rouge and who would publish during his lifetime several books retelling many of the old stories of Louisiana history and legend. During Faulkner's months in New Orleans in the mid-1920s, he and Saxon spent some time together, and it is likely that Faulkner heard, from Saxon or elsewhere, the legends of Bras-Coupé.

But for Faulkner the Bras-Coupé story has new uses. He rewrites it for a new generation made up of people who had only recently (and probably didn't yet realize it themselves) overcome the hysteria of

41. Alan Henry Rose, *Demonic Vision: Racial Fantasy and Southern Fiction* (Hamden, Conn., 1976), 106.

lynching, choosing to focus not on the death of the black hero (as so many of the previous accounts had done) but on his birth. Like Cable's Bras-Coupé, this runaway is encircled by the silence of the other slaves; like Cable's Bras-Coupé, he flees because he doesn't want to die. Like Cable's Bras-Coupé, he undergoes a transformation into hero. This Bras-Coupé, however, does not die. One is meant to understand that he is going to die, of course, but the fact remains that his death is not a part of this story as it was a very important, lavishly detailed part of Cable's story. There it was meant not only to attest to the cruelty of slaveholders but also to satirize the faith of Victorian readers that history had been put safely behind them.

Faulkner's decision to focus, in "Red Leaves," not on the death of a Bras-Coupé but on the transfiguration of an unnamed man into a Bras-Coupé figure has a great deal of import for the way Faulkner understands history, narrative, and authorship in the South of his own time:

> At sunset, creeping along the creek bank toward where he had spotted a frog, a cottonmouth moccasin slashed him suddenly across the forearm with a thick, sluggish blow. It struck clumsily, leaving two long slashes across his arm like two razor slashes, and half sprawled with its own momentum and rage, it appeared for the moment utterly helpless with its own awkwardness and choleric anger. "Olé, grandfather," the Negro said. He touched its head and watched it slash him again across his arm, and again, with thick, raking, awkward blows. "It's that I do not wish to die," he said. Then he said it again—"It's that I do not wish to die"— in a quiet tone, of slow and low amaze, as though it were something that, until the words had said themselves, he found that he had not known, or had not known the depth and extent of his desire.[42]

At dawn, the bodyservant, his wounded arm shrunken and putrid, walks out of the swamp to meet Three Basket and Louis Berry, to ask them for a hatchet with which to cut off the arm. They ignore the request and the servant returns to the swamp. The next morning, "two Indians entered the swamp, their movements noisy. Before they reached the Negro they stopped, because he began to sing. They could see him, naked and mud-caked, sitting on a log, singing. They squatted silently a short distance away, until he finished. He was chanting some-

42. Faulkner, "Red Leaves," 334–35.

thing in his own language, his face lifted to the rising sun. His voice was clear, full, with a quality wild and sad."[43]

In "Red Leaves," resistance is constituted differently and functions differently than in *The Grandissimes*. In this story, written in and for the twentieth century, there is no wilderness swamp where one might survive with or without anyone's help, where one might find other maroons. There is no one to promise a return to Africa. There appears to be no effort on the part of other slaves to help (or to hinder) the bodyservant in his flight or his return. Nevertheless, the unnamed bodyservant's movement from the world of the muted slaves into the wilderness where he learns to speak, through the mediation of a Chickasaw totem, "in his own language," signals Faulkner's discovery of a place and a voice from which the old stories might be rewritten from the perspective of the silenced.

The situation of the bodyservant in the above scene—naked and mud-caked, sitting on a log while the Chickasaws watch him in silence—recapitulates (with some important differences) the situation of the young mute who guards the drums and is often watched by the uncomprehending Chickasaws. The important differences, of course, are that the bodyservant knows the Chickasaws are there and that he sings "in his own language," his voice "clear, full, with a quality wild and sad." He has found, during his flight and through the mediation of the totemic snake, a voice. As the bodyservant is returned to the camp, the omniscient narrator picks his descriptive details strategically: the bodyservant is taller than the Chickasaws, his eyes "luminous," vital with life as he goes toward his death.

Faulkner had spoken often of the significance of silence in writing and for the writer. "I prefer silence to sound," Faulkner claimed in an interview. "The image produced by words occurs in silence."[44] Silence takes many forms in his work. It is often, like voice itself, "black" in its associations. It is a version of his authorial self he evokes in Joe Christmas, who also looks and sounds like a white man but speaks most eloquently of and within blackness. And it is another version of his authorial self he evokes in Charles Bon, who is heard only through

43. *Ibid.*, 338.

44. James B. Meriwether and Michael Millgate, eds., *Lion in the Garden: Interviews with William Faulkner, 1926–1962* (New York, 1968), 248.

(and behind) the white voices that tell his story but who seems, like the author himself, to know the end of the story before the speakers know it.

Any thorough treatment of the subject of Faulkner's conceptualization of the author would need to take up the subject of writing under the aegis of modernism in ways that are beyond the scope of this study. Within the limits of this project, however, one might suggest that the unnamed bodyservant in "Red Leaves" is, for Faulkner, so compelling a representation of the author precisely because of the way he draws attention to the inadequacy of "mastery" as a trope for authorship in the post–Civil War United States. If the Chickasaws, the "masters" of this story, are defined by cultural deciduation, their slaves are associated with germination—mute, teeming, knowing. In "Red Leaves," the context for the bodyservant's voice, what makes it powerful, is the surrounding muteness of his fellows. What this suggests is that, for Faulkner, the essence of sound is silence.

In Faulkner's work, as in Mark Twain's and, to some extent, in George W. Cable's, authorship is less associated with the genealogical control of texts than with the capacity to catalyze historically and culturally viable narratives of identity in the U.S. context. To that end, the authorial voices in these texts "speak" mulatto; in other words, they mediate rather than "master," they embody (or disembody) the "confused and violent origins" of the United States, and they undermine the repressive designs of the Sutpens, the Compsons, the McEacherns, the Hineses; of the Pudd'nhead Wilsons and other Pudd'nheads; of the Grandissimes and the Fusiliers. It may well be that by "speaking mulatto," as by "speaking black," these authors moderate their freedom, but the white man's supposed freedom of self-making (*i.e.*, self-mastery) has always been more a product of New World ideology than New World reality. In the cases of these three authors, a moderation of the dream of self-making is what produces voice; and what these voicings finally signify is the inadequacy of narratives of exclusion in the American context, where cultural paternity is difficult to ascertain and official genealogies, for all their rhetorical power, are at best illusions and at worst lies.

Bibliography

Advertiser (Louisiana). June, 1836.

Alexander, Adele Logan. *Ambiguous Lives: Free Women of Color in Rural Georgia, 1789–1879*. Fayetteville, Ark., 1991.

Anal, Marc. "France." In *Matrimonial Property Law*, edited by W. Friedman. Toronto, 1955.

Anderson, Benedict. *Imagined Communities: Reflections on the Origin and Spread of Nationalism*. Rev. ed. New York, 1983.

Appiah, Anthony. "The Uncompleted Argument: Du Bois and the Illusion of Race." In *"Race," Writing, and Difference*, edited by Henry Louis Gates, Jr. Chicago, 1985.

Appleman, Philip, ed. *Darwin*. New York, 1970.

Atwan, Robert. "The Territory Behind: Mark Twain and His Autobiographies." In *Located Lives: Place and Idea in Southern Autobiography*, edited by Bill Berry. Athens, Ga., 1990.

Ayers, Edward L. *The Promise of the New South: Life After Reconstruction*. New York, 1992.

Baker, Marion. *Historical Sketchbook and Guide to New Orleans*. New York, 1885.

Bakhtin, Mikhail. *The Dialogic Imagination*. Austin, 1981.

Bancroft, George. *The American Revolution*. Boston, 1874. Vols. III–IV of Bancroft, *History of the United States from the Discovery of the American Continent*. 6 vols.

Barbe-Marbois, François. *The History of Louisiana, Particularly of the Cession of That Colony to the United States of America*. Philadelphia, 1830.

Barrow, David. "Mark Twain and the Oral Economy." Ph.D. dissertation, Duke University, 1991.

Baym, Nina. *Women's Fiction: A Guide to Novels by and about Women in America, 1820–70*. 2nd ed. Urbana, 1993.

Beaumont, Gustave de. *Marie, or Slavery in the United States: A Novel of Jacksonian America.* Translated by Barbara Chapman. Stanford, 1958.

Beecher, Reverend Henry Ward. "The Advance of a Century." New York *Tribune Extra,* July 5, 1876, p. 8.

Bell, Michael Davitt. "The Sin of Art and the Problem of American Realism: William Dean Howells." *Prospects,* IX (1984), 115–42.

Bercovitch, Sacvan. *The Rites of Assent: Transformations in the Symbolic Construction of America.* New York, 1993.

Berlin, Ira. *Slaves Without Masters: The Free Negro in the Antebellum South.* New York, 1974.

Berman, Milton. *John Fiske: The Evolution of a Popularizer.* Cambridge, Mass., 1961.

Berquin-Duvallon, Pierre Louis. *Vue de la colonie espagnole du Mississippi, ou des provinces de Louisiane et Floride Occidentale en l'année 1802, par un observateur résident sur les lieux.* Paris, 1803.

Berzon, Judith. *Neither White nor Black: The Mulatto Character in American Fiction.* New York, 1978.

Biklé, Lucy Leffingwell Cable. *George W. Cable: His Life and Letters.* New York, 1928.

Blassingame, John W. *Black New Orleans, 1860–80.* Chicago, 1973.

Bleikasten, André. *The Ink of Melancholy.* Bloomington, Ind., 1980.

Blotner, Joseph. *William Faulkner: A Biography.* 2 vols. New York, 1974.

Boller, Paul F., Jr. *American Thought in Transition: The Impact of Evolutionary Naturalism, 1865–1900.* Chicago, 1969.

Brooks, Cleanth. "Southern Literature: The Past, History, and the Timeless." In *Southern Literature in Transition: Heritage and Promise,* edited by Philip Castille and William Osborne. Memphis, 1983.

———. *William Faulkner: The Yoknapatawpha County.* New Haven, 1963.

Brown, Sterling. *The Negro in American Fiction.* Washington, 1937.

Bruce, Dickson, D., Jr. *Black American Writing from the Nadir: The Evolution of a Literary Tradition, 1877–1915.* Baton Rouge, 1989.

Bryan, Violet. *The Myth of New Orleans in Literature: Dialogues of Race and Gender.* Knoxville, 1993.

Bryce, James. *The American Commonwealth.* 2 vols. New York, 1889.

Buck, Paul H. *The Road to Reunion, 1865–1900.* Boston, 1937.

Buckner, Alice Morris. *Towards the Gulf: A Romance of Louisiana.* Freeport, N.Y., 1972.

Budd, Louis. *Mark Twain: Social Philosopher.* Bloomington, Ind., 1962.

———. *Our Mark Twain: The Making of His Public Personality.* Philadelphia, 1983.

Burke, Kenneth. *The Philosophy of Literary Form: Studies in Symbolic Action.* Berkeley, 1973.

Burrow, John W. *Evolution and Society: A Study of Victorian Social Theory.* London, 1966.

Cable, George W. "After-Thoughts of a Storyteller." *North American Review,* CLVIII (1894), 16–23.

———. "Churches and Charities of New Orleans." New Orleans *Daily Picayune,* February 14, 18, 25, March 3, 10, 17, 1872.

———. Correspondence. George Washington Cable Collection. Manuscripts Department. Howard-Tilton Memorial Library, Tulane University. New Orleans, La.

———. *The Creoles of Louisiana.* New York, 1885.

———. "Drop Shot." New Orleans *Daily Picayune,* February 25, 1872.

———. "The Freedman's Case in Equity." In *The Negro Question: A Selection of Writings on Civil Rights in the South,* edited by Arlin Turner. New York, 1958.

———. *The Grandissimes.* New York, 1880.

———. Ledger-Book. George Washington Cable Collection. Manuscripts Department, Howard-Tilton Memorial Library, Tulane University. New Orleans, La.

———. "Literature in the Southern States." In *The Negro Question: A Selection of Writings on Civil Rights in the South,* edited by Arlin Turner. New York, 1958.

———. "My Politics." In *The Negro Question: A Selection of Writings on Civil Rights in the South,* edited by Arlin Turner. New York, 1958.

———. "New Orleans." *Encyclopedia Britannica.* 9th ed.

Cardwell, Guy A. *Twins of Genius.* East Lansing, Mich., 1953.

Carton, Evan. "*Pudd'nhead Wilson* and the Fiction of Law and Custom." In *American Realism: New Essays,* edited by Eric Sundquist. Baltimore, 1982.

Chase, Richard. *The American Novel and Its Tradition.* New York, 1957.

Chesnutt, Charles. "What Is a White Man?" New York *Independent,* May 30, 1889, pp. 5–6.

Clark, William Bedford. "Cable and the Theme of Miscegenation in *Old Creole Days* and *The Grandissimes.*" *Mississippi Quarterly,* XXX (Fall, 1977), 597–609.

Cook, Nancy S. "Marketing Mark Twain, or, Samuel Clemens and the Selling of 'The Innocents Abroad.' " Ph.D. dissertation, SUNY Buffalo, 1991.

Cox, James. *Mark Twain: The Fate of Humor.* Princeton, 1966.

Croly, David G., and George Wakeman. *Miscegenation: The Theory of the Blending of the Races, Applied to the American White Man and Negro.* New York, 1864.

Curti, Merle. *The Growth of American Thought.* New York, 1943.

Daggett, Harriet Spiller. "The Legal Aspect of Amalgamation in Louisiana." *Texas Law Review,* XI (February, 1933), 162–84.

Degler, Carl. *Neither Black nor White: Slavery and Race Relations in Brazil and the United States.* New York, 1971.

DeVoto, Bernard. *Mark Twain at Work*. Cambridge, Mass., 1942.

————. *Mark Twain's America*. Boston, 1935.

Directory of New Orleans. New Orleans, 1812.

Dixon, Thomas, Jr. *The Leopard's Spots*. New York, 1902.

————. *The Sins of the Father*. New York, 1912.

Dominguez, Virginia. *White by Definition: Social Classification in Creole Louisiana*. New Brunswick, N.J., 1986.

Doyno, Victor. *Writing "Huck Finn": Mark Twain's Creative Process*. Philadelphia, 1992.

Dreiser, Theodore. "Mark the Double Twain." *English Journal*, XXIV (1935), 615–27.

Dunbar-Nelson, Alice. "People of Color in Louisiana." *Journal of Negro History*, I (1916), 361–76; and II (1917), 51–78.

Durham, Robert Lee. *The Call of the South*. Boston, 1908.

Eder, Phanor J. *A Comparative Survey of Anglo-American and Latin-American Law*. Littleton, Colo., 1981.

Ekström, Kjell. *George Washington Cable: A Study of His Early Life and Work*. Cambridge, Mass., 1950.

Ellison, Ralph. "Change the Joke and Slip the Yoke." In *Shadow and Act*. New York, 1972.

Emerson, Everett. *The Authentic Mark Twain: A Literary Biography of Samuel L. Clemens*. Philadelphia, 1985.

Emerson, Ralph Waldo. *The Journals and Miscellaneous Notebooks of Ralph Waldo Emerson*. Vols. XIII and XV of 16 vols. Edited by William H. Gilman *et al.* Cambridge, Mass., 1960.

Everett, Donald E. "Emigrés and Militiamen: Free Persons of Color in New Orleans, 1803–1815." *Journal of Negro History*, XXXVIII (1953), 377–402.

Faulkner, William. *Absalom, Absalom!* New York, 1936.

————. "Elmer." *Mississippi Quarterly*, XXXVI (Summer, 1983), 337–460.

————. *Light in August*. 1932. Corrected Text. New York, 1987.

————. "Red Leaves." In *The Collected Stories of William Faulkner*. New York, 1977.

Fiedler, Leslie. "As Free as Any Cretur. . . ." *New Republic*, August 15, 22, 1955, pp. 7–8.

Fiehrer, Thomas Marc. "The African Presence in Colonial Louisiana." In *Louisiana's Black Heritage*, edited by Robert R. MacDonald, John R. Kemp, and Edward F. Haas. New Orleans, 1977.

Fiske, John. "Manifest Destiny." In *American Political Ideas Viewed from the Standpoint of Universal History*. New York, 1885.

Foner, Laura. "The Free People of Color in Louisiana and St. Domingue." *Journal of Social History*, III (1970), 406–30.

Foner, Philip S. *Mark Twain: Social Critic.* New York, 1958.

Foucault, Michel. *L'ordre du discours.* Paris, 1971.

———. "What Is an Author?" In *The Foucault Reader,* edited by Paul Rabinow. New York, 1984.

Fouchard, Jean. *The Haitian Maroons: Liberty or Death.* [*ca.* 1972]. Translated from the French by A. Faulkner Watts. New York, 1981.

Fredrickson, George. *The Black Image in the White Mind.* New York, 1971.

French, Benjamin Franklin, comp. *Historical Collections of Louisiana.* 5 vols. New York, 1851.

Friedman, Lawrence J. *The White Savage: Racial Fantasies in the Postbellum South.* Englewood Cliffs, N.J., 1970.

Gayarré, Charles. *Romance of the History of Louisiana.* 2nd ed. New Orleans, 1879.

Gellner, Ernest. *Nations and Nationalism.* Ithaca, 1983.

Gerber, John C. "*Pudd'nhead Wilson* as Fabulation." *Studies in American Humor,* II (April, 1975), 21–31.

Gilbert, Sandra, and Susan Gubar. *The Madwoman in the Attic: The Woman Writer and the Nineteenth-Century Literary Imagination.* New Haven, 1979.

Gilder, Richard Watson. "The Nationalizing of Southern Literature." *New York Christian Advocate,* July 3 and 10, 1890, Pts. I-II, pp. 425–26, 442.

Gillman, Susan. *Dark Twins: Imposture and Identity in Mark Twain's America.* Chicago, 1989.

Gillman, Susan, and Forrest Robinson. *Mark Twain's "Pudd'nhead Wilson": Race, Conflict, and Culture.* Durham, 1990.

Gobineau, Joseph A. *The Moral and Intellectual Diversity of Races, with Particular Reference to Their Respective Influence in the Civil and Political History of Mankind.* Philadelphia, 1856.

Gossett, Thomas F. *Race: The History of an Idea in America.* Dallas, 1963.

Gottschalk, Louis Moreau. *Notes of a Pianist.* Edited by Clara Gottschalk. Philadelphia, 1881.

Greenblatt, Stephen. *Renaissance Self-Fashioning: From More to Shakespeare.* Chicago, 1980.

Gribben, Alan. *Mark Twain's Library.* 2 vols. Boston, 1980.

Hall, Gwendolyn Midlo. *Africans in Colonial Louisiana: The Development of Afro-Creole Culture in the Eighteenth Century.* Baton Rouge, 1992.

———. "The Formation of Afro-Creole Culture." In *Creole New Orleans: Race and Americanization,* edited by Arnold R. Hirsch and Joseph Logsdon. Baton Rouge, 1992.

Haller, John S., Jr. *Outcasts from Evolution: Scientific Attitudes of Racial Inferiority, 1859–1900.* Chicago, 1971.

Harris, Trudier. *Exorcising Blackness: Historical and Literary Lynching and Burning Rituals.* Bloomington, Ind., 1984.

Harris, William T. "On the Relation of Education to the Individual, to Society, and to the State." *Wisconsin Journal of Education*, IV (1874), 1–11.

Hearn, Lafcadio. *Chita: A Memory of Last Island*. New York, 1889.

———. "The Original Bras-Coupé." In *Essays on American Literature*. Tokyo, 1929.

Hegel, Georg Wilhelm Friedrich. *The Phenomenology of Mind*. [*ca.* 1807] Translated by J. B. Baillie. 2nd ed. New York, 1955.

Heinl, Robert Debs, Jr., and Nancy Gordon Heinl. *Written in Blood: The Story of the Haitian People, 1492–1971*. Boston, 1978.

Higginbotham, A. Leon, Jr., and Barbara K. Kopytoff. "Racial Purity in Colonial and Antebellum Virginia." *Georgetown Law Journal*, LXXVII (1967–89), 1967–2021.

Higham, John. "The Age of Confidence." In *Strangers in the Land: Patterns of American Nativism, 1860–1925*. New Brunswick, N.J., 1988.

Hildreth, Richard. *Archy Moore, the White Slave; or, Memoirs of a Fugitive*. 1836; rpr. New York, 1969.

———. *History of the United States of America*. Rev. ed. 6 vols. New York, 1880.

———. Review of *Travels in North America, in the Years 1827 and 1828*, by Captain Basil Hall of the Royal Navy. *American Monthly Magazine*, I (1829), 532–40.

Hirsch, Arnold R., and Joseph Logsdon, eds. *Creole New Orleans: Race and Americanization*. Baton Rouge, 1992.

Hobsbawm, E. J. *The Age of Capital, 1848–75*. London, 1975.

———. *The Age of Empire, 1875–1914*. London, 1987.

———. *Nations and Nationalism Since 1780: Programme, Myth, Reality*. New York, 1990.

Hofstadter, Richard. *Social Darwinism in American Thought*. Rev. ed. Boston, 1955.

Holman, C. Hugh. "Ellen Glasgow and the Southern Literary Tradition." In *Southern Writers: Appraisals in Our Time*, edited by R. C. Simonini, Jr. Charlottesville, 1964.

———. "No More Monoliths, Please: Continuities in the Multi-Souths." In *Southern Literature in Transition: Heritage and Promise*, edited by Philip Castille and William Osborne. Memphis, 1983.

Horwitz, Howard. *By the Law of Nature*. New York, 1991.

Horwitz, Morton. *The Transformation of American Law, 1780–1860*. New York, 1992.

Howells, W. D. "Dostoyevsky and the More Smiling Aspects of Life." In *W. D. Howells: Selected Literary Criticism*. Vol. II of 3 vols. Edited by David J. Nordloh. Bloomington, Ind., 1993.

———. "From Mr. G. W. Cable's Aurora and Clotilde Nancanou." In *Critical Essays on George Washington Cable*, edited by Arlin Turner. Boston, 1980.

———. *An Imperative Duty*. New York, 1892.

———. *My Mark Twain: Reminiscences and Criticisms*. New York, 1910.

Hughes, Henry. *A Treatise on Sociology: Theoretical and Practical*. Philadelphia, 1854.

Irwin, John. *Doubling and Incest/Repetition and Revenge: A Speculative Reading of Faulkner*. Baltimore, 1975.

Jefferson, Thomas. *Notes on the State of Virginia*. Edited by William Peden. New York, 1972.

Jehlen, Myra. *Class and Character in Faulkner's South*. New York, 1976.

———. "The Ties That Bind: Race and Sex in *Pudd'nhead Wilson*." In *Mark Twain's Pudd'nhead Wilson: Race, Conflict, and Culture*, edited by Susan Gillman and Forrest Robinson. Durham, 1990.

Johnson, Jerah. "Colonial New Orleans: A Fragment of the Eighteenth-Century French Ethos." In *Creole New Orleans: Race and Americanization*, edited by Arnold R. Hirsch and Joseph Logsdon. Baton Rouge, 1992.

Jordan, Winthrop. *White over Black: American Attitudes Toward the Negro, 1550–1812*. New York, 1977.

Kaplan, Amy. "Romancing the Empire: The Embodiment of American Masculinity in the Popular Historical Novel of the 1890s." *American Literary History*, II (Winter, 1990), 659–90.

Kaplan, Justin. *Mr. Clemens and Mark Twain*. New York, 1966.

Kartiganer, Donald M. *The Fragile Thread: The Meaning of Form in Faulkner's Novels*. Amherst, 1979.

Kelley, Robert. *The Transatlantic Persuasion: The Liberal-Democratic Mind in the Age of Gladstone*. New York, 1969.

Kelly, Alfred, H. "Richard Hildreth." In *Marcus W. Jernegan Essays in American Historiography*, edited by William T. Hutchinson. Chicago, 1937.

Kelly, Joan. "The Social Relations of the Sexes." *Women, History, Theory: The Essays of Joan Kelly*. Chicago, 1984.

Kennedy, John Pendleton. *Swallow Barn; or, A Sojourn in the Old Dominion*. 1851; rpr. Baton Rouge, 1986.

King, Edward. *The Great South*. Edited by W. Magruder Drake and Robert R. Jones. Baton Rouge, 1972.

King, Grace. *New Orleans: The Place and the People*. New York, 1895.

Kinney, James. *Amalgamation! Race, Sex, and Rhetoric in the Nineteenth-Century American Novel*. Westport, 1985.

Kovel, Joel. *White Racism: A Psychohistory*. New York, 1970.

Kreyling, Michael. *The Figure of the Hero in Southern Narrative*. Baton Rouge, 1987.

LaCapra, Dominick. *History, Politics, and the Novel*. Ithaca, 1987.

LaChance, Paul F. "The Foreign French." In *Creole New Orleans: Race and Ameri-*

canization, edited by Arnold R. Hirsch and Joseph Logsdon. Baton Rouge, 1992.

Leavis, F. R. "Mark Twain's Neglected Classic: The Moral Astringency of *Pudd'nhead Wilson*." *Commentary*, XXI (February, 1956), 128–36.

Loggins, Vernon. *Where the Word Ends: The Life of Louis Moreau Gottschalk*. Baton Rouge, 1958.

Low, Seth. "An American View of Municipal Government in the United States." In *The American Commonwealth*, edited by James Bryce. Vol. I of 2 vols. New York, 1889.

Mackey, Charles. *Life and Liberty in America, or Sketches of a Tour in the United States and Canada in 1857–58*. New York, 1859.

Marcus, George E. " 'What did he reckon would become of the other half if he killed his half?': Doubled, Divided, and Crossed Selves in *Pudd'nhead Wilson*; or, Mark Twain as Cultural Critic." In *Mark Twain's Pudd'nhead Wilson: Race, Conflict, and Culture*, edited by Susan Gillman and Forrest Robinson. Durham, 1990.

Martin, François-Xavier. *History of Louisiana from the Earliest Period*. New Orleans, 1827.

McKeithan, Daniel Morley. "The Morgan Manuscript of Mark Twain's *Pudd'nhead Wilson*." *Essays and Studies on American Language and Literature*. No. 12. Cambridge, Mass., 1961.

Meier, August. *Negro Thought in America, 1880–1915: Racial Ideologies in the Age of Booker T. Washington*. Ann Arbor, 1963.

Mencke, John G. *Mulattoes and Race Mixture: American Attitudes and Images, 1865–1918*. Ann Arbor, 1979.

Meriwether, James B., and Michael Millgate, eds. *Lion in the Garden: Interviews with William Faulkner, 1926–1962*. New York, 1968.

Moreau de Saint-Méry, Médéric-Louis-Elie. *Description topographique, physique, civile, politique, et historique de la partie française de L'Isle Saint-Domingue*. Vol. I of 2 vols. Paris, 1958.

Morris, Richard B. *Studies in the History of American Law*. Philadelphia, 1959.

Morrow, Clarence J. "Louisiana." In *Matrimonial Property Law*, edited by W. Friedman. Toronto, 1955.

Mulford, Elisha. *The Nation: The Foundations of Civil Order and Political Life in the U.S.* Boston, 1886.

Nairn, Tom. *The Break-Up of Britain: Crisis and Neo-Nationalism*. London, 1977.

Nevins, Allen, ed. *America Through British Eyes*. New York, 1948.

Norton, Charles Eliot. Review of *The Laws of Race, as Connected with Slavery*, by Sidney George Fisher. *Atlantic Monthly*, VII (February, 1861), 252–55.

Nye, Russell. *The Unembarrassed Muse: The Popular Arts in America*. New York, 1970.

O'Brien, Michael. *Rethinking the South: Essays in Intellectual History*. Baltimore, 1988.

Ott, Thomas O. *The Haitian Revolution, 1789–1804*. Knoxville, 1973.

Paine, Albert Bigelow. *Mark Twain: A Biography*. 3 vols. New York, 1912.

Parker, Hershel. *Flawed Texts and Verbal Icons: Literary Authority in American Fiction*. Evanston, Ill., 1984.

Parrington, Vernon Louis. *The Beginnings of Critical Realism in America: 1860–1920*. New York, 1930. Vol. III of *Main Currents in American Thought*. 3 vols.

Persons, Stow. *Evolutionary Thought in America*. New Haven, 1950.

Petry, Alice Hall. *A Genius in His Way: The Art of Cable's Old Creole Days*. Madison, 1988.

Pettit, Arthur. *Mark Twain and the South*. Lexington, 1974.

Pizer, Donald. "Harold J. Kolb's Study of American Realism as a Literary Form." *Genre*, III (1970), 376–78.

Poole, William Frederick. *Index to Periodical Literature*. New York, 1853.

Porter, Carolyn. *Seeing and Being: The Plight of the Participant-Observer in Emerson, James, Adams, and Faulkner*. Middletown, Conn., 1981.

Price, Richard, ed. *Maroon Societies: Rebel Slave Communities in the Americas*. New York, 1973.

Pugh, Griffith T. "George W. Cable as Historian." In *Writers and Their Critics: Studies in English and American Literature*. Tallahassee, 1955.

Regan, Robert. *Unpromising Heroes: Mark Twain and His Characters*. Berkeley, 1966.

Renan, Ernest. "What Is a Nation?" Translated by E. J. Leonard. In *Cyclopedia of Political Science, Political Economy, and of the Political History of the United States*, edited by John J. Lalor. Vol. II of 2 vols. Chicago, 1883.

Review of *The Grandissimes*. *Atlantic Monthly*, XXXXVI (December, 1880), 829–31.

Ringe, Donald A. "Narrative Voice in Cable's *The Grandissimes*." In *The Grandissimes: Centennial Essays*, edited by Thomas J. Richardson. Special Issue of *Southern Quarterly*, XVIII (Summer, 1980), 13–22.

Roark, James. *Black Masters: A Free Family of Color in the Old South*. New York, 1984.

Robinson, Forrest. *In Bad Faith: The Dynamics of Deception in Mark Twain's America*. Cambridge, Mass., 1986.

Rose, Alan Henry. *Demonic Vision: Racial Fantasy and Southern Fiction*. Hamden, Conn., 1976.

Roussève, Charles Barthelemy. *The Negro in Louisiana: Aspects of His History and His Literature*. New Orleans, 1937.

Rubin, Louis D., Jr. " 'The Begum of Bengal': Mark Twain and the South." In *William Elliott Shoots a Bear: Essays on the Southern Literary Imagination*. Baton Rouge, 1975.

————. *George W. Cable: The Life and Times of a Southern Heretic*. New York, 1969.

————. "Samuel Langhorne Clemens (Mark Twain)." *History of Southern Literature*, edited by Louis D. Rubin, Jr., et al. Baton Rouge, 1985.

Said, Edward. *Beginnings: Intention and Method*. New York, 1975.

————. *Culture and Imperialism*. New York, 1993.

Salsbury, Edith, ed. *Susy and Mark Twain: Family Dialogues*. New York, 1965.

Saxe-Weimar-Eisenach, Duke of. *Travels Through North America*. 2 vols. Philadelphia, 1828.

Schuyler, George. *Black No More; being an account of the strange and wonderful workings of science in the land of the free, A.D. 1933–1940*. 1931; rpr. College Park, Md., 1969.

Shaler, Nathaniel. "The Negro Question." *Atlantic Monthly*, LIV (November, 1884), 696–709.

Sheridan, Alan. *Michel Foucault: The Will to Truth*. London, 1980.

Simpson, Lewis P. "The Fable of the Writer in Southern Fiction." *Prospects*, VII (1982), 249–66.

————. "Home by Way of California: The Southerner as the Last European." In *Southern Literature in Transition: Heritage and Promise*, edited by Philip Castille and William Osborne. Memphis, 1983.

————. *Mind and the American Civil War: A Meditation on Lost Causes*. Baton Rouge, 1989.

Singal, Daniel. *The War Within: From Victorian to Modernist Thought in the South, 1919–1945*. Chapel Hill, 1982.

Smith, Henry Nash. *Mark Twain: The Development of a Writer*. Cambridge, Mass., 1962.

Stahl, J. D. *Mark Twain: Culture and Gender; Envisioning America Through Europe*. Athens, Ga., 1994.

Stanton, William. *The Leopard's Spots: Scientific Attitudes Toward Race in America, 1815–59*. Chicago, 1960.

Stephens, Robert O. "Cable's Bras-Coupé and Merimée's Tamango: The Case of the Missing Arm." *Mississippi Quarterly*, XXXV (Fall, 1982), 387–405.

Sterkx, H. E. *The Free Negro in Antebellum Louisiana*. Rutherford, N.J., 1972.

Stoneley, Peter. *Mark Twain and the Feminine Aesthetic*. Cambridge, Eng., 1992.

Sundquist, Eric. *Faulkner: The House Divided*. Baltimore, 1983.

————. "Mark Twain and Homer Plessy." *Representations*, XXIV (Fall, 1988), 102–28.

————. "Regions and Regionalism." In *The Columbia Literary History of the United States*, edited by Emory Elliott et al. New York, 1988. 501–25.

————. *To Wake the Nations: Race in the Making of American Literature*. Cambridge, 1993.

Tebbel, John, ed. *The Expansion of an Industry, 1865–1919*. New York, 1975. Vol. II of *A History of Book Publishing in the United States*. 4 vols.

Thomas, Brooks. "Tragedies of Race, Training, Birth, and Communities of Competent Pudd'nheads." *American Literary History*, I (Winter, 1989), 754–83.

Tindall, George B. *The Emergence of the New South, 1913–1945.* Baton Rouge, 1967.

Tinker, Edward Laroque, and Frances Tinker. *Old New Orleans.* New York, 1931.

Tischler, Nancy. *Black Masks: Negro Characters in Modern Southern Fiction.* University Park, Pa., 1969.

Tregle, Joseph G., Jr. "Creoles and Americans." In *Creole New Orleans: Race and Americanization,* edited by Arnold R. Hirsch and Joseph Logsdon. Baton Rouge, 1992.

Tribune (New York). Unsigned editorial. August 30, 1879.

Turner, Arlin. *George W. Cable: A Biography.* Baton Rouge, 1966.

———. "Mark Twain and the South: An Affair of Love and Anger." *Southern Review*, IV (1968), 493–519.

———. "A Novelist Discovers a Novelist: The Correspondence of H. H. Boyesen and George W. Cable." *Western Humanities Review*, V (Autumn, 1951), 345–46.

Tuveson, Ernest Lee. *Redeemer Nation: The Idea of America's Millennial Role.* Chicago, 1968.

Twain, Mark. *The Adventures of Huckleberry Finn.* New York, 1987.

———. *The Autobiography of Mark Twain.* Edited by Charles Neider. New York, 1959.

———. "The Character of Man." In *Mark Twain: Collected Tales, Sketches, Speeches and Essays, 1852–1890,* edited by Louis Budd. New York, 1992.

———. "Consistency." In *Mark Twain: Collected Tales, Sketches, Speeches and Essays, 1852–1890,* edited by Louis Budd. New York, 1992.

———. "In Defense of Harriet Shelley." *North American Review*, CLIX, Pts. 1–3 (1894), 108–119, 240–51, 353–68.

———. *Life on the Mississippi: The Writings of Mark Twain.* Vol. IX of 25 vols. Hartford, Conn., 1899.

———. *The Love Letters of Mark Twain.* Edited by Dixon Wecter. New York, 1949.

———. *Mark Twain in Eruption: Hitherto Unpublished Pages About Men and Events.* Edited by Bernard De Voto. 1940; rpr. New York, 1969.

———. *Mark Twain of the Enterprise: Newspaper Articles and Other Documents, 1862–1864.* Edited by Henry Nash Smith. Berkeley, 1957.

———. *Mark Twain's Autobiography.* Edited by Albert Bigelow Paine. New York, 1925.

———. *Mark Twain's Letters.* Edited by Albert Bigelow Paine. 2 vols. New York, 1917.

————. *Mark Twain–Howells Letters*. Edited by Henry Nash Smith and William M. Gibson. 2 vols. Cambridge, Mass., 1960.

————. *Mark Twain's Letters to His Publishers, 1867–1894*. Edited by Hamlin Hill. Berkeley, 1967.

————. *Mark Twain's Notebook*. Edited by Albert Bigelow Paine. New York, 1935.

————. *Mark Twain's Notebooks and Journals*. Edited by Frederick Anderson *et al*. Vol. III of 3 vols. Berkeley, 1975.

————. "Mock Oration on the Dead Partisan." In *Mark Twain: Collected Tales, Sketches, Speeches and Essays, 1852–1890*, edited by Louis Budd. New York, 1992.

————. "The New Dynasty." In *Mark Twain: Collected Tales, Sketches, Speeches and Essays, 1852–1890*, edited by Louis Budd. New York, 1992.

————. "Plymouth Rock and the Pilgrims." In *Mark Twain: Collected Tales, Sketches, Speeches and Essays, 1852–1890*, edited by Louis Budd. 2 vols. New York, 1992.

————. *Pudd'nhead Wilson and Those Extraordinary Twins*. Edited by Sidney E. Berger. New York, 1980.

————. "Reply to the Editor of 'The Art of Authorship.' " In *Collected Tales, Sketches, Speeches, and Essays, 1852–1890*, edited by Louis Budd. New York, 1992.

————. *Selected Mark Twain–Howells Letters, 1872–1910*. Edited by Frederick Anderson, William M. Gibson, and Henry Nash Smith. Cambridge, Mass., 1967.

————. "Turncoats." In *Mark Twain: Collected Tales, Sketches, Speeches, and Essays, 1852–1890*, edited by Louis Budd. New York, 1992.

Twain, Mark, and Charles Dudley Warner. *The Gilded Age: A Tale of Today*. [1873]. *The Writings of Mark Twain*. Vols. X and XI of 25 vols. Hartford, Conn., 1899.

Weimann, Robert. "Realism, Ideology, and the Novel." *Boundary 2*, XVII (Spring, 1990), 189–210.

White, Hayden. "The Forms of Wildness: Archaeology of an Idea." In *The Wild Man Within: An Image in Western Thought from the Renaissance to Romanticism*, edited by Edward Dudley and Maximillian E. Novak. Pittsburgh, 1972.

————. "The Politics of Historical Interpretation: Discipline and De-Sublimation." In *The Content of the Form: Narrative Discourse and Historical Representation*. Baltimore, 1987.

————. *Tropics of Discourse: Essays in Cultural Criticism*. Baltimore, 1978.

Wigger, Anne P. "The Composition of Mark Twain's *Pudd'nhead Wilson and Those Extraordinary Twins*: Chronology and Development." *Modern Philology*, LV (1957), 93–102.

Williams, Edward. *Virginia, More Especially the South Part Thereof, Richly and Truly Valued.* In *Tracts and Other Papers Relating Principally to the Origin, Settlement, and Progress of the Colonies of North America,* edited by Peter Force. Vol. III of 4 vols. New York, 1947.

Williamson, Joel. *The Crucible of Race: Black-White Relations in the American South Since Emancipation.* New York, 1984.

————. *New People: Miscegenation and Mulattoes in the United States.* New York, 1980.

Wilson, Edmund. *Patriotic Gore: Studies in the Literature of the American Civil War.* New York, 1962.

Wood, Forrest G. *Black Scare: The Racist Response to Emancipation and Reconstruction.* Berkeley, 1968.

Woodward, C. Vann. *Origins of the New South, 1877–1913.* Rev. ed. Baton Rouge, 1971.

Yellin, Jean Fagan. *The Intricate Knot: Black Figures in American Literature, 1776–1863.* New York, 1972.

Zanger, Jules. "The Tragic Octoroon in Pre–Civil War Fiction." *American Quarterly,* XVIII (Spring, 1966), 63–72.

Index